Larry Brown

Larry Brown

A Writer's Life

Jean W. Cash

Foreword by Shannon Ravenel

UNIVERSITY PRESS OF MISSISSIPPI   JACKSON

Willie Morris Books in Memoir and Biography

www.upress.state.ms.us

The University Press of Mississippi is a member of the Association
of American University Presses.

First printing 2011

Library of Congress Cataloging-in-Publication Data

Cash, Jean W., 1938–
Larry Brown : a writer's life / Jean W. Cash ; foreword by Shannon Ravenel.
p. cm. — (Willie Morris books in memoir and biography)
Includes bibliographical references and index.
ISBN 978-1-60473-980-0 (cloth : alk. paper) — ISBN 978-1-60473-986-2 (ebook) 1.
Brown, Larry, 1951–2004. 2. Authors, American—20th century—Biography. I. Title.
PS3552.R6927Z55 2011
813'.54—dc22
[B]   2010053721

British Library Cataloging-in-Publication Data available

For my son, Gordon W. Cash

and

for my friend, Keith R. Perry

Contents

Foreword

Shannon Ravenel

Larry Brown's story, "Facing the Music," begins, "I cut my eyes sideways because I know what's coming. 'You want the light off, honey?' she says. Very quietly."

I first read those words in May 1987. I was on an airplane headed for Washington, D.C., to attend the huge annual American Booksellers Association convention. Algonquin Books, by then almost five years old, had paid for a booth at the convention, and our small staff would be taking turns tending it.

In those days, I never got on a plane or train without a stack of the latest literary magazines, which I read looking for candidates for inclusion in *New Stories from the South*, the annual anthology Algonquin had introduced the year before. "Facing the Music" was in the fall–winter 1986 issue of *Mississippi Review*. I read the story in one amazed gulp. And then I read it again. Who was this Larry Brown of whom I, a supposed expert on contemporary southern short fiction, had never heard? The story didn't strike me as the work of a beginner, but the only information the contributor's note gave was that the author was a captain in the Oxford, Mississippi, Fire Department.

In Washington, the Algonquin staff gathered for dinner at the hotel restaurant. With us was one of our investors, Julian Scheer, a newspaperman and former public relations manager for NASA. As soon as we sat down, Julian leaned over to me and said, "I have just come across the best short story I have ever read." "Was it," I asked, "by a fireman from Oxford, Mississippi?" Julian's mouth dropped open. "How did you guess???!!!" I reminded him that he'd asked me for a list of the ten best American literary journals because he wanted to subscribe to them. *Mississippi Review* was at the top of that list, and I knew he always read it as soon as it arrived.

The next day, at the convention center, when I was doing my turn in the Algonquin booth, I noticed a young man staring at us from a little distance away. He was pacing, as if working up his nerve. When he finally approached, I read his name tag—"Richard Howorth, Square Books, Oxford, MS." After introducing himself, he said he wanted to tell me about a new writer from his hometown. "Is it Larry Brown, the fireman?" I asked. I got a second stunned expression. I told Richard I wanted to include "Facing the Music" in the 1988 volume of *New Stories from the South*, and he gave me Larry's address and phone number.

I don't usually telephone writers because I am not great on the phone and because I figure writers prefer to read what a person has to say, at least at first. So I wrote a letter to Larry Brown—but I wrote it right away and asked him to call me, collect. And that was the beginning of Algonquin's long relationship with a man I consider one of the best American writers of the twentieth century.

The last line of "Facing the Music" is "She turns the light off, and we reach to find each other in the darkness like people who are blind." What goes between those opening and closing sentences is the powerful stuff Larry Brown dealt with in all his work—human need, human pain, human courage. He was a writer whose creative impulse was to turn his gaze directly onto men and women challenged by crisis and pathology and to compel his readers to face that music with him.

The story of Larry Brown's determination to become a writer and of his own struggles and triumphs is a great one. Jean Cash has turned over every stone in recounting that story and given what she's found the beauty of expression his life deserves. I miss Larry as a person, and I miss having new work from him to read. I'm grateful to Jean for capturing his being in this brilliantly illuminating biography.

Preface

I met Larry Brown at an April 1989 conference on southern literature sponsored by the Arts and Education Council of Chattanooga, Tennessee, where he appeared just after publishing *Facing the Music*. Larry was introduced as a "rising star" among southern writers and diffidently yet enthusiastically presented a lecture and a reading from his first novel, *Dirty Work*. Later published by Algonquin as *A Late Start*, Brown's talk shows his honesty as a creative artist. He in effect tells the world of his working-class background, his alcoholic father, his supportive mother, his years as a fireman, and his desire to make a better life for his family by becoming a writer. I remember seeing Larry later in an elevator at the hotel; he looked young (he was not yet thirty-eight) and was dressed in clothes he favored throughout his life—blue jeans, a casual shirt, a tweed jacket, and cowboy boots. The most appealing part of that memory is the smile on his face.

What impressed me then and continues to impress me is that Brown, without the benefit of formal education, honed a talent and achieved success in a field that is today primarily occupied by college graduates, often products of programs offering master's degrees in fine arts. To me, his portrayal of the lives of working-class rural Mississippians seems both authentic and unique.

I bought *Facing the Music* in Chattanooga and had Larry sign it. From that time forward, I read each of Larry's works as it appeared, noticing the development of his skill and craft; however, not until the publication of *Father and Son* in 1996 did I realize the extent of Larry's genius. As I read the novel through the evening and into the night, I soon realized that *Father and Son* discredits Poe's notion that the novel, as genre, is too lengthy to be read in a single setting. I finished reading about two o'clock in the morning, and I will never forget my reaction to Glen Davis's final words: "I'm sorry." I believed both him and Larry. From that point on, I began to teach the novel regularly.

Since then, I have been an advocate of Brown and his work. I gave my first conference paper on him in 1999 at the annual meeting of the Philological Association of the Carolinas; in that paper, I established correspondences between *Father and Son* and a song by Bruce Springsteen, "Adam Raised a Cain." That was the first of my many presentations on Larry's fiction and his life. In 2001, I began to plan a collection of essays devoted to Brown and his work. A year later, I published an article on Larry Brown and Flannery O'Connor in the *Flannery O'Connor Review*; the next year, I wrote an extended entry on him for a volume of the *Dictionary of Literary Biography*. I began to correspond with Larry and received his assistance in these projects. He approved of the O'Connor essay and made minor corrections to the manuscript of the biographical essay for the *Dictionary of Literary Biography*. Larry was also enthusiastic about my idea of collecting and editing essays on his work, even recruiting two of his friends, Gary Hawkins and Rick Bass, to contribute. In 2008, the University Press of Mississippi published this collection, *Larry Brown and the Blue-Collar South*, which I coedited with Keith Perry. The essays address Brown's fiction, its relationship to that of his forebears and contemporaries, its use of sympathetic characters who seek meaning in hostile environments, and the issue of art versus family.

When I attended the annual Faulkner Conference in Oxford in the summer of 2000, I again met Larry Brown after he read "A Roadside Resurrection." I was immediately mesmerized by the story's humor and its power. I last saw Larry Brown in person in the fall of 2003, when he read "A Roadside Resurrection" at a Milledgeville, Georgia, celebration of O'Connor's life and work. His reading that night was vastly more sophisticated than the one I had heard three years earlier. He completely captivated his audience.

Like Larry's family, friends, and other acquaintances, I was shocked and grieved to learn of his death in November 2004. When someone as talented as Larry dies as the age of fifty-three, we all feel regret. In the summer of 2005, I approached his widow, Mary Annie Brown, about writing Larry's biography. She agreed.

During my years of research into Larry's life and writing, I was most surprised to find that he wrote a huge number of letters to friends and acquaintances; thinking back, however, I should not have been so shocked. He answered the first letter I wrote to him in 2000 and reported its content to his editor, Shannon Ravenel, describing me as a "girl" at James Madison University who was teaching *Father and Son*.

I have remained a strong advocate of Larry and his work, seeking to convince other college teachers and the world at large of the literary viability of his writing. This biography will help to fulfill that goal.

Larry Brown

Introduction

Picture Henry David Thoreau sitting by Walden Pond, a cigarette in one hand, a can of beer in the other, a fishing rod at the ready, a writing pad nearby. This is Larry Brown, a Mississippi writer who loved the world he grew up in and never really left it. Fishing, hunting, working on his land, and relishing the beauty of North Mississippi were important to him throughout his life. In appearance and manner, Brown seemed a typical inhabitant of the area. Rugged, weathered, and gentle, he was a humorous yet warm and sensitive human being. His appealing Mississippi accent and intelligent gaze immediately marked him as a person of stature in spite of his relatively small physical size. Larry Brown was about five feet, nine inches tall; he said he never weighed more than 140 pounds. He favored casual dress, often wore a billed cap, and usually held a cigarette in his hand. Glennray Tutor, an Oxford artist who became a close friend of Brown's, remembered him as "one of the kindest people I have ever known in my life. He was a gentleman, for one thing, but he was kind-hearted as well, and I knew that right off the bat. He tried to please you and make you happy. He was brought up in the old Mississippi country way of things."

A man of ambition, Brown pursued every activity in his life with incredible determination. He was driven to succeed as a U.S. Marine, as a husband and father, as a fireman, and later as a writer. Writing provided a positive outlet for this sometimes troubled man. Brown's widow, Mary Annie, has said that he was happiest when writing and was often depressed when he was not writing or enjoying his life at Yocona and Tula. When not writing, he sought relief from his depression in Oxford, where he frequently partied with his many friends.

Larry Brown developed numerous friendships. Nobody disliked

Brown, who in the late 1990s had business cards printed that read "Larry Brown, Human Being." According to Mary Annie Brown, "With Larry, what you saw was what you got. Friends were very important to Larry because if you were Larry's friend, you were Larry's friend forever. Larry never saw bad in anybody. You had to prove yourself bad. He trusted everybody. He believed everything anybody told him. [In friendship, Larry] showed the gentleman he was supposed to be." His longtime friend and fellow novelist Clyde Edgerton elaborated, "Larry's friendship had a preciousness to it. By that I mean I felt that he would go a long way to avoid any conflict, that loyalty occupied a throne of sorts. His confiding in me about personal subjects automatically led to reciprocity. But it wasn't that I felt like he was confiding in me only. I, and I think many other people, sensed that he thrived on friendships that were as similarly close and loyal to other people. The possibility of conflict seemed remote. The possibility of him offering humor, helping you clear land, etc.—was always there, in spite of disagreements, differing opinions." Brown pursued these friendships through both personal contact and extensive correspondence.

With the publication of *Facing the Music* in 1988, Brown became one of the most touted of the new group of working-class writers who emerged in the South as the literary descendants of Harry Crews, a Floridian whose background in many ways resembled Brown's and whose novels offered sometimes shocking portraits of lower-class life. Crews was one of Brown's literary heroes, as his essay on Crews in *Billy Ray's Farm* clearly demonstrates. According to Brown, he "read everything Harry Crews has ever published. I reckon all of his novels and even his first story, which was published in about 1963" (Parsons 3). In his 2000 essay, "The Rise of Southern Redneck and White Trash Writers," Erik Bledsoe charts the evolution of Crews and his followers, asserting that although "lower class whites have a long tradition in Southern fiction," they had never received serious treatment; the middle-class writers who introduced such characters gave them three roles: comic characters, villains, or victims (70). Because these writers, William Faulkner among them, were looking at these characters from the outside, they were fair game for stereotyping. In Bledsoe's view, Faulkner saw these whites as comic until they began to gain economic power: "The narrative perspective of the Snopes Trilogy is that of the middle classes who watch in horror as they lose ground to the white trash that seeks to displace them" (72).

Bledsoe correctly asserts that the younger writers who followed in Crews's footsteps—Dorothy Allison and Tim McLaurin as well as Brown—"were born in and write about the Rough South, a term coined by documentary filmmaker Gary Hawkins and more commonly referred to as the world of redneck or white trash" (68). Bledsoe goes on to claim that these writers (I would add William Gay and Tom Franklin) force readers "to reexamine long-held stereotypes and beliefs while challenging the literary role traditionally assigned poor whites" (68). Brown's "writing does not drift far from the poor-white world of his upbringing. But unlike Faulkner, he does not fear that world" (75). Edgerton said that Brown "has a deep love of the earth. He loves people and things in a way that keeps him anchored to his own good sense. His writing shows that he's in touch with something at a deep level that few writers ever make it down to" (O'Brient, "Writer" L6).

What clearly separates Brown from other Rough South writers is the story of how he became a writer. Crews, Allison, McLaurin, and Franklin honed at least some of their writing skills in academic environments. Though these authors grew up in families that resembled Brown's, they went on to college, where they learned both how to write and how to transform their lives into viable fiction. Brown remained at home, where he imbibed the richness of local culture and taught himself how to write.

Brown refused to bow to the convention that "You can't go home again." He lived nearly forty of his fifty-three years in a decidedly rural area of North Mississippi, just ten miles from Oxford. There he divided his time between his house in Yocona and his land in Tula, his private Walden. He bought six acres there in 1990 and cleared the field and pond, created spillways, and stocked the pond with "black crappie, channel catfish, and a hundred Florida bass" (*BRF* 9). North Mississippi provided Larry Brown with a rich proving ground from two perspectives: that of the rural area encompassing Yocona and Tula in which he spent the greater part of his life, and that of the small city of Oxford, which was developing as an artistic center at the same time that Brown was teaching himself to write. Although his family lived in Memphis from the time Brown was about three until his early teens, the rural parts of Lafayette County were essential to Brown's outlook on life and to his fiction.

Most of North Mississippi remains rural. Oxford is the only sizable town in Lafayette County, and much of the rest of the area remains sparsely settled farmland. A two-lane highway, Route 334, branches off University Avenue in Oxford. The community of Yocona, where Brown spent his adult life, is about ten miles southeast of Oxford. Tula, the picturesque village where Brown's mother grew up, is about two miles further down Route 334. The village of Yocona was established in the 1830s and named for the river that runs through the area—the same waterway that gave Faulkner the name for his fictional Yoknapatawpha County. The river remains a favorite spot for local residents fishing for white bass in the spring, and the area's farmers continue to raise corn and soybeans as well as cattle and horses. For more than one hundred years, when cotton was the primary crop in the area, a gin operated at the center of Yocona, which also had a country store that today operates as the Yocona River Inn, a popular restaurant (Miles, "Yocona" 1A). The Brown homestead, where Larry's son, Billy Ray, continues to farm and to operate an organic dairy, is less than a mile from the restaurant. Billy Ray has described the area as "about the best place in the world for a kid to grow up" (Miles, "Yocona" 1A). The calm of the landscape provided Larry Brown with some of his Mississippi settings, and the stories of area inhabitants were vital to his fiction.

Tula's history differs somewhat from that of Yocona. Tula was settled in the late nineteenth century and got a post office in 1889. According to Jenny Wilson, "At its height, Tula had seven stores in operation, a major and constable, three churches, a sawmill, a grist mill, a big new schoolhouse, and even a hotel" (n.p.). In 1890, Professor Charles C. Hughes founded the Tula Normal Institute and Business College, which thrived for a few years before becoming the Tula Consolidated High School. After the school burned in 1922, the community languished. Today, the town has neither store nor post office, but it has the kind of rural ambiance favored by Brown. When he looked for work and books, however, Oxford attracted him: the Oxford Fire Department and the Oxford–Lafayette County Library became central to his life.

Oxford was in many ways the ideal place for a young writer of Brown's determination in the early 1980s. The town had finally thrown off the shame that surrounded it and the University of Mississippi when the school resisted African American James Meredith's attempts to enroll in 1962. By 1980, the town and the university were experiencing a renaissance in the arts and in the general quality of life. The university had an outstanding library, and the community made extensive use of the public library. Larry Brown; his mother, Leona Barlow Brown; and his siblings had been enthusiastic users of the library from the time they moved back to Lafayette County from Memphis in 1968 (Fitts interview).

The first step in Oxford's rebirth arguably came with the university's new outlook on William Faulkner. Beginning in 1973, Evans Harrington, John Pilkington, Ann Abadie, and later Doreen Fowler organized and held annual conferences that drew scholars from all over the world to meet and discuss the works of one of the greatest writers of American fiction. The preeminent scholars of Faulkner's work who came to Oxford included Joseph Blotner, Michael Millgate, Cleanth Brooks, Andre Bleikasten, and Elizabeth Kerr. After Faulkner's widow, Estelle, died in the mid-1970s, the university bought Rowan Oak from his daughter, Jill Faulkner Summers, and opened the home as a literary shrine. From 1988 until his death, Brown often read and spoke at the annual Faulkner Conference.

In 1977, the university established the Center for the Study of Southern Culture under the direction of William Ferris, who later served as the director of the National Endowment for the Arts during Bill Clinton's administration. With the help of Charles Reagan Wilson and Ann Abadie, the center began to offer a multitude of enriching events, among them conferences devoted to southern writing and music. The University of Mississippi today holds the most extensive collection of blues recordings in the world. The *Encyclopedia of Southern Culture*, sponsored by the center and published by the University of North Carolina Press in 1989, added much to the reputation of the university and the town. Ole Miss introduced a southern studies major and enhanced its program in creative writing under the direction of Evans Harrington, who hired Mississippi novelist Ellen Douglas to teach at Ole Miss one semester every year. In 1982, Barry Hannah, a Mississippi native who had begun his writing career outside the state, came to the university as a writer-in-residence. He subsequently became a permanent member of the faculty, heading the creative writing program, which began to offer a master's degree in fine arts in 2001. Hannah helped to launch the careers of young writers such as Donna Tartt and Steve Yarbrough. Though Brown did not study creative writing with Hannah, Hannah was one of the first writers whom Brown asked to evaluate his early fiction. Willie Morris came to the university in 1984 as a visiting writer-in-residence; because of his connections in New York, other writers, among them William Styron and George Plimpton, visited the campus to present readings and interact with students.

Another major development on the Oxford literary scene came on 14 September 1979, when Richard Howorth, a native of Oxford and University of Mississippi graduate, and his wife, Lisa, also an Ole Miss alumna, established a bookstore on the Square. The store, at first located on the second floor of a downtown building owned by Richard Howorth's aunt, soon became a center for readers and writers of fiction. Thirty years later, Howorth operates not only Square Books (now located on the corner of Lamar and the Square) but also Off-Square Books and Square Books Jr. (for children). To visit the main store is to trace the history of Oxford's literary life over the past three decades. Nearly every contemporary writer of note has given a reading at either Square Books or Off-Square Books. In the early 1980s, Brown began to patronize Square Books; the Howorths soon recognized his talent and became his friends and promoters. In 1992, Marc Smirnoff, a former Square Books employee, founded a literary magazine, the *Oxford American*, that provided an outlet for many southern writers, including Brown. For several years, John Grisham served as its publisher, with his name and the magazine's high quality adding to the town's overall reputation.

A second significant connection between Square Books and the

Center for the Study of Southern Culture was the 1993 creation of the Oxford Conference for the Book. Brown was a frequent reader and panelist at these annual conferences, which drew writers and book enthusiasts from all over the world and thus helped to create what Rob Gurwitt has described as "Oxford's reputation as a literary center of the South." Complementing the town's literary expansion was an interest in contemporary music; since the 1980s, Proud Larry's, Ireland's (later Murff's), City Grocery, Long Shot, and other bars and restaurants have provided outlets for country and folk, heavy metal, blues, and other musical genres. Brown, always a lover of music, soon became a part of this scene, developing his wide-ranging interests. Although he had long owned a guitar, he gradually became more adept at playing and began to write songs. The debut of a local radio program, Thacker Mountain Radio, on 15 October 1993 represented still another important artistic development. Bryan Ledford and Caroline Herring first hosted the show, which continues to offer music and author readings every week from fall to spring. Now hosted by Jim Dees, Thacker Mountain was picked up by Mississippi Public Broadcasting in 2002, bringing the show and the southern writers it has featured (including Brown) to a wider audience.

His birth, adolescence, and early writing in the rich atmosphere of Oxford and its surrounding countryside were important to Brown's development as a writer; equally important were the significant southern writers whom he, a lifelong reader, discovered on his own. The serious writers he found used their particular locales to examine concerns regarding the realities of human existence. Brown frequently praised these writers and acknowledged that reading and studying their work had helped him train himself to write what he hoped would be viable and enduring work. Ironically, however, Brown set out to make serious money from his fiction but, like his literary heroes early in their writing lives, ended up admired but little read by a popular audience. In response to frequent questions about which writers he most admired, Brown most often mentioned Crews, Faulkner, and Cormac McCarthy, whose works Brown began to read long before he started writing. He also commonly cited Flannery O'Connor, John D. McDonald, Raymond Carver, Charles Bukowski, and Stephen King. According to

Brown, these writers taught him "how to make strong characters, how to move them around and motivate them. I learned that story was all-important, and I learned about narrative hooks. I learned about using the language, and the different things you can do with it" (Ross 89).

The first serious writer whom Brown claimed was Crews. In an unpublished essay about his first visit with Hannah, Brown wrote that he was awed to learn that Hannah knew Crews: Hannah "led me over to a wall, and there it was. A picture of him, Big He of southern Florida and Bacon County, Georgia, The One, Harry Crews. . . . This guy actually knew Harry Crews, my own personal candidate for Great Writer of the Century. I've read everything I could get my hands on that was written by him. I know all about his lifestyle. To me he is the greatest. It is my most fervent wish to one day be able to speak to this man. He is everything I want to be. His thoughts and attitudes so closely parallel mine that I guess I have been influenced unduly by him" (Rankin Papers).

Brown next turned to McCarthy. In an unpublished 1986 interview, Brown explained that after discovering McCarthy's novel *Suttree* in the Oxford–Lafayette County Library, he went out and "got all [McCarthy's] books. His prose and his dialog is just so exact, so lyrical, he finds words that I've never heard of, words that I don't even know exist, and he uses them, he knows how to use them. Also, his work is so funny in places that [it] just makes you laugh out loud. And some of it's so sad it can almost make you cry. But he's deeply into natural horror. The horror is all real. That's what's so scary about it. The things he writes about can happen. . . . Child of God [is] just a great, great book, but it's very, very scary. A lot of people wouldn't be able to handle reading it" (Brown Collections). After reading *Blood Meridian* in the mid-1980s, Brown wrote a letter of appreciation to McCarthy, receiving a brief reply. Brown again wrote to the elusive author in November 1988, sending his hero a copy of *Facing the Music*. McCarthy thanked Brown for the book and offered encouragement: "Congratulations on the completion of [*Dirty Work*] too, I hope these books get attention for you. It's a tough business, I'm sure I don't have to tell you" (Brown Collections). In October 1988, Brown wrote to a friend, Jake Mills, "I think if there's anybody in the country who's in the place Faulkner used to be, great and unknown (relatively) it's Cormac McCarthy. He'll get the Nobel one day, if there's any justice in the world" (Brown Collections).

Faulkner also stood near the top of Brown's list of literary idols for the obvious reasons that Faulkner is so closely associated with Oxford and that Brown was born and lived near the town for most of his life. Throughout his life, Brown carried a talisman from Faulkner's home, as he told Edgerton in 1991: "I got two pieces of cloth from Faulkner's favorite chair a while back. One of them is hanging up in front of my typewriter for luck. The other one I kept cutting small pieces off of for friends for luck, for instance gave one to a boy who does a lot of hunting to put on his gun, then fucked around and lost the rest of it except for one thread that I keep in my pocket. And this other big piece, of course. It's brocade or some shit" (Edgerton Papers). As early as his appearance at Ole Miss's 1988 Faulkner Conference, shortly after the publication of *Facing the Music*, Brown told about first reading Faulkner's work as a result of a friend's accident. Brown and other boys bought their injured contemporary a copy of Faulkner's *Big Woods*; all of the friends eventually read the book.

In *On Fire*, Brown describes his first visit to Rowan Oak: "I had never gone there until sometime in the late seventies when a film crew from New York was shooting something, probably a documentary, in the yard and wanted some rain, only there was no rain that day" (172). Brown continues, "I like to walk around the old wooden fence, and look at the trees, and think about what he did with his life. I figure he didn't pay much attention to what the world thought. He just went on and wrote his novels and stories and eventually won the Nobel Prize" (174). Brown also derides the town's notion that Faulkner "didn't have nothing"—that is, no money. In Brown's view, Faulkner's talent was vastly more important.

Thus, a combination of talent and determination, location, and the influences of other writers helped Brown move toward becoming an author. Until he was nearly thirty years old, however, he did not realize that he would join his literary heroes.

CHAPTER ONE

Origins, 1951–1969

Larry Brown emerged from a troubled, working-class background, but he rose to success through a combination of personal determination and talent, clear insight into what makes us human, and the support of the strong, ambitious women in his life—his mother, Leona Barlow Brown; and his wife, Mary Annie Coleman Brown. Both of Brown's parents were farm people who grew up in the Yocona-Tula area of Lafayette County. His family on both sides had long lived in the North Mississippi countryside outside Oxford. Leona Barlow Brown was a descendant of the Davis family; other clans to which Larry Brown was related included the Hipps, the Sharps, the Sockwells, the Franklins, and the Johnsons.

Except for his ten years in Memphis and two years in the marines, Larry Brown lived in Tula or Yocona for virtually all of his life. He loved the area, telling Jonathan Miles in 1996, "There's a lot of sky out here" ("Yocona" 1A). Brown extended this theme in *On Fire*, writing, "I live out in the county, out here in the land of the Big Sky country. I live at the edge of a river bottom and the clouds can go all mushroomy and marshmallowy late in the afternoon and loom up big and white in the sky so that they can capture your attention. We have our own catfish pond, and we feed our fish. . . . We live a life in harmony with nature and are glad we're here" (26–27).

According to Lafayette County records, the Davises were the third family to build a house in Tula, then called Poplar Springs. The first Davis in Mississippi was Allen, born in 1750. His son, Vincent, was Leona Barlow Brown's great-grandfather. According to Leona Brown, her grandfather, Robert Davis (1839–1932) married Martha Susan Oswalt, from Choctaw County, in 1853. The Civil War profoundly affected the Davises, like most southerners: Robert Davis was wounded during the conflict, and according to family lore, his wife "sat on the only pair of scissors they had to keep the soldiers from stealing their scissors." Robert and Susan Davis's daughter, Mattie (d. 1970), married Joseph Barlow (d. 1922), and the couple had many children, several of whom died before reaching adolescence. The family lived in Tunica, in the Mississippi Delta, where Leona was born in 1921. In 1988, Larry Brown told his friend, Clyde Edgerton, that after the birth of his mother, "my grandmother forbid [her husband] to come to her bed any more. . . . [H]e was going to leave them and move to Arkansas." One of Leona's brothers "was nearly grown and was going to have to farm the place they had and support the family. Then my granddaddy died suddenly" (Edgerton Papers). Now widowed and caring for eight children, including thirteen-month-old Leona, Mattie Barlow "had no choice but to come back to the hills, to her family" in Tula (Leona Barlow Brown interview). Mattie was a strong, independent woman whom Leona described as "a mighty good manager to have raised all of us on that old clay farm." Mattie also looked after her father during those years, and at his death, her siblings agreed that she should inherit his 106 acres in the Tula area. Later in life, Mattie wrote a regular column on news from Tula for the *Oxford Eagle* and authored at least one historical article on the town, probably in the early 1950s. According to her cousin, Jenny Wilson, Mattie was "a very eloquent writer." Years later, Leona Brown wrote a brief prose poem, "Mama," in tribute to her mother:

> She greatly influenced
> My life. Her motto was "Do
> Unto others as you would have
> Them do unto you." She loved
> Her church, and attended at every
> Opportunity. She supported
> Her children in whatever
> They attempted to do.

The Brown family, too, had deep roots in Lafayette County. Larry Brown's great-great-grandfather, Confederate lieutenant Samuel L. Paschall (1839–1862), died of disease during the war and was buried in Richmond, Virginia ("Discipline" 189). The Paschalls had come to Lafayette County from South Carolina between 1838 and 1842 and had intermarried with the Green, Brown, and Watts families. Larry's grandfather, Max Watts Brown (1895–1964), fought in World War I "at some tender age"; a photo of Max from that time sat on Larry's desk. Samuel Paschall's daughter, Anna (1862–1933), married the Alabama-born James Oren Brown (1858–1942), and together they had seven children, including Larry's grandfather, Max Watts Brown, who was raised in Tula. Max married a fellow Tula resident, Vera Sharp (1898–1984), in 1919, and the couple's four children included Willis Knox Brown (1922–1968), Larry's father. After running a store in the Old Dallas area of Lafayette County, Max Brown moved to Memphis, where he spent the rest of his life. Vera took the children and left Max but never divorced him: Larry Brown wrote to Edgerton in 1990, "Max lost his family due to his drinking like Daddy lost his, but I hope I don't continue the tradition" (Edgerton Papers).

While in the first grade at the elementary school in Tula, Knox Brown began to pass notes to Leona Barlow; however, Leona recalled, "Knox was mean. He got in a fight with the principal, who expelled him from school." Knox subsequently attended school in Yocona, but he continued to write notes to Leona. By the time Knox joined the U.S. Army in 1941, he and Leona were informally engaged. Leona refused to wear his ring, however: "I wanted to get married before he left; he said, 'No,' that he might come back without any arms and legs." Leona spent the war years working in an Oxford five-and-dime, riding into town with the mailman on Fridays, and briefly taught in Tula's elementary school. Leona and Knox corresponded regularly throughout the war, and after he returned physically unharmed in 1945, the couple married. The newlyweds settled in Potlockney, located about twelve miles outside Oxford, near Tula. Knox Brown Jr. was born on 12 December 1947, followed by Joy on 30 June 1949, William Larry on 9 July 1951, and Darrell on 3 February 1953.

Knox Brown's experiences in World War II had dramatic and traumatic effects on both him and his son. Larry wrote that his father "had been an infantry soldier for four years, had fought at the Battle of the Bulge, had fought with his division all the way across Europe, had been at Berlin when it fell, had been wounded physically only once. It's taken me a long time to understand this, but it left emotional scars on him that were never to heal. He would never mention the war when he was sober, but when he was drinking, which was frequent in the years of my growing up, he would begin to talk about it, about the horrors he had seen, and he would eventually break down" (Brown Collections). Knox Brown told his son "terrible, frightening things about the friends he had seen killed, and the cold they fought in, and the overwhelming amount of death he had seen on both sides. My mother told me once that shortly after they married, he woke her up in the middle of the night while he was having a horrible nightmare, thinking he was back in it again, fighting in hand-to-hand combat with bayonets and gunstocks. He had never once talked about that particular skirmish, because it must have been one of his most fearsome memories" (Brown Collections). In 1994, Brown recalled that his father "went through some heavy shit in the war. . . . It was tough for him. . . . He was a good man. I know he never really got over the war. His experience was so fucking incredible, he couldn't shake it" (Steven Campbell 8). After his father's death, Larry enjoyed reading Knox's wartime letters to Leona: "It was just neat to see those letters that had come across from Europe to her, to know that they were dating, going together. This was a long time before I ever was" (Rankin, "On" 95). Knox Brown's war souvenirs also made a deep impression on his son: Larry recalled, "We have his bible that he carried with him. . . . He had German rings, photos, a silver cigarette case, a Solingen switchblade" (Edgerton Papers). In addition, the family "had a piece of pink granite that [Knox] chipped out of Hitler's actual fireplace with his bayonet" (RS).

The Brown family's first home in Potlockney "was really just a little shack, and there are still plenty of little shacks very similar to it scattered around the countryside [around Yocona]. Just small unpainted houses with chimneys of poorly laid bricks, and tin on the roofs, and chickens in the yards" (Brown Collections).

Even in Larry's early years, the family's lack of money and his father's alcoholism posed constant problems. Brown's mother related to him an incident that had occurred when Larry was a baby and she was pregnant with his younger brother:

> Mother and Daddy had saved ten dollars toward her doctor bills, and one night he went out and bought a bottle of whiskey with it, and came in drunk. . . . I can imagine her grief and her outrage. . . . She took the bottle and broke it over the table, spilling the whiskey everywhere. He took handkerchiefs and soaked up the whiskey, recapturing some of it so that he could strain it through the cloth and drink at least a little of it.
>
> I've never forgotten that story. It's the epitome of desperation, in what must have been a desperate time in their lives. One of the questions about human nature that interests me is how people bear up under monstrous calamity, all the terrible things that can befall them. I believe in the resilience of the human spirit while I understand that some do break under stress. (Brown Collections)

The family lived in Lafayette County until Brown was three years old, when his "father took us away from Mississippi . . . because he couldn't make it sharecropping. He worked at Fruehauf Trailer Company [in Memphis] for a long time. Then he painted houses some and worked at the Mid-South Fair" (190). The family found life in Memphis little better than life in Mississippi, although Leona recalled receiving considerable help from family members: "Knox's mother was [living in Memphis], and a sister and a brother, and I had a sister up there who helped me tremendously. . . . [I]f she hadn't helped me, there would have been a lot of days when I couldn't have gone to work. The kids were sick, ill, whatever. I [worked] and [Knox] didn't, just very seldom." Larry Brown, too, remembered that his father often was unemployed during the family's time in Memphis: "The solution to him taking his paycheck on Friday and being drunk the whole weekend, even spending or losing the grocery money, had been not to work at all. . . . My mother supported us all" (Brown Collections). Brown also described life in Memphis as "a series of rented houses. . . . We lived in one place until we couldn't pay the rent, and then we moved to another place.

Memphis was full of streets and houses, full of schools" (*LS* 3). Larry certainly contributed to the family disorder, as he wrote to his editor, Shannon Ravenel, in 1989: "I used to make my little brother so mad he'd chase me with a knife with snot running out of his nose. Shot him in the butt with a BB gun one day, cut his hair while Mama was gone to work" (Algonquin Files).

In the early 1990s, Brown wrote to Edgerton that "most of my early life was fear. I know that sounds bad, but it was bad. [Knox Brown] picked up our television one time and threw it completely through a window. And you know how big and heavy TVs were back then. I don't know how many cars he wrecked. A bunch. One burned. He got drunk one time and blew up some fucking rubbers, laughing like hell. My grandmother, his mother, had a goddam fit. We didn't know what they were. I remember him sitting on the bed, blowing them until they busted, laughing his ass off. She couldn't do anything with him. Nobody could. He used to sit in the kitchen of our old house and shoot mice with a BB gun. I loved him so much, but I'll never be as scared of anything in my life as I was of my daddy" (Edgerton Papers). According to Mary Annie Brown, the drunken Knox frequently "went after" Larry, and his siblings tried "to hide Larry to keep [Knox] from hurting Larry. The kids had to run across the streets of Memphis in their pajamas with [Knox] drunk coming after Larry." Larry remembered "weekends of drunken madness and terror." He saw his father "in handcuffs and in patrol cars more than once. I can remember the excitement in my mother's voice each time he promised to quit [drinking]. I can see myself in nothing but my pajamas when I was seven or eight running down the sidewalk, running away from him barefooted because we feared for our lives. Nobody seemed to be able to do anything with him. Nobody seemed to be able to make our world any better" (Brown Collections). And what Brown saw "within my own family when I was a child made deep and lasting impressions on me" (*LS* 3).

Nevertheless, Larry loved his father, whom he believed "did not set out to be mean and drunk and cruel to us" (Brown Collections), and had other, more positive memories of his father and his childhood: "I was always building stuff, building stuff out of wood. He was always trying to help me, show me the right way to build something. I can remember getting aggravated with him and wishing that he'd go and leave me alone. I wanted to do it myself; I didn't want somebody to do it for me. I wanted to saw the stuff and get the nails and all. He'd always have to show me where I was going wrong" (Rankin, "On" 93). Another bright spot was the Memphis Boys Club, which offered an annual Halloween party and classes in art and pottery making, among other entertainments. Brown participated in the club's wrestling and gymnastic teams (Rankin, "On" 93) and proudly attended its annual father-son dinners.

Leona Brown served as a positive counterpart to her war-damaged husband, keeping the family together. In Memphis she made sure that all of her children attended school, driving them there every morning. Because Knox was so often unemployed, Leona Brown held a number of jobs during these years, working at Katz Drugstore on Lamar Street and at the Camp Electric Company near Sun Records, among other places.

Despite his mother's efforts, Larry Brown found himself discontented with life in Memphis, with the sound of trains on nearby tracks, the houses built too close together, and the lack of woods and streams for hunting and fishing: "It's one thing to have a life in a place, and to be happy in it is quite another" (BRF 10). Brown also regretted that he "couldn't have a dog in Memphis, couldn't have one on the city street up there. Just out of the question" (Rankin, "On" 96). But Brown also had positive memories of city life—"the freedom of impossibly long summer days, steel skates, cops on motorcycles, Elvis Presley, the Fairgrounds" ("Writing"). Brown also had a paper route for five years in Memphis.

Life in the Tennessee city also helped to shape Brown's views on African Americans. His mother recalled that at the time, "there were no blacks in Memphis schools." But one African American father, a lawyer, "was determined his little boy was going" to attend the previously all-white Peabody School, where the Brown children were enrolled. The boy was admitted, but he was so afraid that white kids would steal his lunch money that "he would put his money down in his shoes. . . . Larry was just so disturbed about that. [He wondered] why they would do all that."

In both Memphis and Mississippi, Larry Brown and his siblings were avid readers. Brown told Dorie LaRue that he had "always been a big reader all my life"; from the time he was "a little kid," reading was "one of the main pleasures I had in life" (40). He "started reading way before I went to school" (*RS*). Brown often recounted both his mother's passion for reading and her desire to build her children's enthusiasm for it. She was "big on reading. She passed it on to all of us and we picked it up real early." She read "old trashy novels once in a while [and] a lot of romance stuff, those little thin paperbacks you see. She had boxes and boxes of stuff. She read the Bible a lot, too. She read a lot of magazines. Whenever she was sitting down—if she wasn't cooking or ironing or washing or something, taking care of us—when she was sitting down, she was reading something" (Rankin, "On" 92). Leona Brown confirmed her son's assessment: "When we lived in Memphis, we were just a short distance from the library up there, so as soon as they all started school, they got their library cards, and we went once a week and got books. And everybody read. All my children. And we still do" (*RS*).

Knox Brown, conversely, read little. Larry recalled that he never saw his father read anything other than a newspaper and that the older man "didn't like to be around anybody who was reading. I can remember [Leona] sitting there in a chair reading a magazine, as he walked into the room, she'd pull up the cushion and hide the magazine 'cause she knew it'd aggravate him" (LaRue 40). On another occasion, Larry shared his belief that his father did not think "very much of reading. And I *might* even go so far as to say he thought it was not too good a thing to be doing" (*RS*). Said Leona Brown, "My husband did not want me to sit around and read. He could not stand it."

Despite her husband's objections, Leona encouraged her children to follow her reading habits: "When they learned to read, they realized what you could learn, what you could memorize and keep within yourself. What you read. You know, you don't ever forget when you see the printed word. You may hear something and it goes in one ear and out the other, but when you read it, you've got it. It stays with you" (*RS*). She also believed that reading helped keep Larry and his siblings out of trouble: "When they were children, they stayed at home. They were not allowed to roam around anywhere while I was at work. [Reading] was a good pastime for them. Kept them from fighting a good bit, too, all four of them like that" (*RS*). As his mother had hoped, reading opened up new horizons for Larry: "My mother instilled the love of reading in me early as well as in my brothers and sister. For this, among other things, I am eternally grateful to her. What she allowed me to see was that there were other worlds that existed far beyond. . . . [A]ll you had to do was sit down and open a book. . . . There was another world inside books that was always waiting, one where children fought the campaigns, and men fought bulls or great fish or the Blue fought the Gray. . . . The library was full of books like that. You could have as many as you wanted as long as you brought them back in two weeks or maybe three. It was a pretty good deal for a kid who needed to be somewhere else in his mind a lot of the time" ("Writing").

Larry Brown's informal education further expanded when he was about ten years old and his mother bought the family a set of encyclopedias: "I actually read a lot of literature without knowing what I was doing because Mother bought a set of encyclopedias and there was a set of ten classics that came with it. There was Edgar Allan Poe and Mark Twain, and Zane Grey, and Herman Melville, and *Grimms' Fairy Tales*, and Greek mythology, the *Iliad* and the *Odyssey*, and Jack London. That's eventually what brought me to writing—loving to read" (Bonetti et al. 235–36). Reading the *Iliad* and the *Odyssey* "got me thinking in terms of myths and dreams; I was really into Greek mythology, all the battles and gods, what each one did and what each one was responsible for. They formed the core of my belief about storytelling" (Ketchin, "Interview" 138). In addition to such classics, Larry read "boy-and-dog stories, like James Street's *Good-bye, My Lady* and Jim Kjelgaard books about dogs, like *Big Red*. Books about hunting dogs, about labs, bird dogs, and cat hounds. Fred Gipson's *Old Yeller*, *Savage Sam*. Anything that was about hunting and dogs, I was really into that. And I liked, and still do like, a lot of stuff about Westerns, about cowboys and Indians and all that" (Rankin, "On" 92). Another book that made a deep impression on Brown was William Faulkner's *Big Woods*: "I read every word of it, not even knowing that he was already dead, or anything about the legacy of work he had left behind him, or even that he was from Oxford. But I remember right now how I felt when I read how the big bear's track slowly filled with water and went out of sight, like the huge old bass the boy had seen in a pool slowly recede into the depths without any motion of his fins. I didn't know then that I wanted to be a writer. . . . Mr. Faulkner to me is like a great god sitting out there somewhere, high above" (Brown Collections). But the book that Brown described as the most influential in his boyhood was the Bible, because of the emphasis that his mother put on religion (Rankin, "On" 92). He "was raised in the Methodist church in Memphis. That's where all my cousins, aunts, and uncles went" (Ketchin, "Interview" 130). He went to church "every Sunday and prayer meeting on Wednesday night, Methodist Youth Fellowship on Sunday evenings" (Rankin, "On" 92).

Brown's childhood exposure to other cultural media was limited: "I never saw a real play that I can remember as a child. We had music, though. Even my daddy liked Hank Williams, and we listened to Marty Robbins, Elvis Presley. We had no art in the house. I liked to draw and did it pretty well, but quit. I learned to play the violin, but I'm left-handed and they tried to force me to play it right-handed, so I never had a chance at that. . . . But I don't remember much culture in my early life besides *The Lawrence Welk Show* on Saturday nights" (Day 191). That early exposure gave Brown what became a lifelong love of music, which, his wife later recalled, "was in his blood." Late in his life, Brown wrote that he had bought his "first little cheapie guitar on credit" in the early 1980s. Twenty years later, he was "still just a three-chord player, but the firsthand realization of the difficulty encountered in trying to learn how to progress in musical skills only makes me even more in awe of somebody who can get up on the stage any night he wants to and make his guitar sing anything he wants it to" ("Whole" 98).

Movies also played a role in Brown's childhood. His favorite movie as a boy was *Shane*; he saw it for the first time in Memphis as a reward for being "a safety patrol boy" (Rankin, "On" 92). Despite the growing popularity of television in American homes of the 1950s, Brown's family did not have one while living in Memphis, although young Larry sometimes got to watch while visiting his paternal grandmother's home: "The first television I remember watching was one my grand-mother had, a big, old cabinet about four feet high, but the picture tube was only about twelve inches in diameter and it was round. The whole thing was full of tubes; you had to turn it on and let it warm up" (Rankin, "On" 92).

Brown found relief from life in Memphis during summer vacation visits with his maternal grandmother in Tula. Mattie Barlow let each of Leona's children come in turn, and Larry and his siblings enjoyed the visits immensely: "It was always our favorite thing to do, to come down here and get to stay about a week, take a vacation and come down here" (Rankin, "On" 92–93). In addition to providing enjoyment, these visits reinforced Brown's Methodism: his grandmother and ex-tended family "were all big on" religion and the church (Rankin, "On" 92).

Visits to Tula also provided Brown with the opportunity to listen to stories told by community elders at the local store: "I grew up around a lot of old people, which I think is a big advantage. They tell such great stories. I used to talk to all these men up here at Tula. . . . They used to talk about World War I" (Rankin, "On" 94). From Norman Clark, who owned the store in Tula, as well as Brown's father and his father's friend, Paul Coleman, young Larry heard stories about World War II. When the subject turned to hunting or fishing, Larry and the other boys would chime in. Mattie Barlow "could also tell good stories" (Rankin, "On" 95). These conversations probably stimulated an essay that Brown wrote while in fifth or sixth grade "about a trip down here to Mississippi. . . . That's probably the earliest attempt I can remem-ber to write anything. But I never had any active desire to pursue it" (Rankin, "On" 93).

The Brown family's time in Memphis ended in 1964 when relations between Knox Brown and his wife and children reached a critical point: Larry Brown remembered, "My mother finally had to choose between him and us. He finally succeeded in driving away my older brother who was about fifteen then. He hitchhiked nearly a hundred miles to Mis-sissippi, and he swore that he would not come back as long as my fa-ther was there. Some relatives of ours took him in, and my mother had to decide, and in a few days we were on our way back to Mississippi, and we left [his father] behind in Memphis" (Brown Collections). The family began its "new life on our own in Tula" (Brown Collections), which at the time had about 150 people, a store, two churches, and a high school (*BRF* 15). Larry was thirteen years old.

Knox Brown Sr. soon followed the family back to Mississippi, where Leona Brown met with him without her children's knowledge. She and her children began to discuss the possibility of reuniting the family. Knox Jr. rejected the idea of allowing his father to return, while Larry at first was "undecided": "I had lived in fear of him for most of my life, and now that fear was gone. I had a dog for the first time, and woods and fields and creeks to explore, and places to fish. What I had was a whole new world, the Mississippi world I had wanted to go back to all my life. I was afraid if we took him back, things would be better for a while and then they would revert to the way they had been before. Finally my vote was no. I loved my father, as children will even when they are being abused, but I remembered the weekend my brother left. It had been the worst of all, and it wasn't that far in the past" (Brown Collections). Over both sons' objections, Leona took back her husband. Larry spent the evening of Knox Sr.'s return in the woods: "I knew it was probably hurting my father, but I couldn't face him yet, and I knew that if they tried to come after me, all I had to do was melt away into the woods, and stay there until he was gone" (Brown Collections). Knox stopped drinking, found a job at the Chambers Stove Factory in Oxford, and bought a car; Larry got a gun and spent his nights "roaming the woods with dogs and a flashlight, climbing trees, crossing rivers, completely happy for the first time in my life" (Brown Collections).

The reunited family's happy rural life was cut short when Knox Brown Sr. began drinking again: according to Larry, "He didn't come home one Friday afternoon, and we knew it had started again. The promises were quickly made again, and just as quickly broken, and it was only a short time before the law was involved in our lives again. . . . [T]he law was dispatched to pick him up one night for being drunk" (Brown Collections). The situation simmered until Knox Brown had a horrific argument with his oldest son: according to Larry, "My brother took an old single barreled shotgun of mine, put a shell in it, cocked it and put it in my father's face and told him he would kill him if he didn't stop this madness. It worked. My father got sober and stayed sober until his death April 19, 1968." The image of that confrontation remained "forever etched" in Larry Brown's memory (Brown Collections).

Even with her husband employed, Leona Brown continued to work outside the family's home: "I got off at twenty minutes to six at Sears and [Knox] got off at 4:30. Well, he had supper cooked every night. [Their children] were all sitting on the couch when I walked in the door. They had their T-shirts on—they weren't allowed to go to the table without a T-shirt on—and their hands washed and their hair combed. And when I walked in the door they rose and were headed for the kitchen. I didn't hardly have time to wash my hands before they were at the table ready to eat."

Knox Sr.'s death ended this brief period of order in the Brown household and traumatized Larry: "I think my father dying when I was 16 probably had a lot to do with my attitude. I think when that happened my world pretty much fell apart and changed. He was sitting at the breakfast table early one morning, I guess around six o'clock. He had to be at work at seven at Chambers. Me and my brother woke up, or I woke up, and there was nobody in the house. I asked my little brother, Darrell, where everybody was, and he said that Daddy had gotten sick and they had to take him to the hospital. It was only just a few moments until Mother and Knox, Jr., and Joy all rode up in the car. She came in the house and said, 'Boys, I got some mighty bad news for you. Daddy had a heart attack and died at six o'clock this morning.' When that happened all kinds of things happened. You got this figure that's the head of your household, depend on him, look up to him, and in a flash, he's gone" (Rankin, "On" 96–97). On another occasion, Brown recalled that with his father's death, "the world changed suddenly on me in an unthinkable way" (Day 192).

Despite Knox Brown Sr.'s flaws, Leona Brown truly loved him, as Larry recognized. In *A Late Start*, he wrote, "I remember what my mother said at his funeral—that she was so proud to have been his wife. Her love for him, even in the face of what she lived with in her marriage to him of a little over twenty years, is a testament to the strength of the human spirit, and maybe my early life is why I write so many things about drinking and trouble and violence. I know those things well, and I don't have to imagine what life with them is like" (3). Larry also remembered the huge crowd that gathered at his father's memorial service: "The church wouldn't hold half the people at his funeral" (Edgerton Papers).

Soon after the family's return to Mississippi, Larry's great-uncle had given the fourteen-year-old a twelve-gauge single-barreled shotgun (*BRF* 13). Knox Brown Sr. never hunted, probably because he had seen too much killing in World War II. But, Larry remembered, after his father's death, the older men in Tula "put their heads together . . . and came up with a plan to educate me in the fine points of guns and dogs" (*BRF* 16). Larry became particularly close to two of these men, Ontis Mize and Sam Jones. Larry's son, Billy Ray Brown, remembered seeing his father cry only three times, one of which was at Jones's funeral.

After moving back to Mississippi, Larry and his siblings attended school in Yocona, which they found quite different from the Memphis city schools. Joy Brown came home one day and reported to her mother that there was a hole in the school floor. In 1965, Lafayette County opened a new consolidated high school, to which it admitted black students. The four Brown children graduated from this new school. Larry Brown always spoke disparagingly of his high school years, often attributing his lack of interest in school to his father's death or to his passion for hunting, which formed "a major part" of Larry's life "from the time I was 14 until I married and raised a family, probably from 1964 until about the late 80s. . . . It was a major influence on my growing up" (Rankin, "On" 96). In addition, he worked to help support his family: "The first job I ever had was chopping cotton for $4 a day from six to six. Hour for lunch. Later I picked it for two cents a pound. I started working in a grocery store when I was about fourteen or fifteen" (Day 190).

One of Brown's first friends at Lafayette High School was Lynn Hewlett, a seventh-grader from Taylor, Mississippi, who was a year behind Brown. When Yocona and Taylor had separate high schools, they were intense rivals, but after the schools united, Hewlett said, Brown "was one of the guys who crossed over pretty quick. It didn't take him but a little while." The teenaged Larry was

> a little old wiry tough guy, but he was friendly and it didn't take him long to make friends. To a lot of people, he was quiet, and I could see how people thought he was quiet. He was one of those guys who didn't do a lot of excess talking. He didn't just babble for the fun of it. If he said something, it usually meant something. . . . He was thinking all the time.
>
> He had a sense of humor and a little way about talking, just his mannerisms, the way the talked. It always tickled the fool out of me, just listening to him. He had this little dry wit that, if you didn't know him, you wouldn't even hardly know what he was talking about.
>
> He was never bad about talking about people in a negative way, but if somebody had kind of got on his raw side, sometimes he'd say some kind of little remark that they wouldn't even understand. It would just be gouging the devil out of them, and they wouldn't even realize what he had said. That rascal had a whale of a sense of humor.

On one occasion, Hewlett, Brown, and a third friend, Mike Foster, decided to help along the courtship between two older local residents. The boys went out and painted "Wilbur loves Dorothy" on the side of the old Tula schoolhouse, dangling Brown by his feet from the roof to do the painting.

Though Hewlett remembered Larry's mother "very, very well," he could not remember seeing Knox Sr. "more than once or twice. At that time, you didn't quiz people—I was raised to keep my mouth shut. I always knew there was something going on there, but you didn't ask about it. . . . I saw a picture of his daddy somewhere right after he passed away and, had the man still been alive, I don't know whether I would have recognized him."

Brown's high school grades were average at best; for example, he received a B+ in English during his freshman year, but his grades in the subject dropped to a B– the following year and a D as a junior. As a senior, he failed the course: he "loved reading and had all my life, but I didn't see how English was going to help me get a job after I got out of school, which was all I wanted to do" (*LS* 4). He earned similar grades in other classes, including a B- in typing, although he subsequently put that skill to great use. Brown believed that "the only reason I even passed the 11th grade" was that "a little old girl, my teacher, a first year teacher just out of college, felt sorry for me" because of his father's death that year (Rankin, "On" 97). The F in English meant that Brown "didn't graduate with the rest of my class. Very, very bad on my mother. She had already given me my class ring, and people had given graduation presents, and all that. . . . I was pretty crushed about that, but it was my own fault. Been studying by myself, and my term paper on deer hunting got an F. Most of the time I stayed out in the woods, out with my dogs coonhunting, when I should have been home doing my homework" (LaRue 55–56). Nevertheless, IQ tests showed his intelligence to be above average. Brown attributed his poor performance as a student to "a combination of losing my father when I was sixteen and never having any interest in school to begin with. The only interest I had was in getting out of school, getting a job and buying a car, because I didn't have any way to go anywhere. I always had to catch rides with somebody else. I was just itching to get out on my own and start making a living. I didn't think the future looked very bright at that point anyway because the [Vietnam] war was going on. It was so bad, and all the boys I grew up with were worrying about it. We'd already had some friends who'd gone over and been killed. I pretty much knew that I was going to have to go into the service at the height of the Vietnam War. I didn't have any long range plans. I didn't see too much reason to worry a whole lot about what happened in school" (Bonetti et al. 236–37).

According to Hewlett, however, Brown was not as poor a student as he always claimed: the two teenagers "were kind of alike, I guess. All I was looking for was to get by, and he was, too. . . . I think he could have been a good student if he had wanted to be." Moreover, Hewlett believes that Brown never knew how intelligent he was: "I don't think he would have ever admitted that in public, or maybe even to himself."

In March 1990, Brown's twelfth-grade English teacher, Glenda Lester wrote him a letter, identifying herself as "a voice from the past": "I have been following your career as a literary genius—in spite of the fact that you failed high school English. I like to think that if I had passed you, you would not have worked so hard to get where you are today" (Brown Collections).

Brown retook English in summer school, earned a B, and received his diploma on 11 July 1969. He had no desire to attend college, and his family did not encourage him. In 1988, Brown recalled that he had done no writing at all before 1980 other than "stuff your teacher wanted you to write" (Pettus, *Conversations* 3). The idea of becoming a writer had "never crossed" his mind (LaRue 40).

CHAPTER TWO

Marine, Husband, Father, and Fireman, 1969–1980

At eighteen, just out of school, and only partly educated, Larry Brown had little to look forward to other than being sent to Vietnam. While waiting for the draft to catch up with him, Brown got a job at the Chambers Stove Factory in Oxford, where he remained for a year and a half. He underwent the mandatory physical exam for military service, was classified 1-A, and had his name entered into the lottery for draftees, which was based on potential soldiers' dates of birth. In 1970, according to Brown, "my birthday came up number one. . . . So the lady who ran the draft board called my mother and she told her, she said, 'Now Larry's got about two weeks before the army drafts him, he's gone you know, so if he wants to join another branch like the Navy or the Air Force or the Marines, he'd better do it now.' And I just decided that since I was going to have to go anyway, I'd join the Marines. I figured they were about the toughest thing going. That's what I wanted to join" (Pettus, "Interview" 10). He knew little about the marines until after he joined and began training, but he did know that he could sign up for two years rather than the four that the army required. After he made his choice, the marines "came to my house and signed me up. They made house calls back then" (Watkins 2D). In "Discipline," Brown recalled, "Like a dumb ass I joined up before Christmas and got to spend it" in basic training at Parris Island, South Carolina. His "only solace was Jesus and the church services we were allowed to attend" (180).

He found basic training far more grueling than he had expected and even at times cruel and sadistic, later describing it as "like serious camp for adults" ("Discipline" 177). Recruits learned to fire M60 machine guns, to throw hand grenades, to use dynamite to kill, to fight with knives, and to kill a man "by crushing his larynx through an ingenious use of your elbows and forearms and hands" (177). Off-duty marines constantly fought among themselves and with men serving in the other military branches. Much of the tension was racial, pitting blacks, whites, Indians, and Hispanics against each other. When the situation became intolerable in 1972, Brown recalled, the "commandant ordered every enlisted man in the entire Corps to start taking human relations classes, where we sat down in classrooms and faced each other, black and white and red and brown, and talked about what pissed us off the most about each other" (185).

The drill instructor of Brown's platoon fit the stereotypes about marine sergeants. A Vietnam veteran, he was tough, fit, and able to "put fear into your heart. . . . He'd get right up in your face telling you what a miserable piece of human work you were and you couldn't say anything" (Brown, "Discipline" 178). Instructors and the training itself reduced all recruits to the same basic inferior status with the goal of breaking them down to build them back up. Once broken, Brown and the other recruits learned "the fine art of killing. How to conduct warfare as well as ceremony, and administer large doses of discipline" (178).

The training included rope climbing as well as scrubbing the floor of the barracks every morning, with Brown and the other men on their hands and knees using hand brushes. Brown persevered because he could not endure the shame of going home in disgrace: "I knew I was there until it was over. Whatever it took to stay" ("Discipline" 182). On one occasion, a drill instructor told Brown that his gun was dirty and "slapped that damn thing out of my hands. It hit the ground, hit the sights, the trigger guard, all that shit. And that's the only time I ever felt like trying to break. Just 'cause it hurt me that he had so little regard for *my* weapon that I had tried to keep so clean and care for like a baby" (Rankin, "On" 97).

Many of Brown's fellow recruits could not take the pressure: Brown's platoon started with seventy-five men but graduated only thirty-two (Dees, "Rough Road" 12). Only later did Brown realize the importance

of marine discipline: "I can see now that the [drill instructors] had a
job to do. If some goober from Mississippi broke down weeping at a little verbal harassment in South Carolina, what the hell would he do in a
firefight in Southeast Asia with incoming bullets ripping the shrubs to
shreds" ("Discipline" 182); nevertheless, Brown always looked back on
his time at Parris Island as a negative experience: "Man that was a bad
place, there. That's where you don't want to go" (Pettus, "Interview"
10).

In the summer of 1971, after completing his training, Brown went to
Camp Lejeune in North Carolina as part of a guard company (Brown,
"Discipline" 183). Riding around the post in a Jeep, he "carried a 12
gauge pump shotgun and .45s, checked doors, roads, buildings, walking a post for four hours at a stretch with an M-14, big heavy bastard
that weighed eleven pounds, rested and wrote letters between shifts,
drank beer, read" (185). Even while he was in the marines, reading remained "one of my favorite things to do. Whatever base I was on I
went to the library, man, and got me some books. Yeah. Sure did" (RS).

Brown never felt that he became a good marine, calling himself a
"shit bird," corps slang for anyone who could not quite make it: "I just
couldn't help being a shit bird. I didn't want to be a shit bird. I tried
not to be one. I ran. I lifted weights and shined my boots, but none
of my inspections were completely good. I could spit shine fine, but I
couldn't make up that bunk exactly the way they wanted me to. I could
get my rifle clean, but then I'd display my underwear the wrong way.
I was never on time for 4 A.M. mess duty, not one single time in two
weeks, and kept getting yelled at by the cooks. The shit bird just lived
in me" ("Discipline" 185).

In addition, Brown found life at Lejeune extremely dull: "We had
no wheels, we couldn't get out of town, we couldn't get any women"
("Discipline" 188). The high point of his stay in North Carolina was
a visit to his paternal aunt, Maxine Caudle; her husband, Julian; and
their daughter, Cathy, in Columbia, South Carolina. The Caudles took
him to Myrtle Beach, where he swam in the ocean for the first time:
"We had cold beer and they fed me well. I spent that good weekend
with them, and then went back to Lejeune to walk some more posts
and wrote more letters to friends and family back home, trying to save

a little money to send to my mother who needed it badly, since she was trying to get my little brother into college so that he could stay out of the shit I was already in" (186). The visit was important not only to Brown but also to his aunt, who wrote to him in 1988, "I'll never forget your visit when you were stationed in NC. It meant lots to me that you made the time to come see us" (Brown Collections).

Brown and others at Lejeune were waiting for permanent orders. Most of the men hoped to be sent to the Mediterranean; few expected to be sent to Vietnam, where the war was winding down, and in fact only four or five men from his training platoon went (Bonetti et al. 237). According to Brown, when the government starts "withdrawing troops, they withdraw the Marines first. So nobody much out of my platoon" saw action in Southeast Asia (Shoup and Denman 88). Early in the fall of 1971, Brown was ordered to report to the marine barracks in Philadelphia. Brown described it as "the oldest post in the Corps. It's where they were founded in 1775 at Tun Tavern. It was dress blues duty, white cap and gloves, all spit and polish, all pomp and ceremony like the ads on TV" ("Discipline" 188). Before heading to Philadelphia, Brown took a thirty-day leave, flying home for a reunion with family and friends. He felt like something of a hero on the flight home, since he "could smoke on the plane while . . . having cocktails, and the stewardesses liked Marines in their snazzy uniforms and bright shoes, and would sit on the armrest of your seat with their good legs rubbing up against you and talk to you" (189).

Brown enjoyed his return to Mississippi, catching up with his family and friends. In addition, he recalled, "I squirrel hunted all the time I was home. One golden uninterrupted month of beautiful fall. My old friend Sam Jones and I went out and killed fox squirrels and grays every day" ("Discipline" 189). Brown and his friends spent their evenings in the way Brown always preferred, driving the sandy back roads, listening to music, and drinking beer. When he returned to duty, he left with the feeling that it "was okay to be a soldier" (190). He "was ready to go rejoin the herd, maybe stay with them forever" (190).

In Philadelphia, Brown met wounded Vietnam vets being treated at the veterans' hospital: "We had this NCO club behind our barracks, next to the mess hall where we ate. That's where I spent just about all my off-time because I didn't have a car when I was up there. Didn't have much to do. It was a huge Navy base, but the Marine contingent was very small—a couple of hundred Marines or so. We did guard duty and that kind of stuff. But there were all these boys who were attached to the Fourth Naval hospital there. They had all lost limbs in Vietnam. They were all in wheelchairs" (Stroup and Denman 85).

In Philadelphia, Brown also met John B. Edmiston, who "took an immediate liking to Larry; he was an imminently likeable guy. In the Marines, we all called Larry 'Mudcat,' actually short for 'Mississippi Mudcat,' and Mudcat is the only name by which I heard him referred." Edmiston recalled that Brown took some ribbing about his accent, but by and large, "the Marine Corps was a place that valued a guy for his 'cool' and his competence and toughness, and Larry had all 3." However, according to Edmiston, he and the other marines who had not been sent to Vietnam "were ashamed of our lack of battle scars. . . . We were ashamed enough to talk about it. We did feel like 'shitbirds.'" The first time Brown and Edmiston had liberty together, Brown drank so much alcohol that he "got sick and threw up. He was so ashamed of himself and apologized profusely to us." In one of Brown's unpublished novels, "Mama's Waiting," the narrator recalls his time in the marines in Philadelphia, no doubt drawing on Brown's experiences: "Marine Barracks Philadelphia is the oldest post in the Corps, and it looks it. I spent a weary thirteen months up there, marching in parades and christening ships, wearing dress blues for special occasions, mostly getting shitfaced at Tun Tavern II. It was our own personal bar right behind the barracks and you could get a beer for a quarter. Mixed drinks were fifty-five cents. Needless to say, you can throw a cheap drunk in there. I threw one almost every night" (Brown Collections).

Edmiston also recalled an occasion when some Turkish soldiers came to train at the barracks: "Someone conceived of the idea of staging arm wrestling contests between Marines and Turks, and whichever side won got drinks bought for it by the losing side. Competitors were matched based on relative weights. The Marines won every contest, and so we drank for free that night, compliments of the Turkish Armed Forces. Larry and the rest of us enjoyed that very much. . . . [O]nly a couple of the Turks spoke English, so they had to interpret for both groups. Larry was not allowed to ask questions because the Turks who spoke English had a hard time understanding him. . . . When he was embarrassed, as on that occasion, he'd get a grin on his face and his dimple would stick out. We teased him about that, too."

Brown's years in the marines ended on a sour note, however, after he got into a barroom brawl.

What they got me for was I got in a fistfight with a bunch of Puerto Rican sailors. The damn fight was over with I reckon and we's all standing out there.

All these sailor boys come running by, and somebody said something I don't know what it was.

But one of 'em just reached out—great big ole tall guy—and hit me right in the damn nose just as square and hard as he could hit me, man. Almost knocked me down.

We chased 'em over to their damn barracks and was screaming for 'em to come out and fight. Called 'em chickenshit, motherfuckers, all that.

They later hung two of 'em for possession of marijuana. Our Admiral said, "No, no, no, you can't hang these people on American soil."

They said okay. Backed their damn boat out into the Delaware River and ran 'em up the damn yard arm and hung 'em and redocked.

Big thing over it. (Dees, "Rough Road" 12)

Brown's tour of duty ended in the fall of 1972, and he returned to Mississippi. As he looked back on his stint in the marines, Brown generally viewed it as a positive experience, telling Orman Day,

It was good for me. It gave me some discipline and let me know I could do things a lot of people couldn't do, because if you kept fucking up you were out of there. It was [also] the first time I ever saw reverse discrimination. This black sergeant looked at my admission papers the first night I was there and said: "You look like a backwoods motherfucker. Get yo ass to the back of the line." . . . It was a bad place to wake up in the morning. But I'm glad I went. It challenged me harder than anything ever had up to that time. I would've probably stayed in if I hadn't gotten into some trouble near the end of my enlistment that was none of my fault. There was a life there, but I decided it wasn't the one I wanted. I missed home too much. (193)

In late November 1972, Brown moved into his mother's trailer in Tula and returned to his job at the stove factory. On his first day home, he renewed his acquaintance with Mary Annie Coleman, whom he had first met when she was fourteen or fifteen: "She thought I was a smart-ass the first time she met me," which was right after he had been in a minor automobile accident. Brown and a friend, Danny Hipp, "were going to town one afternoon in my mother's car and I hit this wet curve . . . and spun out of control, spun in a ditch. I landed in his lap and blew out two tires." Mary Annie and her father, Preston Coleman, "came along to help me and I'd done called the wrecker and she thought I was getting smart with her daddy. And I said, 'It won't do any good to pull it because two of the tires are blown. The wrecker's on the way, but thank you anyway.' . . . She claims I got smart with her daddy" (RS).

Living in rural Mississippi, the Brown and Coleman families had known each other for many years. During the Great Depression, her father had sawed logs for his paternal grandfather for fifty cents a day. Preston Coleman and Knox Brown Sr. also had a long history together: on one occasion, Larry Brown recalled, the two men had gotten "in a fist fight down at Tula, drunk over a gambling debt or something. They used to be wild around here, have these gambling matches and they'd get to drinking and get in these fistfights. They'd all been good friends all their life, but they'd get in a fight and it would be over in five minutes" (Rankin, "On" 96).

Mary Annie and a friend who was also Brown's cousin went to visit Larry at his mother's trailer on his first day home. He was emptying his duffle bag but was too embarrassed to pull out his underwear in front of her (RS). By that time, Mary Annie was "eighteen and had great legs" (OF 66). She had graduated from Lafayette County High School while Larry was in the marines and was living with her parents on their sixty-acre Yocona farm. An only child, Mary Annie had grown up helping her father: "I was raised as a boy, just about, where Daddy had two tractors, and we farmed, and he was on one and I was on the other all summer long. In the morning we got up early, you went to the field, you did what had to be done, and you'd come home and you'd be so tired you'd eat your dinner and go to bed" (*RS*). Larry had similar recollections of Mary Annie's upbringing: "She used to run these cows around this place with a stick. And I think I can remember her driving this tractor up and down. . . . She'd get on that tractor and drive it just like a man when she was fourteen years old" (*RS*). Preston and Esther Lee Coleman were poor but loving: according to Mary Annie, "If my mother and I went somewhere, before the day was out my father was there because he wanted to be around us" (*RS*).

Larry and Mary Annie had their first date on New Year's Eve 1973 (*RS*). Less than nine months later, on 17 August 1974, twenty-three-year-old Larry Brown and nineteen-year-old Mary Annie Coleman married. According to Mary Annie, they had gotten engaged a few months earlier when he gave her a ring while they were sitting in a porch swing at her mother's house. Brown remembered the decision to get married somewhat differently: "Actually she proposed to me. Something like, 'Are you ready to get married?' or something like that. That was . . . in her daddy's living room" (*RS*). On the day of the wedding, Mary Annie "woke up at three o'clock in the morning . . . and started crying and cried until I walked down the aisle." One of the newlyweds' first purchases was a record album by Willie Nelson and a stereo system to play it on.

Despite their youth, the two had already forged a strong bond that would persist throughout their marriage in spite of the difficulties they encountered. Jonathan Miles, who viewed the Browns as surrogate parents, believes that Larry could not "function" without Mary Annie and that she "was the love of his life"; for her part, Mary Annie described herself as having "worshipped that man." She "fell totally in love with him, his wild side, because I was so different from him" (*RS*). At the time, she had no conception of what he would become: "I didn't marry Larry the writer. That came later" (*RS*). According to Miles, Mary Annie provided much-needed stability in Larry's life; he benefited not only from her love but also from her organizational, secretarial, and accounting skills. Miles believes that Mary Annie "put up with a lot because she adored him. . . . Sometimes he didn't deserve her; it was hard when she was sitting there at City Grocery drinking diet Cokes all night while he was saying, 'Just one more.'" But Larry could also be romantic: novelist Steve Yarbrough recalled that for one of the couple's anniversaries, Larry took Mary Annie out to a "pasture somewhere [at Tula] on a hill, and Mary Annie had no idea why they were going out there, and he had prepared this table with champagne and candles." When Larry was away from home, he always missed Mary Annie, and he preferred that she travel with him, in part because, as he admitted to Clyde Edgerton in December 1989, "I know I look at too many women. It's best for me to keep Mary Annie with me at all times, and that's what I've been trying to do lately" (Edgerton Papers). In October 1989, Larry wrote to Edgerton that Mary Annie "loves me, I know, more than any other woman ever will" (Edgerton Papers).

The Browns started out their marriage living with Mary Annie's parents, but Larry soon went out and bought a trailer so that he and his wife could have their own place on her parents' land. According to Mary Annie, Larry did not consult her before making the purchase: "He went and bought it, and I never did see it [until] after they brought it out here and set it up" (*RS*). After Preston Coleman's death in the mid-1970s, the Browns moved back into Mary Annie's family home with Esther Lee Coleman and her mother.

On 5 June 1975, Larry and Mary Annie welcomed their son, Billy Ray, into the world. A daughter, Delinah, followed two years later but died shortly after her birth. The loss profoundly affected Larry Brown: "When our baby died in 1977, I didn't think I would survive. It was a very rocky time . . . tough. . . . You never get over it" (Ketchin, "Interview" 129). The couple had two more children, Shane, born on 14 August 1979 (and named for the character in the movie Larry Brown had loved as a child), and LeAnne, born on 29 June 1982.

Larry Brown's wife and children were essential to his existence. Steve Yarbrough recalled, "Larry would kill for his family. Now like most of us, he may have had times when he wished he could crawl into a hole. But I never had the impression that he was trying to escape from his family." Billy Ray remembered his father as always busy:

even when Larry was at home, "he was doing something. He wasn't just sitting around the house, laying on the couch. He was working. . . . Constant work, constant work, especially in the early, early years. . . . When he got time, we would go hunting or fishing."

After Larry Brown began to write, his children would hear him typing late at night. Billy Ray remembered that Larry "wrote all over the house. He might write at the bar, or he might go to the dining room and write. He might write at the kitchen table, he might write in his room—in the bedroom—and he might write out there across the carport, what he called the cool pad. He wrote at any hour, anywhere. You could just hear it." LeAnne concurred: "He just typed away all night long while we were sleeping."

Larry loved his children dearly and had a special bond with each of them. Billy Ray shared his father's love of farming and animals: he recalled, "I couldn't ask for a better father. He really was good, you know. We knew that he loved us. He would tell us that he loved us. Some men can't do that. He never did have a problem with that." Shane, who shared his father's love of music, was the only one of Larry's children to attend college and believes that Larry "was always proud of me going to school." Because she was the only daughter and because she had health problems as a child, LeAnne was close to her father in a different way from her brothers, but she too remembers her father as devoted to making life better for his children: "I know the reason he worked so hard was for us. If it weren't for him, we wouldn't have been able to have the things that we had." However, because of his constant work, Larry had minimal involvement in his children's school activities: according to LeAnne, "I was big into softball, and he probably came to one game in all the years. I can remember it too because I was shocked that he was there. I don't know if he went to too many of Shane's ball games." Mary Annie confirmed LeAnne's assessment: "He was never around the kids that much. I mean, he did help raise LeAnne more than he did the boys, because LeAnne was born premature, hole in her heart. But I'm the one that's in charge of the kids. He likes to be off at Tula, and I like to be home with the kids, and that's the way it's been all our married life" (RS). Brown's drive to publish, Mary Annie said, "caused more problems than anything in our marriage. We got to the point where [she and their children] were second to anything and everything. I raised the children, and he wrote, and that's just the way it was."

In 1974, Larry left his job at the stove factory and took a paid position with the Oxford Fire Department, "a more respectable profession than he had expected to attain" (Skube M3). Brown later recalled that being a fireman "looked like it might be a pretty exciting job to have, too. Something that would be pretty interesting, to learn all this stuff about how to be a firefighter and go and put out fire and do all that kind of stuff" (RS).

Jerry Johnson, who joined the Oxford Fire Department shortly before Brown, described him as a dedicated fireman who performed his job well: "I remember watching him one day. We were out in the County and he was out keeping a hose on a gas tank. When he got through, he removed his helmet, and it was all sunk in, sort of melted. I asked, 'Didn't that get hot?' He said, 'Yeah, but I couldn't leave that tank alone.'" Brown recalled being terrified during his first years at the department: "The scariest thing, though, is driving that fire truck to a fire for the first time. [Your] legs are shaking on the gas and clutch. The lights are going, the siren is going, and you're running red lights and people are getting out of the way and you just hope you get it down the street, thinking 'What the f——k do I do now?'" (Dees, "Rough Road" 12–13). Mary Annie Brown was more sanguine about her husband's new job, however: "I don't think I ever worried about him once. I trusted him" (RS). According to Johnson, Brown both read and wrote at the station, activities that did not go over very well with some of the other firemen, who were more inclined to spend their time playing poker, washing the trucks, telling stories, watching television, or pitching horseshoes. Nevertheless, Brown felt a camaraderie with the other members of the squad: "These men are like a family to me, and the only thing I can relate it to is being in the Marine Corps, where everybody, black or white or brown or tan, wore the same uniform, all assembled for a common purpose, a brotherhood. This thing's the same thing" (OF 3).

Even after he began work at the fire department, Brown's salary was not adequate to support his family, and he constantly sought to supplement his income. He recalled, "I pulled a twenty-four shift at the fire department in Oxford ten days a month, and on the other days I drove nails or sacked groceries or cleaned carpets, whatever it took to make a few extra dollars to feed my growing family, heat the house, pay the bills everybody has" (*BRF* 21). During the 1970s, according to Mary Annie, Larry's part-time jobs included bricklaying, surveying, working for a telephone answering service, and running a "little country store" in Tula (*RS*). In 1986, Brown told an interviewer that he had "just started this job the other day. I'm working part-time down at this Oxford Answer Phone. It's getting close to Christmastime and I've got to have a little extra money" (Brown Collections). In addition to providing the family with extra money, holding so many part-time, blue-collar jobs taught Brown "that I didn't want to work with my back for the rest of my life and wanted to use my mind instead. I didn't want to remain poor. I wanted my children to have better opportunities than what I had. I wanted to work for myself. I saw people work their whole lives in factories standing on concrete, forty hours a week and I didn't want that life. I wanted more than that from life. I thought I could find it in writing. And I did. I have great sympathy for the good people of the working class. . . . I consider myself a working-class person who lucked out" (Day 192–93).

Work was not the only activity that took Larry Brown away from his family, however. Early on in their marriage, recalled Mary Annie, "we didn't have enough money for him to buy anything to drink. So he couldn't drink" (*RS*). But Brown's success as a writer improved the family finances and gave him both the means and an excuse to go out drinking and socializing. Brown explained to Don O'Brient that bars were "where I get a lot of my stories. There's so much material there. I just watch what goes on and later on I find a place to put that stuff in my novels. It's fascinating watching somebody come in sober and then see how they behave when they get intoxicated" ("Writer" L1). Larry's fondness for partying caused tension on and off throughout his marriage, since Mary Annie could not "understand why [he] wouldn't want to be" at home with his family (*RS*).

Furthermore, Mary Annie believed that because he was a writer, people excused Larry's behavior. On one occasion, when Larry and a friend had been out drinking for most of the day and were "really wasted," Mary Annie found him and attempted to get him to come home. When she asked the bartender to cut him off, the bartender said, "'Who are you to ask me to cut Larry Brown off?' I said, 'Well, being married to him for so many years gives me the right.' And he said, 'Well, I'm not cutting him off.' [She said,] 'Okay, if he leaves here tonight and he hurts someone or he hurts himself, I'll own your butt and this bar's butt by the time I'm through. There's no reason not to cut him off'" (RS). Mary Annie then left the bar without her husband.

Larry recognized his problems with alcohol and believed that they were "part hereditary," recalling his father's alcoholism. Brown also understood that both heredity and his example would make his children prone to drinking problems: "I hate that, but there ain't really nothing I can do about it, and I'm not no good example because they've grown up seeing me drink all their life. I ain't been a good role model" (RS). Toward the end of his life, he realized that his drinking had harmed his writing: "I wasted so much damn time, man, sitting on a bar stool. God, that's what kept me from working. . . . I just can't do both of them at the same time. It's just counterproductive for me. And not good for me, either" (RS).

Brown struggled with his alcoholism as well as his fondness for marijuana throughout his adult life, although his time as a fireman helped him control the problem, since he would work twenty-four-hour shifts. All of Larry's close friends knew about his drinking: recalled Oxford artist Glennray Tutor, "Larry was an overindulger in alcohol and marijuana. . . . He drank all the time, every day, unless he was trying to go on the wagon. His favorite drink was Crown Royal chased with a peach schnapps but also working in some beer along with it and some weed. He could hold it pretty well, but by dawn he was pretty well gone." Tutor believes that Brown drank so much because as "an artist—a writer, a musician, or a painter" he had "this perception . . . of super strength and the world is coming in to him with all these faceted realities [and] he can't handle it all. He finds alcohol or whatever it is to put blinders on." Alcohol helped Brown "get away from the 'highs.' . . . What he was doing when he was drinking or smoking [marijuana], he was taking a vacation. That was a break from being high."

Brown often wrote to his close friend Clyde Edgerton about his drinking exploits, many of which involved Paul Hipp, who was both Brown's friend and his second cousin. In January 1989, Brown wrote to Edgerton, "Me and Paul have this ritual about once a week, sacred" (Edgerton Papers). The ritual involved what Brown described as beer-drinking rides through the "gloam." In 1989, Brown wrote that he and Hipp were "gonna do a little gloamriding after while. We haven't done any in about three or four weeks. . . . Been 'havin' myself. Ain't been acting ugly in the words of my mama" (Edgerton Papers). By the following June, however, Brown had been trying to control his drinking, with mixed success, as he wrote to Edgerton: "Went on a bad binge Friday and woke up Saturday morning with some kind of bad kidney pain or something. . . . I've been drinking too much for a long time anyway, just wouldn't admit it. I don't have to have it ever day. But I've had it every day I guess since I quit the fire department" the preceding January (Edgerton Papers).

Edgerton saw Brown's drinking as "part of the way he dealt with the world and himself" and confronted his friend about his alcohol abuse early in 1991: "I told Larry in a letter . . . that I thought he had a drinking problem and that I worried about his health and thought he ought to do something about it. Now *ought* can be a big word between friends, . . . and it's a very difficult thing for a southern male (or perhaps any male or female) to warn his friend about alcohol use because alcohol can be an apparent (or maybe real) glue to relationships, and by seeming to chastise you risk diluting a friendship by suddenly being seen as a parent. But I decided it was worth the risk. My warning did not seem to hurt our friendship, but then again, I was never sure. Larry often reported to me when he was cutting back on his drinking, but he didn't let me know when he started back."

Edgerton's warning had at least some effect on Brown, who responded that his friend's letter

hit me pretty hard. But I don't love you any less. I couldn't. That's not something you can turn off and on like a light bulb. . . . I know that alcoholics deny that they've got the disease, too. So I guess I'll have to see if I can quit. . . . Nobody knows any better than I do that I drink too much. But to be called an alcoholic by somebody that you love and highly respect. That's sobering. But I don't think I'm ready to start attending an AA meeting yet.

All that said, I appreciate your concern about me. I hate I've worried you. . . .

Well anyway. I'm thinking hard about everything you said. I know you wouldn't have said them if you hadn't been worried.

Hey, you can give me advice any time you want to. You don't have to have an invitation. Big brothers don't. (Edgerton Papers)

Nevertheless, Brown continued to drink. According to his editor, Shannon Ravenel, on one occasion in Atlanta in 1993, Brown got so drunk that he was unable to read at a bookstore panel with Edgerton and two or three other Algonquin authors. The incident prompted Brown to write Edgerton a letter of apology and again to try to stop drinking:

I know I've caused you worry over me. I know I was drunk in Atlanta. I'm bad ashamed about it, the hotel, the bookstore, all of it. Mary Annie said I was drunk when I got on the plane that morning. I've been knowing it's been hurting me for a long time. It's caused me to make a lot of mistakes. The wrecks, the women. I know how to act when I'm sober.

Sunday morning Nov. 7th, I decided to stop. 13 days isn't long I know but it's a start. I haven't had a drop, not even a beer. And it's been years since I went that long without a drink. . . .

But stopping requires a pretty big change in lifestyle. No more bars, no more drinking with my buddies. But I was losing big blocks of time, Unc. I was losing whole nights where I didn't know what happened, how I got home, where I'd been or who with. (Edgerton Papers)

The pattern of attempts at sobriety followed by bouts of drinking and drug abuse continued. In February 1994, he wrote to Edgerton about a night spent drinking and "smoking dope" in Washington, D.C.; nine months later, however, Brown reported that he had not "had a drink in 46 days now." In 1997 and 1998, Brown made another serious attempt to stop drinking but soon fell off the wagon: "I guess I had a pretty good time in Montana, all things considered. I just got so homesick halfway through. So I drank some. I made it 510 days without a drink. But I figured I'd start back eventually, sometime. Sooner or later" (Edgerton Papers).

Billy Ray Brown was aware of his father's drinking problem "since the time I can remember. . . . When he was drinking, he was drinking for days, but if he was not drinking, he didn't want anybody opening a beer around him. He could not be around it. He could not. . . . He fought it all his life." Billy Ray believed that drinking heavily made Larry miserable: "When he was not drinking he seemed to me to be a lot happier. He'd get a lot of work done. When he drank a lot, he didn't get much done."

LeAnne Brown, too, knew that her father drank, but during his lifetime, she believed that "he chose to be that way, to make the choices that he made. And [after his death], I realized he's an alcoholic. . . . On many occasions he tried [to quit]. But when the traveling was going on, it wasn't going to happen. He was going to be by himself, he was going to get down, he was going to get depressed, and he was going to drink. He just didn't like to be away from home for long periods of time."

Jonny Miles understood that Brown was an alcoholic and watched as he struggled but failed to gain control of his drinking. In one instance, Brown had promised to go to a beauty pageant in which LeAnne was competing, but he simply could not stop drinking and kept saying, "Just one more." Miles went to the pageant but left Brown at the bar. Miles believes that in addition to a genetic predisposition toward alcoholism, Brown also suffered from depression and drank to ward off the symptoms.

Larry and Mary Annie Brown's marriage was also strained by Larry's repeated infidelities. A close acquaintance of the Browns believes that many of these incidents resulted from Larry's alcohol problems: he "would get to a point when he was drinking when he would have no control over himself. Larry never went anywhere intending to pick up a woman. He was very passive. What would happen was, for whatever reason, he would get himself completely blind drunk and at one o'clock in the morning a woman would come up and pick him up and take him home with her." The friend does not think that Brown "ever picked up a woman in his life." In the early 1990s, however, Brown had an extended affair with one of his students at Bowling Green, moved out of his family home, and contemplated divorce. And even earlier, in the late 1980s, he briefly left his family:

> I had been out one night, drinking, and Mary Annie had cooked a supper for me that I hadn't been there to eat. Later on, when I finally came in, and had fixed my plate and was about to carry it out to the living room, words were said. I had told her I'd be home in time for supper. She was hot over my going out drinking instead. I said something smart and she doubled up her little fist and caught me square in the jaw with a decent right hook. It didn't hurt that bad . . . but of course I dropped my plate on the floor, food everywhere, gravy, all that. I told her I'd be packing my shit immediately, which I did. There was one brief and insane struggle over a .22 rifle. I took all the bullets away from her. . . .
>
> Four days were all I could stay away from them. I crawled back in the window one night and I've been there ever since. (OF 24–25)

Larry subsequently remained committed to Mary Annie, telling Judith Weinraub in 1990, "I've got a happy marriage and I'm crazy about the girl I'm married to. I couldn't ask for anybody better" (F4). Similarly, he told Kay Bonetti, "I'm very much concerned with family connections, relatives, and all that. That's like a nest you go back home to every night. You have these people around you who are going to be with you all your life—the person you picked to marry, and your children" (Bonetti et al. 244). According to Mary Annie, by the last three or four years of his life, her husband had mended his ways: "I think down deep he knew he had to turn it around, that it was not the way that he needed to go; it was a life that he didn't want to lead. And he finally got his priorities in order. They left him for a while but he got them back. And now he seems happier than he's ever seemed in his life" (RS).

CHAPTER THREE

Literary Apprenticeship, 1980–1987

In *A Late Start*, Larry Brown described his decision to become a writer, recalling that in 1980, "when I was twenty-nine, I stopped and looked at my life and wondered if I was ever going to do anything with it" (3–4). Because he had long been a reader of popular fiction, he decided to change his life by trying to become a writer. He believed that he could teach himself to write salable fiction—and make more money—in the same way that he had learned such skills as carpentry and fire-fighting. He aspired to the kind of success achieved by many of the writers whom he was reading in the late 1970s, among them John D. McDonald, Louis L'Amour, and Stephen King. He wanted to make sure that his three children would not start their adult lives "working in a factory" (5). He told Judith Weinraub, "I was trying to put something on the bestseller list to make some money. I thought that maybe this might be a little easier than all the other backbreaking things I was doing" (F1).

In October 1980, when Brown "was working at Comanche Pottery on my days off, working the regular shift at the fire department, . . . the question kept occurring in my mind about giving it a try. There was not really any big fanfare about it. It was something I had been think-ing about on my own for a long time" (Rankin, "On" 93). One day, he picked his wife, Mary Annie, up from work and told her that he had gone to see his sister, Joy Brown Mooney, and retrieved Mary Annie's "old portable Smith-Corona electric" typewriter (*LS* 4–5). Then, she said, he announced, "'I'm gonna start writing.' And I said, 'Oh yeah, well, okay.'" From that day onward, he wrote "constantly, every day, all the time" (*RS*). Mary Annie did not initially take seriously Larry's new ambition: "I thought it was a whim at first, but he kept at it, month after month. I knew he was serious. He was so determined to make it. . . . We got used to doing things without him around because he was always writing" (O'Brient, "Writer" L6). Mary Annie ultimately gave her husband her full backing: in Larry Brown's words, "She believed that I wanted it badly enough, and she was willing to support and stand by me" (Weinraub F4). She was skeptical about his prospects for success "because Larry doesn't express his feelings real well" but also believed that "usually, whatever he wants to do, he does" (Watkins 1D).

Brown's first idea was a novel "about a man-eating bear in Yellowstone National Park, a place I'd never been to, and it had a lot of sex in it" (*LS* 4–5). Writing steadily when he was not working one of his other jobs, Brown finished the manuscript, "The Wages of Sin," in five months. In 1991, Brown admitted, "Of course, I didn't know what I was doing. I didn't even know about double-spacing. I typed that whole novel single-spaced, 327 pages" (Summer F-4). He sent "The Wages of Sin" to Everest House Publishers in New York City, which rejected the novel in May 1981. Undeterred, Brown next tried Random House, which also rejected the work with the suggestion that he send it "to a paperback publisher" (Brown Collections). At around the same time, Brown also sent out "a few horrible short stories," all of which were immediately rejected (*LS* 5). At the time, Brown "didn't have any idea about how much work was involved. I surely didn't think it would take seven years before my first book was published" (Ross 4).

Brown continued to believe that if he "wrote long enough and hard enough, I'd eventually learn how" (*OF* viii). When he was not working one of his jobs, he "could usually lock myself away in a room, sometimes for ten or twelve hours, sometimes for as much as five or six thousand words" (*LS* 7). Said Mary Annie, "He was so determined to make it he would stay right there with it all the time. He might come in and sit down and eat with us. To this day he usually doesn't eat with us, because if he's writing, leave him alone, let him write. He'll eat when he gets hungry. So we've always done everything without him around because he was writing" (*RS*).

Between 1980 and 1983, Brown wrote four other novels and numerous short stories. His second novel, "The Patch," "was about a couple of old boys in Tennessee who were going to plant a big patch of marijuana and make a lot of money" (*LS* 7). Everest House rejected it in November 1981. After Donald Cleary of the Jane Rotrosen Agency in New York rejected Brown's third novel, "All God's Children," a tale of the supernatural, he burned the manuscript behind his mother-in-law's house in Yocona. Mary Annie "watched him burn [it] one day, page by page. Stood right out there at that burning barrel and pitched one page in at a time. He just came out of his room and said, 'This is no good.' He just didn't think he had it" (*RS*). His fourth novel, "Mama's Waiting," is written from the first-person point of view and features a young boxer just released from the marines. Cleary rejected it, too.

New York readers also rejected "When the Rain Comes," Brown's fifth novel, but finally offered the author some encouragement. On 23 July 1984, Cleary wrote, "I enjoyed WHEN THE RAIN COMES. You write well. You evoke the backwoods setting effectively. You have an unusual cast of characters. But I do not believe I could place it for you. . . . The setting is quite distant from the lives of usual hardcover book buyers. For such a setting to be viable (in our opinion), the story must transcend the setting in scope and impact. I don't believe this story does" (Brown Collections). Gordon Lish suggested that Knopf might publish the book if it were revised. For help in understanding Lish's suggestions, Brown sought out Evans Harrington, a professor of creative writing at the University of Mississippi. Harrington "almost did a hot swoon when he saw that letter from Alfred A. Knopf. But he was great. He showed me where I'd gone wrong and how to correct it. So I retyped the whole damn thing (a tornado hit our house in the meantime; a tree took the back off like God had taken a knife to it) and got it ready and sent it back" (LB to SR, Algonquin Files). Lish rejected the manuscript again in May 1984.

Larry then sent the novel to Random House, where Gary Fisketjon, later Cormac McCarthy's editor at Knopf, read the manuscript. On 5 June 1984, Fisketjon told Brown, "You write very well indeed, and your scenes of 'deep tonk' are as strong as any I've ever read. . . . But obviously I'm returning the manuscript. My reason is that your characters and plot are limited in a way that your prose isn't. . . . In any case I'm glad to have read this, and will be pleased to read anything else you've written or will write in the future. You have considerable talent and power" (Brown Collections).

In hindsight, Brown recognized that his early novels did not "need to be published. They're just not good enough. I can see now that everybody else was right years ago. See, I just didn't know it myself. That's the process you go through" (Pettus, "Interview" 8). Among the more than two hundred rejection letters he received and saved, however, were other words of encouragement, particularly from readers at the magazines where he was sending stories. In 1981, Jeannie Jagels at *Outdoor Life* "wrote me a letter back about one of my early efforts, telling me why they couldn't publish it, telling me, gently and kindly, why it wasn't good enough. She was the first saint I met in the publishing business, and the publishing business is full of saints" (*LS* 6). Ted Klein at *Twilight Zone* liked Brown's stories but "said he could always tell where they were heading too soon." The two men "carried on a correspondence for several years. [Klein would] always write me a personal letter about each of my stories" (Brown Collections).

Not surprisingly, Brown questioned whether he would succeed as a writer, wondering "if it ever will be, if the rejection slips will ever stop coming, how much longer it will take to learn what I want to learn. The most frightening thing to think is that it might never come, but I never allow myself to think about that very much" (*OF* 153). The constant rejections affected Mary Annie as well: "Those were hard. To see him work so hard, and then those slips come in. They'd be just little short sentences like, 'Well, we're sorry, but not this time. Try us again.' Things like that" (*RS*).

In 1982, Brown received his first acceptance when *Easyrider*, a motorcycle magazine, published "Plant Growin' Problems." According to Jerry Johnson, Brown "brought the magazine into Station 3 and said, 'Look here, I'm published.'" When Brown's mother, Leona, went to a local newsstand to buy a copy, the shocked owner asked, "Mrs. Brown, I know you're a nice lady; why are you buying this magazine?"

"Plant Growin' Problems" seems tailor-made for publication in a rough and somewhat seedy bikers' magazine. The protagonist is a biker, Jerry Barlow. (Brown also used Barlow, his mother's maiden name, in "92 Days.") A corrupt sheriff, overweight in the stereotypical style of southern lawmen, discovers Barlow's illegal crop of fifteen marijuana plants in the Georgia backwoods and plots to use a rattlesnake to kill him and then take the marijuana. But the tables turn, the sheriff dies, and Barlow makes his getaway on his bike. Though clearly written and containing considerable suspense, the story lacks depth and sophistication. But it earned him $375 (Brown Collections).

Nearly two years passed before Brown's second story was published. "Boy and Dog" appeared in the fall 1984 issue of *Fiction International* and earned him about seventy dollars (Harold Jaffe to LB, Brown Collections). Brown later included the story in *Facing the Music*, and Gary Hawkins dramatized it in *The Rough South of Larry Brown*. In 1985, Klein finally accepted one of Brown's stories, "Nightmare," for *Twilight Zone*, paying him $150 (Brown Collections). That same year, Brown also published "The Rich" in the *Mississippi Review*. Payment was typical for a small literary magazine: five free copies of the issue "plus a small check (amount not yet determined) for your trouble" (Rie Fortenberry to LB, Brown Collections).

In addition to consulting with Ole Miss's Harrington, Brown looked for other ways to improve his writing. He had long been a patron of the Oxford–Lafayette County Library, but his visits took on a new purpose. Head librarian Dorothy Fitts recalled that "he used to come in here all the time, reading on his lunch hour, checking out books, then coming back again after he got off work" (Herbst 8). Brown "checked out books on writing by the armload and read them cover to cover"; he also read essays by writers who had succeeded after long struggles, finding their examples "tremendously heartening" (*LS* 6, 7). He later described that period as one in which he was "plugging along all by myself there without any kind of guidance—just what I could get out of books about writing and what I could learn from reading, trying to see how good writers put it together" (Ross 89).

Brown soon realized that he needed to seek help in a more formal way. In the fall of 1982, Brown approached Barry Hannah, a newly arrived teacher of creative writing at Ole Miss, "in Dino's Diner. He had stories in hand, was so respectful and sincere I read them and talked to him at my house on Johnson Avenue. We visited an hour."

Brown recorded his version of Hannah's assistance in an unpublished essay, "Ten Minutes with Barry Hannah," expressing his gratitude for the more experienced writer's time and guidance. Six weeks after, as Brown put it, he "inconsiderately pressed six of my short stories" on Hannah, Brown went to Hannah's house to pick up the stories. Brown was thrilled when Hannah told him, "I read some of your stories, Larry, and I'm impressed." Brown also noted the books "all over his living room. There were titles of the highest literary content. Here was truly the domain of a genuine writer and I was talking to him about my writing." Brown immediately began to create his own library, ultimately amassing more than 550 books (Brown Collections). Hannah advised Brown that the best way to improve his writing was to keep writing.

Despite his encouraging words, Hannah was secretly skeptical about Brown's future as a writer. Brown's stories at the time "were so bad, I'd duck out the back of the bar when I saw him coming down the walk with the inevitable manila envelope. I couldn't stand hurting his feelings. I loved his sincerity. I didn't give him a cold prayer in hell as to a future in literature" ("Larry Brown" 11). Hannah's attitude soon changed, and in the fall of 1987, he suggested that his agent, Liz Darhansoff, take on Brown as a client. Ravenel approved of Brown's relationship with Darhansoff, telling him that the experienced New Yorker was "tough, aggressive, and with good taste" (Algonquin Files). Like Ravenel, Darhansoff read "Facing the Music" and immediately recognized its power ("Go, Little Book" 46), and in October 1987, she agreed to represent Brown. Hannah also encouraged his publisher, Seymour Lawrence, to offer Brown a contract, although he did not take it.

In the spring of 1982, Brown's took another step to educate himself more formally as a writer by enrolling in a class at Ole Miss taught by Ellen Douglas (the pen name of Josephine Haxton). According to Douglas, when Brown "came to interview for my graduate writing class at Ole Miss, he had not had any college. He had been admitted as a special student. I asked him if he had done any writing and he said, 'Yes, ma'am,'—he had that Mississippi deference to older women. I asked him what he had written and he said about a hundred short stories. And he said he had drafts of three novels. I said, 'Come to class.' The main thing I did was point him in the direction of writers he needed to read. He already knew how to write a sentence" (Skube M3). After reading some of his fiction, Douglas provided Brown with some constructive criticism. As Brown explained, "I was writing mystery stories and horror stories and stories about people killing each other over just hatred or little trivial things, and [Douglas] said, 'I don't have any problem with the way you construct a sentence, but your subject matter is what you've got to find and these are the people you've got to read and understand. . . . You start reading "Heart of Darkness," and you start reading "An Occurrence at Owl Creek Bridge," and you start reading "A Good Man Is Hard to Find" and you'll find out what the things are to write about.' And she was right" (Manley 127).

Brown credited Douglas with introducing him to several major writers, including "Conrad and Dostoevski and Ambrose Bierce. She'd assign us all these stories out of the *Norton Anthology of Short Fiction*. I had never encountered these stories before. I had never heard of Katharine Anne Porter before, I had never heard of Flannery O'Connor before. And I found all these wonderful writers, some of them had been dead a long time. I really had my eyes opened to what was going on" (LaRue 43). The class included eight students, at least half of whom were townspeople rather than graduate students directly affiliated with the university. Enrollees included an older woman from Memphis whom Ellen Douglas remembered as writing a memoir and Oxford residents Anne Odell and George Kehoe. The class read three of Douglas's novels, including *White Cloud/Black Cloud*, as well as O'Connor's "A Good Man Is Hard to Find" and "Everything That Rises Must Converge," Porter's "Theft" and "Flowering Judas," and Eudora Welty's "A Worn Path" and "Place in Fiction." O'Connor had a particularly strong impact on Brown, and he later designated her "one of his idols" (*LS* 3). He told an interviewer that he had "read just about all of Flannery O'Connor's stuff. I think she's a great writer" (Brown Collections), and in 1988, when Shannon Ravenel sent him a tape of O'Connor reading, he enthusiastically thanked her: "I hear that old voice from so many years back. And that voice so good. Thanks, Shannon. It instantly became one of my most prized possessions" (Algonquin Files). He especially appreciated O'Connor's assertion that writers' early experiences are all they need as subject matter for their fiction. O'Connor's viewpoint made Brown realize that he had "plenty of material for a long time" but that he did not yet know how to use it (LS 3).

Douglas also encouraged her students to expand their vocabularies and presented Brown with the opportunity to have other students read and critique his writing. Brown later thanked Odell for being "kind to me early on, to me and my work. I haven't forgotten that and I never will. You and some others in the class gave me lots of encouragement when I needed it. A few people were highly critical. I haven't forgotten who they were either. They were the least skillful writers in the class. I've found out that it's like that all over. The bad writers envy and despise the good writers" (Odell Papers).

Although Douglas later said that she could not teach Brown much because "he taught himself by reading voraciously," Brown believed that Douglas had been an integral part of his development as a writer: she was "a great teacher. She had all this accurate insight into your manuscript. And she kind of pointed me in the right direction" (LaRue 43). She helped transform him from a writer who sought popular success, money, and fame to an author who strove for literary excellence, and "about that time that I began to discover what kind of writer I wanted to be" (Bonetti et al. 236). For her part, what Douglas herself found most "important and memorable" about Brown's work "is his own voice, his honesty, the way he 'faces the music' (to borrow one of his titles) of the human condition."

In 1984, Brown took a writing class at the public library in Memphis taught by John Osier, a novelist and professor at Northwest Mississippi Community College. During this class, Brown wrote a story, "Old Frank and Jesus," that would become part of his first published volume, Facing the Music. When he read the story to the class, it was the first time he had ever read anything aloud (LB to SR, Algonquin Files). Brown later recalled that he "had to drop that class two thirds of the way through when the tornado . . . partially demolished our home. . . . It was a bad time, but Tom Jenks, who was then a fiction editor at

Esquire, read 'Old Frank and Jesus' and began writing me and encouraged me to send him more work" ("'That Fellow'" 7).

In Osier's estimation, Brown came to the class already in possession of many of the qualities that would lead to his writing success: in addition to his natural talent, which he had honed through his voracious reading, he had "tremendous drive" and "that burning in the belly, that fire. [He saw writing as] something you have to do. It's like a compulsion." Osier also saw Brown as possessing a "basic inner integrity or honesty to pull [feelings and insights] from deep inside himself" as well as the "ability to observe people accurately . . . to tap into his own inner emotions but also observe people and see them and . . . to be able to write from deep within [himself] but to be able to write honestly and almost expose [himself]."

Brown found the time between 1983 and 1986 frustrating. He had learned to distinguish good writing from popular fiction and had decided to write literature rather than more popular books that might have made him quickly and easily rich, but success remained elusive. Brown described himself during that time as "real impatient. . . . I thought I ought to have it a lot sooner than what came. And I just didn't understand that I hadn't put in enough time yet" (*RS*). He "had learned by then that the price of success for a writer came high, that there were years of a thing called the apprenticeship period, and that nobody could tell you when you'd come to the end of it. You just had to keep writing with blind faith, and hope, and trust in yourself that you would eventually find your way, that the world would one day accept your work" (*BRF* 19).

During this period, Brown discovered "that there was a bookstore in Oxford which I didn't know" (Rankin, "On" 94). Square Books further broadened Brown's literary horizons: "I got to looking at the titles. I'd heard something about Raymond Carver and there were his books on the shelf. So I started going back to the bookstore and buying books. That was the first time I think I'd actually bought books. I'd always used the library before" (94).

Brown developed a close relationship with the owner of Square Books, Richard Howorth. Howorth had worked with Brown's mother, Leona, and knew other members of the family but did not meet Larry until he began visiting the bookstore. Howorth remembered that "when we had book signings, he'd come in and sort of hang around. I don't know that he felt real comfortable. But gradually he began to feel at home, and was one of the regulars who came in. For a long time, I didn't know he was a writer" (Skube 4). Brown's reading interests differentiated him from most of the store's other customers: said Howorth, "Your casual reader doesn't just stroll in off the street and buy books by [Raymond] Carver and [Harry] Crews" (Watkins, "Hot" 1D). Howorth "hadn't seen anybody like Larry and haven't since." John Evans, owner of Lemuria Books in Jackson, described the relationship between Brown and Howorth as "a bookseller's fairy tale. It is just what this business is all about. It is truly the essence of the heart and soul of the bookseller in making a difference within people and for people." Such connections, Evans believes, demonstrate "the real purpose of my occupation and Richard's occupation. . . . I think it's so fortunate and very uncommon. . . . They were peers. It was personal."

In the late 1980s, Brown telephoned Howorth and "said that he was depressed. He'd been sending out a lot of stories and they'd been rejected in a lot of places. He just wanted to know what he was doing wrong. I said, 'Come over and we'll talk about it.' He came over. It was a rainy Sunday afternoon. He brought two or three stories which I had not read. I had never asked to read his stories, and he had never asked me to read them" (Brown et al. 51). The first story Howorth read was "Facing the Music," which Brown wrote in 1985. Howorth knew immediately that his friend would succeed as an author: "When I began to read it, a bolt of lightning hit me directly in the spine. I knew then that it would find an audience" (51).

Howorth began to encourage Larry "in a lot of ways. . . . I always wanted him to go straight to the *New Yorker* or the *Atlantic*." Brown had already realized that he needed to get his work accepted by reputable magazines and journals, and Howorth tried to help place "Facing the Music." Howorth took Brown to a Jackson party at which he met Evans and Richard Ford, a native of Jackson who had published several successful novels, including *The Ultimate Good Luck* (1981). Brown told Ford, "I'd had a few stories published, and I told him about ['Facing the Music']. They had already read it at *Esquire*, an associate editor [Tom

Jenks] had read it, and sent me back a letter and said if he owned the magazine he'd publish it in a minute, but he didn't think his boss, who was Rust Hills, would go for it" (Brown Collections). Ford responded, "'Send me the story, and if it's good enough, I'll try to help you with it'" (Brown Collections). Ford kept his word, trying to get the story published in *TriQuarterly*, to no avail.

According to Mary Annie Brown, Howorth subsequently became her husband's best friend in Oxford. Larry Brown corresponded not only with Richard Howorth but also with his wife, Lisa, even though he lived only twelve miles from the couple. He wrote to the two separately, Richard Howorth recalled, "not because there were great secrets, but because he gave his friends individual attention. Thick envelopes would arrive with several pages. . . . One of the best feelings in the world was to come home to find among the dreck of daily mail one of Larry's fat, wonderful letters" (Howorth Papers).

Like her husband, Lisa Howorth, an artist and writer, met Brown in the early 1980s when he began to patronize Square Books. She and Brown "both were night owls. We loved the nightlife, the live music scene in Oxford. Larry and I would be the geezers in the group at times; we would invariably show up for some of the live shows with some of the young musicians around town. . . . We bonded in a lot of ways over silliness. We talked a lot of ridiculous talk about dark things we'd done or dark things that we had thought up to do that would be outrageous. We just laughed a lot." On some occasions when Brown was too drunk to drive after a night of partying in Oxford, Lisa recalled, he would sleep in the swing on the porch of the Howorths' Victorian home just off the Square.

Toward the end of his life, Brown often called Lisa on her cell phone late at night. He had cut back on his visits to Oxford's bars, and "he would call from out in his 'cool pad,' as he called it, and say, 'I'm taking requests; what do you want to hear?' He would have his guitar, and I would name a couple of songs, and he'd say, 'No, I don't know that, can't play that,' and finally I'd say, 'What about "Streets of Laredo,"'" not knowing that it has about nine hundred verses, of which Larry knew every one and sang them." When Lisa Howorth was writing a book, *Yellow Dogs, Hushpuppies, and Blue Tick Hounds: The Official Encyclopedia of Southern Culture Quiz*, Brown provided her with information about different types of dogs, and she "used the descriptions verbatim that he gave me because they were so complete and so interesting. You could always go to Larry for something like that."

On 12 September 1986, after seven rejections, "Facing the Music" was accepted by Frederick Barthelme, a novelist and longtime teacher of creative writing at the University of Southern Mississippi, for publication in *Mississippi Review*. In his formal letter of acceptance, Barthelme wrote, "This is one of the best stories to come our way in a long time—wonderfully written and straight from the heart" (Brown Collections). According to Brown, Barthelme paid thirty dollars for the story (Watkins, "Hot" 1D).

Numerous other rejections found their way to Brown's mailbox during this time. Between August 1985 and January 1987, "Samaritans" was rejected by nine publications, including *Ploughshares*, the *Texas Review*, and the *New Yorker*. Between March 1984 and December 1986, "Old Frank and Jesus" was rejected by the *Paris Review*, the *Antioch Review*, *Esquire*, and ten other periodicals. The *New Yorker* rejected "Kubuku Rides," calling it "awfully monotonous" despite its "effective" ending (Brown Collections). Brown later reflected on how much these rejections frustrated him: his work "wasn't being rejected because the story wasn't good, it was being rejected because it hurt people too bad to read it. Because it was too honest. And too brutal some say. And the only way I can really defend myself against any of that is to say, 'Well, yeah it's brutal, but I think that it's honest.' And what I think you've got to do is share this experience with these people. That's what I'm writing about. That's what the story is about. And you just can't tack a happy ending on things" (128).

Early in 1986, Larry took six months off from writing to build a ranch-style house on the Coleman family's sixty acres. He had already started to write the novel that became *Joe* but decided that he could not continue to write while working full time at the fire department and building the house. He hired some of his fellow firefighters to help and the crew started "in March and [had] it framed up, the roof on and the windows and doors in, in a few weeks" (*OF* 71). While he was building the house, the idea for *Dirty Work* came to him: "I got an idea about a guy whose face was disfigured from a rocket attack in Vietnam and he wouldn't come out of his room. That was all I had. It was just driving me crazy to get to work on it, but I couldn't until I had all the sheetrock hung, and the wallpaper and paint, trim, the cabinets, all the million things that go in a house. But the day that I had a table to put my typewriter on, and a chair to sit in—we hadn't even moved in yet—I sat down and started writing *Dirty Work*" (Bonetti et al. 250).

One feature of the house was a utility room across the carport that Brown later converted into a writing room: his cool pad. There, Brown was "completely isolated from the main part of the house. That's where I do my work. I felt like I had to have that if I was going to build a new house. I had to have a place I could go to. I've got three children and they keep the television going all the time and something's going on all the time in the house, so this is where I stay when I work" (Pettus, "Interview" 8). Brown later added on a patio constructed in "a herringbone pattern, just like the one in the sidewalk in front of William Faulkner's house" (*OF* 23).

"Facing the Music" appeared in the fall–winter 1986 issue of the *Mississippi Review*, where it caught the attention of Shannon Ravenel, senior editor of Algonquin Books of Chapel Hill. When Ravenel first read the story, she "didn't recognize the author's name [but] the story was so good, so accomplished, so sure-footed, I figured it had to be by some established writer who didn't usually frequent the little mags" ("Go" 44).

On 3 June 1987, Ravenel wrote to Brown to tell him that she wanted to nominate his "wonderful" story, "Facing the Music," for inclusion in both *Best American Short Stories* and *New Stories from the South*. She also asked if he had enough stories for a collection of his own writings. Brown answered, "I've got a hundred. How many would you like to see?" (Weinraub F4). Brown was immensely grateful to receive Ravenel's letter, writing back,

> You've made me very happy because this is the best letter I ever got. . . . It's wonderful that this is going to happen, and I'm thrilled about appearing in the anthology of Southern stories. My hopes and dreams are finally coming true, and I want to thank you for helping.
>
> I've been wanting to publish a book for a long time, and a collection of stories would be the best thing that ever happened to me, but

I'll be totally honest with you. I've written 100, but I wouldn't want to show 90% of them to you because they are apprentice work, and not good enough to publish. The other thing is that the other nine or ten I want to send you are not like, or maybe not as good as "Facing the Music," but what I'm trying to say is that maybe some of them have too many dark resolutions and unhappy endings, although I think they are honest. Many of them have been rejected over ten times, but "Facing the Music" was rejected seven, so maybe that doesn't mean anything. (Algonquin Files)

On 16 June, Brown sent Ravenel manuscript copies of eleven of his stories: "Facing the Music," "Samaritans," "Old Frank and Jesus," "Kubuku Rides (This Is It)," "The Rich," "You Can't Go on Like This," "The End of Romance," "Discipline," "Cats," "Boy and Dog," and "Nightmare." Ravenel read the manuscripts and was impressed: she wrote to the author, "I had to read them slowly—partly because I was taking notes, but mostly because they affect me so strongly. You are a powerful and talented writer. Very powerful. Very talented" (Algonquin Files). She also reconsidered the idea of publishing a volume of his short stories, suggesting that he publish a novel first. A novel, she believed, would create less negative critical reaction than "a collection of powerful—and depressing—stories," since critics would accept "powerful grimness far more readily in novel form than in short story collections. There IS something almost lethally debilitating about reading one gut-raking story after another—the short story form delivers its punch with far more accuracy and force than the novel does" (Algonquin Files). Ravenel advised Brown to publish the best of the stories in magazines, write and publish a novel, and then release the collection of short stories a year later. She cautioned him against changing his subject matter "to get into print" before closing with the words, "I would love to be your editor and have the pleasure of watching over your work for as long as that seems useful to you" (Algonquin Files). When he received Ravenel's letter, Brown showed it to Richard Howorth, who "like to flipped. We partied until late that night" (Algonquin Files). Brown's dreams were finally about to be realized.

CHAPTER FOUR

Facing the Music, 1987–1989

The publication of his first few stories won Brown an audience not only nationwide but also in Mississippi. In late 1986, as he recalled in an unpublished interview, Richard Howorth's sister-in-law, Mary Hartwell Howorth, "contacted me and asked me to read" at Yoknapatawpha County Arts Festival hosted by the Center for Southern Studies at Ole Miss (Brown Collections). The event was probably his first public reading in Oxford, and according to Brown, "The date I believe is Nov. 8th. I'm gonna be kind of juggling time that night. I'm working at the fire station that day, and I think it's supposed to start around 7, so I've gotta take off that night at 7, and try to get up to the courthouse and settled in time" (Brown Collections). Glennray Tutor, an Oxford artist whom Brown had met earlier, attended the reading. Tutor remembered that the two men talked and then "somehow we just began hanging out with each other." Tutor believes that Brown pursued their friendship because he wanted someone from a similar background with whom he could discuss the nature of artistic expression: "It's almost a magic thing that happens—I mean, how somebody like Larry, how somebody like me, somebody like Elvis Presley can come out of complete cultural impoverishment, and yet there's some kind of magic starlight inside of them that leads them into artistic endeavor. . . . Just think about the enormous energy or effort required of a person to realize they've got something, a creative gift. The effort required to go ahead and do something." Brown put up a print of one of Tutor's works "over my typewriter. My motivation wall. Alongside Barry Hannah, Cormac McCarthy, Jack Butler" (Tutor Papers).

The connection between the two men was not merely artistic but also social. Tutor and his son, Zach, often fished with Larry, and Tutor and his first wife, Barb, became frequent visitors to the Brown home in Yocona. Tutor also became one of Brown's correspondents.

At the festival, Brown read "Facing the Music" in what Tutor described as "an unusual setting for a reading, the Courthouse, and I remember that it was pouring rain that day. All this provided a striking backdrop for what I felt was a very powerful reading" (Ravenel, "Two" 4). Barry Hannah introduced Brown, who read a paragraph from Raymond Carver's introduction to the 1986 edition of *Best American Short Stories*, which contained "Facing the Music." Before reading the story itself, Brown also told listeners that "Facing the Music" had been "rejected seven times before it was accepted. . . . There was a time when I began to wonder if it would ever be published, but I'm lucky to have friends who support me, and who read the story and believed in it. One of those friends is Richard Howorth, and this story is dedicated to him" (Brown Collections).

During 1986, Brown was promoted to the rank of captain in the Oxford Fire Department. By 1988 and 1989, he had to work only "ten shift days a month" and found it "wonderful to finally have those other twenty days a month to write" (*LS* 1). But "there was *always* the Fire Department; every third day there was always the Fire Department to go to, that was just regular clockwork" (*RS*). He continued to read during his off time and began to keep a journal at the station. Though his colleagues jokingly called him "Faulkner" (Holland B3), they were also "pretty excited" about his success: "The boys at the fire department and my family have been knowing about it for years because I've been doing it for so long. . . . [T]hey're glad to see me finally break on through. So, they're excited, they're happy for me. I've got a lot of people pulling for me" (Pettus, "Interview" 9). In October 1987, Brown reported that station gossip was "that I got a $25,000 advance and am going to make $100,000 the first year, and I'm going to quit in just a few more days. I know all the lieutenants are hoping it's so. They all want my job" (LB to SR, October 1987, Algonquin Files).

Beginning in about 1987, Larry, Mary Annie, and Larry's mother, Leona Barlow Brown, operated a small store in Tula. Larry described the business as "just a little country store in a little country community. . . . There's farm land all around here, woods all around, so there's a lot of logging going on too. . . . Tula Grocery, heaps of ham and cheese and baloney sliced, . . . money loaned, checks cashed" (LB to SR, Algonquin Files). The store also served the community as a post office, with Leona Brown as postmistress. The store became an enormous burden to Larry, particularly after he committed to writing, and by the end of 1988, he had given it up, writing to Shannon Ravenel, "I got about two truckloads of weight off my head getting rid of the store. . . . I'm free again. I'll never put myself in a situation like that again" (Algonquin Files). Brown apparently paid off the forty-five hundred dollars he owed on the store and then turned operations over to his mother (Edgerton Papers). Leona Brown remembered, "He handed me the keys one day and said, 'Mama, I'm outta here.' I guess he thought he had it made."

Despite Larry Brown's nonliterary activities and Ravenel's advice that Brown finish and publish a novel before launching a collection of short stories, *Facing the Music* became Brown's first published volume when Algonquin released it in the fall of 1988. According to Ravenel, "Ultimately, another fan of Larry's, Dudley Jhanke, who was at that time doing Algonquin's marketing, said, in essence, to hell with conventional wisdom about introducing new writers with novels. These stories are too strong to keep in manuscript" ("Go, Little Book" 45). Before the collection came out, two more of the stories included in it were published in other venues. "Kubuku Rides (This Is It)" appeared in the *Greensboro Review* in 1988 and received the journal's annual prize for fiction; the story was also included in the 1989 edition of *Best American Short Stories*. And "Samaritans" was published in the *St. Andrews Review* in 1988. Although Ravenel tried to get popular magazines such as the *Atlantic* and *Playboy* to accept Brown's stories and thus increase the collection's potential audience, editors at the magazines "were taken with the strength of Brown's writing" but found his stories "'not quite right for our magazine[s].' Not quite cheerful enough, is what [they] meant" ("Go, Little Book" 46).

With publication of *Facing the Music* set for June 1988, Algonquin launched a promotional campaign. Ravenel solicited and obtained what she called "a truly remarkable set of endorsements from Jack Butler, Harry Crews, Ellen Douglas, Barry Hannah and Willie Morris" ("Go, Little Book" 46). Louis Rubin, who cofounded Algonquin Books of Chapel Hill with Ravenel, advertised the collection at the University of Mississippi's 1987 Faulkner Conference, and Ravenel took several of Brown's stories to a Southeastern Booksellers Association meeting in Atlanta, where Clyde Edgerton and Jill McCorkle read them. Ravenel wrote to Brown on 15 September 1987, "Everybody talked about how powerful a writer you are. . . . You would have been very proud. I was" (Algonquin Files). Algonquin publicist Mimi Fountain sent numerous reviewers the book's galleys or the bound volume, "shamelessly [using] the fireman-turned-writer hook. And it worked. *Facing the Music* received more than thirty national reviews" ("Go, Little Book" 46). The first published assessment appeared in the *Kirkus Review* and was quoted on the book jacket: the reviewer called the stories "raw and gritty" and declared the appearance of Brown's work "one of the more exciting debuts of recent memory."

In October 1987, Brown received the contract to have Algonquin publish a collection of ten of his stories. Brown was to get a two-thousand-dollar advance, 10 percent royalties on the first five thousand copies sold, 12.5 percent on the next five thousand copies, and 15 percent on all further copies sold. For Brown, the contract represented "a dream come true. A lot of people around Oxford are glad and happy for me, and even out here in the nether regions some people are, like, wow. My oldest boy is so proud of me. Mary Annie's scared of it (success or recognition or whatever's coming), but I'm not" (LB to SR, Algonquin Files). Brown suggested that the collection be titled *Facing the Music* because "most of the characters are having to face something, the fireman, Mr. P., Frank in the bar, Angel, the guy breaking up with his girl" (LB to SR, Algonquin Files). Ravenel immediately approved of the idea, writing to Brown, "It's what I wanted all along, but I didn't want to push" (Algonquin Files). Brown signed and returned the contract on 29 October (Algonquin Files). Five months later, Brown sent Ravenel a photograph to be used on the volume's back cover, explaining, "This is me. I hope you like the picture. . . . This was taken on the balcony at Square Books. Mary Annie watched from the window of her office in the courthouse, top window, far right. Photo credit: Jack Cofield" (Algonquin Files).

On 27 June 1988, the *Oxford Eagle* published a front-page story on the publication of *Facing the Music*. The article's author, Nina Goolsby, quoted novelist Ellen Douglas, who had taught Brown at Ole Miss, lauding his "unerring comic sense, . . . sensitive ear for talk, . . . unsentimental commitment to his characters and, above all, . . . intimate, ruthless, loving connection with the world." According to Hannah, Brown "rediscovers real stuff, like great writers do. He's been out there, and reports it beautifully. He is a master." And Morris declared Brown's work "direct, powerful, and singularly honest" (1).

Brown was thrilled by the Goolsby's article, writing to Ravenel, "I'm about to get a little recognition in the local paper. I can't believe it after all this time. This is the *Oxford Eagle*. . . . [T]he editor and owner [is] Nina Goolsby. . . . She called over here this morning and woke Mary Annie up having a fit for my picture so she could run the press release in the paper tomorrow. . . . That local publicity will be good, could help us sell some more books. I went up to her house and she came to the door in her housecoat and curlers—'Oh Lord don't look at me!'— just thrilled to death. So I'll be famous locally tomorrow" (Algonquin Files).

Brown also spent his time during 1987 and 1988 working on a play, ultimately titled *Wings*, that he had written for a 1985 contest at Ole Miss. Brown "took some vacation time . . . and locked myself in a room for seven days and wrote it. I doubt if it even got a complete reading [by contest judges] because it was from a local writer. I just said so much for that; I didn't know anyplace else to send it." Two years later, however, Oxford's Hoka Theater began staging plays and "invited submissions from local writers. I don't know how many scripts they got but they picked mine. It just needed some work. It had some flaws that needed to be changed and corrected" (LB to SR. Algonquin Files). Plans to stage the play fell through, however. Brown also sent the play to literary agent Nat Sobel, who returned it with the comment, "There's nothing wrong with the writing in WINGS, but I think you have a way to go as a dramatist in making this work. There are no surprises to this rather straightforward story and nearly all the really dramatic moments (except for the accidental killing) happen off-stage" (Sobel to LB, August 1987, Brown Collections). In January 1991, Brown learned that *Wings* would be published in *Mississippi Writers: An Anthology*, edited by Dorothy Abbott, telling Edgerton, "My old play's going to get published in this Mississippi anthology thing. I corrected the proofs yesterday, going to mail them off tomorrow. I thought they were only going to publish one act, but they're doing the whole thing. It's probably a little inferior to most of my work. It's five years old. But I still like parts of it. I'm not making anything off it. Maybe somebody will stage it one of these days" (Edgerton Papers). Despite Brown's hopes, however, the play was never produced.

In January 1988, Brown read "Samaritans" at Ole Miss, the prospect of which "pretty much scared" him "shitless. I've been taping myself and timing myself and all that, but they're going to tape me, too, so it's scary. But it is an honor, and I can't turn it down. It also might sell some books for us" (LB to SR, Algonquin Files). Two months later, Brown did another reading in one of William Ferris's classes at the university: Ferris "got up and made this five minute spiel about the prodigy I was and how proud of me they were and what I'd published and what I was going to publish and then introduced me as Larry *Farmer*. Jesus, Hurt me to my soul. I just went on and did it. But if he pulls some shit like that at the Faulkner conference, I'll walk out. After telling them what my name is. I guess he was thinking about Farmer Brown, I don't know. Christ, I don't blame you for laughing. I'd probably laugh too if it happened to somebody other than me" (LB to SR, Algonquin Files). Brown found no need to walk out of the 1988 Faulkner Conference, where he read "Samaritans" and "Old Frank and Jesus" on 3 August. He was introduced by Rubin, who, Brown told Ravenel, "said some nice things about me. And you, too. He gave you all the credit. Accurately" (LB to SR, Algonquin Files). Though Brown feared that some "imprudent academic" would make him look like a "dumbass," he received "two rounds of thunderous applause" (LB to SR, Algonquin Files).

The next day, Brown held his first book signing, at Oxford's Square Books. According to Susie James, writing in *Mississippi* magazine, a state publication, "the writer sat at one of the tables in the café up-stairs, signing books and receiving encouragement from his mother, Leona Brown, and his wife, Mary Annie" (80). One of those in atten-dance at the signing was John Grisham, a Southaven, Mississippi, law-yer who had just written his first novel, *A Time to Kill*. Grisham recalled that he and a friend, Bill Ballard, frequently traveled to Oxford to visit Rowan Oak and Square Books, and "during one of our road trips, we just happened to be at the bookstore when Larry was publishing *Facing the Music*. . . . There was a big, huge crowd, and it was very, very hot. . . . There was a lot of excitement and driving home and for a couple of days after that, I found that [experience] to be very, very inspirational, because here was a guy who had a dream, and he was determined to write, and he had written far more than I had." On another occasion, Richard Howorth recalled that Grisham, Brown, and several other writers were "signing books at the same time, and Larry had a long line of people to get to sign his books, [but] nobody was at [Grisham's table]. And Larry said to John, 'Don't worry—I know what you're go-ing through. It'll be better next time,' or something like that." The two writers continued to encourage each other. On 8 August 1989, Grisham wrote to Brown, "I enjoyed reading *Facing the Music* and I look forward to reading *Dirty Work*. I hope you sell a million copies. And if you do, and if I sell a million copies of *A Time to Kill*, then maybe we can retire to the balcony at Square Books and spend our time drinking cold beer, watching co-eds, and talking about future books" (Brown Collections). Though *A Time to Kill* did not sell well, Doubleday published Grisham's second novel, *The Firm*, in 1990; even before the book was released, Paramount Pictures purchased the film rights. Learning of Grisham's good fortune early in the year, Brown wrote to Clyde Edgerton, "A guy I know, John Grisham, who published his first novel last year, who lives in Southaven, MS, just sold his second unpublished draft to Para-mount for $600,000. . . . Can you imagine? The lucky pup" (Edgerton Papers). According to Howorth, in the year between the writing of *A Time to Kill* and the writing of *The Firm*, Grisham and his wife, Renee, "studied methodically the best-seller lists . . . to kind of see what made books best sellers. They probably made a judgment about where their particular niche was in the best-seller market." Both men "started out trying to make money by writing books, but John went about it in a much more businesslike fashion, whereas Larry . . . became a captive of literature, a 'fool for literature.'" Lisa Howorth remembered that people in Oxford were "happy for that to happen to John, too, but it wasn't quite the same as Larry, the homeboy from out in the country making it." The two writers began their careers with opposite motivations: Grisham looked to achieve success as a literary writer, while Brown wanted to make money. In effect, they switched positions, with Grisham becoming an enormous popular success and Brown becoming a literary novelist.

Brown and Grisham maintained a casual relationship, often appearing together at Oxford literary functions. Both authors read at the High Cotton Writers' Conference at Ole Miss in June 1991, and they were the headline speakers at the Living South Festivals held in June 1992 and 1993 and participants in the first Oxford Conference for the Book the following April. Stephen King came to Mississippi to participate in the conference, and Larry and Mary Annie Brown attended a dinner Grisham hosted for King. Grisham and Brown joined Hannah and Morris in reading at Robert Khayat's installation as the University of Mississippi's chancellor in 1996. Brown provided the keynote address at the dedication of the Oxford–Lafayette County Library on 13 April 1997, but a quotation from Grisham graced the cover of the program: "A public library is a building that indicates what a community thinks of itself."

Brown had mixed feelings about Grisham, and many of their mutual acquaintances believe that Brown was somewhat jealous of Grisham's huge financial and Hollywood success. In 1991, Brown told Edgerton about a French visitor to Oxford who asked him how "it felt to be rich and famous. I said Go ask John Grisham" (Edgerton Papers). Four years later, Brown was somewhat annoyed when Wayne Pond at the National Humanities Center in Chapel Hill, North Carolina, asked him to try to persuade Grisham to do an interview in the Soundings series: "That's amusing. Like I've got his phone number or some way to get in touch with him. You don't get in touch with him. He gets in touch with you. If he wants to" (LB to JM, Brown Collections). According to Brown's son, Billy Ray, however, his father did not "have any bitterness that I know toward anybody, especially anybody else writing." In contrast, Brown's surrogate son, Jonathan Miles, believes that Brown was jealous of Grisham's success, as is indicated by a song, "Come Back Home, Johnny Grisham," that Brown wrote in 1998. According to another of Brown's friends, Tom Rankin, Brown "would sing [the song] late at night, only to me, or to Jonny [Miles]. He didn't want to hurt John Grisham's feelings, [but], [i]t was as close as you get to Larry's parody of Grisham's life."

Grisham has never made any public statements showing anything but respect and admiration for Brown. Grisham describes his fellow author as "always likeable because there was no pretension. He was a country boy, and for that reason people may have discounted him at some point. But when you read his stuff, you realized there was a lot of talent there but also the perseverance, the determination. . . . Larry was a sweet guy without a mean bone in his body. There was not a pretentious bone. He always felt comfortable in his own skin. He never tried to become somebody else, and that was what was so endearing about him." On one occasion when Grisham was visiting New York City in the mid-1990s, after several of his books had been made into movies, a store clerk asked him, "'Where you from?' I said, 'Oxford, Mississippi.' She said, 'My favorite writer's from Oxford, Mississippi.' I kind of . . . held my breath and I said, 'Well, who's that?' And she said, 'Larry Brown, of course.' I burst out laughing."

In late September 1988, the weekend before *Facing the Music's* official release, Larry and Mary Annie Brown traveled to Nashville, Tennessee, for the annual meeting of the Southeastern Booksellers Association. Ravenel advised the author that he did not need to dress up for the occasion, since writers wore pretty much whatever they wanted: Brown bought new cowboy boots in celebration of the event (SR to LB, LB to SR, Algonquin Files). Brown participated in an autograph session at the Opryland Hotel and gave a reading and told Ravenel that he and his wife "had a *great time* in Nashville. Mary Annie was so happy. She loves to feel included in all this stuff. Thanks for being so nice to her, for making her feel so good" (Algonquin Files).

The Nashville conference was also significant because it was where Brown met Clyde Edgerton, who would soon become his closest literary friend. Shortly after returning home, Brown wrote to Ravenel to express his excitement about his new acquaintance: "It was sure fine meeting Clyde. When he comes to Oxford, I hope he's got time to come out and stay with us some. I want to cook him some fried catfish and some boiled shrimp. And I'm supposed to take him to the Hipp cemetery. I hope it doesn't rain and muddy up the roads before then. No way we'll make it up there if it does. He is a *really* nice guy" (Algonquin Files). Edgerton recalled that even before the conference, he had "read the story 'Facing the Music' and knew he was an extraordinarily talented writer." Seated next to each other at a dinner, the two men "realized without saying it I suppose that our backgrounds of hunting and fishing as kids in the south was something we shared—our mutual love of southern land and food and our raised eyebrows at some things modern." In Edgerton's memory, Brown then called to ask "how to get the blinking red light to go out on his [hotel] phone, and I recall that it was a serious phone call but the call turned into a kind of pointed satire of things 'hotelish.' He remembers me telling him not to eat the outsides of cheese balls because they were plastic. We realized I suppose without saying it that we shared a kind of humor in the process, a kind of dark humor in some cases. We didn't talk about it of course. We didn't say 'We share a kind of dark humor,' but we did laugh about things right much, little stories, incidents, etc., from then on."

Brown and Edgerton were indeed much alike, although Edgerton had much more formal education, including a master's and a doctorate in English from the University of North Carolina at Chapel Hill. Algonquin had published Edgerton's novels, *Raney* (1985) and *Walking across Egypt* (1987), just before Ravenel discovered Brown's writing, so Edgerton could both empathize with Brown and offer advice about adapting to his new role as writer. Brown looked up to Edgerton, usually addressing him as "Big Brother" or "Unc"; Edgerton often called Brown "Little Brother." In March 1990, Brown described Edgerton as "one of the few people I know who's got his head on straight" and said, "I listen to you more than I do anybody" (Edgerton Papers). Brown visited Edgerton in Durham, where the two men went flying in Edgerton's plane and fishing, and Edgerton traveled to Brown's home in Tula, where "Larry would entertain me by taking me to ride in the truck for beer drinking and listening to music and talking, just talking, or just riding without a whole lot of talking, more or less soaking in the country, the land and trees and creeks and an unspoken imagining of the spirits in the trees and land and what all the animals might be doing, what all sorts of adventures were there for anybody willing to take it all on in some fun way, mainly fishing or hunting. . . . Our conversations were usually about what was at hand in front of us: fish, his cabin, the pond." Nevertheless, according to Edgerton, their relationship "was more a friendship through letter writing than hanging out."

The Algonquin connection also brought Brown relationships with other authors whose works the press was publishing, including Jill McCorkle, Kaye Gibbons, and Lewis Nordan, though he never developed the close friendships with them that he maintained with Edgerton. McCorkle recalled a "wonderful company of . . . writers being launched by Algonquin" ("In the Company" 1) during the late 1980s and early 1990s. Though she was not as close to Brown as Tom Rankin and Edgerton became, "being Algonquin writers together in those early years was kind of like being related and there was an automatic connection." McCorkle "admired [Brown] tremendously, both the work on the page and the man who had worked so hard to get himself there." Brown often appeared at conferences with both McCorkle and Gibbons, and he invited both women to participate in his Lila Wallace Reading Series in Oxford. He read and enjoyed *Ellen Foster*, telling Ravenel that Gibbons was "a very good writer. The voice is wonderful, so authentic and funny and sad. A mighty brave little girl" (Algonquin Files). The feeling was mutual: in 2006, Gibbons told Mike Segretto that "Larry Brown's work deserves the widest possible audience. He was incapable of writing a weak sentence."

Brown also formed a friendship with Tim McLaurin, one of the first contemporary southern writers Brown met through his connection with Square Books. Brown was still working at the Oxford Fire Department when McLaurin came to town in September 1988 to read from his first novel, *The Acorn Plan*. Brown "was drinking coffee with some of my partners at our kitchen table, and he walked in wearing jeans and a jean jacket, and some kind of feed store cap. He said he was looking for Larry Brown. He was a husky guy with a thick brown mustache, and he had a country accent that sounded kind of like mine. . . . I invited him to sit down and have a cup of coffee with me, which he did. Later I . . . drove him down to William Faulkner's house, and from that day forward we were friends" ("Remembering"). Soon after returning home to North Carolina, McLaurin wrote to Brown that he "enjoyed meeting you last week in Oxford. . . . I got a copy of your book in Memphis and read it in one night. It knocked me out. I mean it. Your book crackles with energy, and it is written beautifully. The stories made me look at myself, and at many people I know, and kept me thinking" (Brown Collections).

Early the following year, McLaurin was diagnosed with a rare form of cancer, multiple myeloma. Brown had written a blurb for McLaurin's new novel, *Woodrow's Trumpet*; after seeing the published volume, Brown called McLaurin to offer congratulations but instead learned of his illness. The news "shocked" Brown, and he told a mutual friend, Jake Mills, "I don't know how much good words are going to do him but I'm going to try and write a letter with careful words to at least let him know I'm thinking about him and worrying about him" (Brown Collections). Brown and McLaurin remained in touch, and in June 1990, while recovering from a bone marrow transplant, McLaurin wrote that a recent letter from Brown "was the funniest thing I've read in a long time. You were writing at 1:30 in the morning while steadily nursing a fifth of Crown Royal. You had your music on and were flying right after having driven the back roads with beer and schnapps. In the middle of one serious paragraph, you stopped dead sentence and wrote, 'I love me some music'" (Brown Collections). The friendship endured until McLaurin's death in 2002.

During this period, Brown also met another up-and-coming writer, Rick Bass, a petroleum engineer who had produced two works of nonfiction before publishing his first collection of short stories, *The Watch*, in early 1989. Bass came to Oxford to read from the collection, but Brown was on duty at the fire department and could manage only brief visits with Bass between calls. Brown later returned "to the bookstore just as Bass was getting ready to leave." Brown "burst in and he seemed real glad to see me. We got us a mutual admiration society going right quick. I bought one of his books and he signed it real nicely for me.

I didn't get to talk to him long. But he's a very nice guy" (Edgerton Papers). In July of that year, the two met again when Bass returned to Oxford to read from his nonfiction book, *Oil Notes*, and they subsequently maintained their friendship through correspondence and visits whenever Bass was in Oxford. According to Bass,

> Usually we went out to his "cool pad," other times hung out in his house, other times to the pond at Tula. Sometimes at parties in town, occasionally at the Howorths, and often, riding around in the dusk. Sometimes to eat catfish, and often to have dinner at Ajax or City Grocery Bar, always loud and crowded. In the bars a switch would go on, he would be supported and hobnobbing would surround him, he would be swarmed. He would be a little apologetic because it disrupted our private time but it was good for him and he liked it; he'd be a little sheepish but he would breathe it in like the cigarettes he smoked. He would inhale it and be comforted by that attention. And it was certainly his due. Those who swarmed him took something away, as well—something vital and wild. He knew it, they knew it. It was very interesting.

Facing the Music was officially published on 30 September 1988. The front cover of the first edition features blurbs by Jack Butler and Brown's idol, Harry Crews, while the back cover bears comments from Ellen Douglas, Barry Hannah, and Willie Morris as well as the photograph of Brown standing on the balcony of Square Books. The original hardback version quickly sold between three and four thousand copies (Algonquin Files).

Brown initially promoted the book with readings in other Mississippi cities, including Amory, Columbus, and Jackson, and described some of the experience in a letter to Ravenel:

> I read "Kubuku Rides" at Amory, mostly to a bunch of grayhaired ladies. Freaked a few of em, I guess. They paid me $200 to read to about 20 people. [Columbus] went really well. I read "Old Frank and Jesus" to about 130 students. Plus [Mary Annie] and I spent the night before with the president of [the Mississippi University for Women] and his wife. They were real nice. Gave us the whole top floor of their house.

They even baked a *cake* with the cover of FACING THE MUSIC reproduced in icing. I told them it was about the nicest thing anybody'd done
for me. Know how many copies of my book they had in the whole town
for sale? 2. It was a good reading, though. They beat their hands silly. I
was awed by the response. (Algonquin Files)

When Brown read at Lemuria Books in Jackson on 28 October, he was
"underwhelmed at the response. But," he reported, bookstore owner
John Evans "has sold about 70 of the 100 he ordered, so I was happy"
(LB to JM, Brown Collections).

Brown's promotional efforts on behalf of *Facing the Music* were
limited because he was still working at the Oxford Fire Department,
he was concentrating on completing *Dirty Work*, and he had already
become reluctant to travel to promote his books. In April 1989, however, he went to Chattanooga, Tennessee, for the Biennial Conference
on Southern Literature, which sought in part to advance the work of
new southern writers. The experience was novel for Brown, who at
thirty-seven years old had traveled little outside Mississippi except
while he was in the marines; in addition, Brown's participation earned
him twenty-five hundred dollars plus expenses from the Chattanooga Arts Council (Brown Collections). On 8 April, Brown gave a talk,
"A Late Start," and read from the manuscript of *Dirty Work*. Edgerton
later wrote to Brown, "Your reading and talk were something—both.
You knocked them and me dead" (Brown Collections). In "Chattanooga
Nights," an essay included in *Billy Ray's Farm*, Brown recalled, "I was
pretty excited about going. I was also intimidated by the whole thing
because I was still pretty green about the situation a young writer finds
himself in if people like his books, the travel and the speaking engage-
ments and the readings and the bookstores. . . . The conference was the
first well-paying gig I ever had, and the money they were giving me was
a lot more than a whole month's salary at the fire department" (29–30).
Downtown Chattanooga's Radisson Hotel was "the nicest place" (31) in
which either he or Mary Annie had ever stayed, and both of them were
thrilled with their new success. Moreover, the conference brought him
into the orbit of several heavyweights in the southern literary world:
"It was pretty stunning to me to see Ernest Gaines and Louis [Rubin]

going down the street just talking like regular people. My eyes got big seeing William Styron and Andrew Lytle and Horton Foote in the flesh" (32). Brown also met and talked with Madison Jones; although Brown did not know who Jones was, the Mississippian appreciated the older and more experienced author's kindness (32).

Less than a month later, Brown gave a reading and workshop at Delta State University in Cleveland, Mississippi. Bill Hays, a professor of English there, subsequently told Brown, "Your workshop and reading were as good as any we have ever had at Delta State. I thought the afternoon session was especially good. There were many good questions from our people, and your answers were thoughtful, honest and clearly without the pretension that often occurs in such programs" (Brown Collections).

That May, Brown made his first trip to New York City and won his first major award. Brown traveled to New York to promote his forthcoming novel, *Dirty Work*; to meet Peter Workman, who had recently bought Algonquin Books, and others who worked in the press's New York offices; to meet his agent, Liz Darhansoff; and to attend an organized reading of "Samaritans" at a small Symphony Space conference on the short story, for which he earned fifty dollars. Back home in Yocona, Brown wrote to Edgerton, "The thing on Broadway was fine. It was sold out, 900 people paid ten bucks a head." The meeting with the publishing staff had also been a success: "I . . . met Workman and all, gave my little reading. I even got a pretty good round of applause from the salesmen. Of course they made me leave the room after that, so they could talk freely about DIRTY WORK." And he had enjoyed meeting Darhansoff, whom he described as "really nice. Like a different person over the phone. God she's rich, ain't she. . . . She was really sweet in person, though." But Brown was glad to be home: "I ain't nothing but a homeboy, ain't no need pretending I'm anything else" (Edgerton Papers). His designated escort on the trip, Ina Stern, a member of Workman Publishing's marketing department, recalled that Brown indeed appeared uncomfortable in the big city and that he seemed particularly dismayed with the way she drove her small car around Manhattan: "We criss-crossed the island, running yellow lights and zig-zagging between traffic lanes and trying to avoid cabs and buses, honking at everything that came into our path. I casually pointed out all of the wonderful sights of New York as we whizzed by them and I tried to explain to Larry that that is how you drive in New York" ("Go, Little Book" 48). After the ride, Brown suggested a stop for a drink. He and Stern had several, ending up at the Fulton Fish Market, and Brown did not return to his hotel until nearly two in the morning. When he described his night out to Mary Annie, "It didn't sit well with her atall," even though "I didn't do anything wrong" (Edgerton Papers).

On the way to New York, Brown spent several days in Chapel Hill, visiting with Edgerton and the staff at Algonquin. Brown was impressed with the size of the town and had a pleasant stay there despite his homesickness. He also apparently did considerable drinking: Edgerton subsequently wrote to Brown, "We enjoyed having you. I didn't mind you getting drunk—you were on vacation—you were very calm and nobody cared. I was glad to have you. . . . I felt like you were family in a good way" (Brown Collections).

Before his trip, Brown learned that *Facing the Music* had earned him the Mississippi Institute of Arts and Letters Prize, a ten-year-old award that brought with it one thousand dollars in cash. In a 23 May *Oxford Eagle* article, Brown said,

> It's the most important thing that's ever happened to me. I knew I had been nominated a couple of months ago. I was really stunned when they called to tell me I'd won. . . . I said, 'Are you kidding?' I just couldn't believe it.
>
> I had always hoped for something like this. But I never thought it could come on the first book, and I was up against some good books. (David Smith, "Local" 1A)

Other authors whose works had been nominated included Will Campbell, Ellen Douglas, Ellen Gilchrist, Beverly Lowry, Margaret Walker Alexander, Stuart Stevens, Frederick Barthelme, Hodding Carter III, and Elizabeth Spencer (1A). Brown received the award at a "black tie banquet" held at the Mississippi Art Museum in Jackson, giving a brief acceptance speech and reading "Facing the Music." Brown told the audience, "I set my goals high early on, and although I've never lowered them, I've had to learn patience, and maybe the most important thing: if you want to be a writer bad enough, nobody can stop you." He concluded, "This is the proudest moment of my life, and it's because of the literary heritage that we have here. I was born here, raised here, I still live here. I've been to quite a few places, and they're okay to visit, but I haven't found any place yet that suits me any better than this one. For my state to honor my work like this—my state: Mississippi—means more to me than I can say" (Brown Collections).

In June 1989, Brown attended the annual meeting of the American Booksellers Association in Washington, D.C., though he hated the idea of going and wrote to Ravenel on 27 April, "The more I think about it, the more it sounds like a bad idea for me. I have this terrible fear of getting embarrassed in front of people because I don't know enough about literature to talk about it like I do. I don't run around with any intellectuals and don't want to know any. I damn sure don't want to try and sound like one" (Algonquin Files). While there, Brown held a joint press conference with Gibbons to talk about their soon-to-be-published novels, *Dirty Work* and *A Virtuous Woman*: "Brown told reporters he 'grew up in Mississippi listening to people tell me stories' and that he likes to use the first person narrative method because it 'reminds me of listening to those stories. . . . I try to write about the south that I live in now'" (Glendenning, "Booklovers" L7).

Brown reluctantly read again at the Faulkner Conference in Oxford at the end of July: he had "tried to decline, saying truthfully that I didn't want people to get tired of hearing me, but they kept on and on until I finally relented. Clyde [Edgerton] was coming down anyway, to visit with me and just attend the Conference, so we worked it out in a way that won't cost him anything to attend. He'll enjoy it. I'm going to cook him some catfish and shrimp one night and take him to the oldest graveyard that I know of, one where the stones go back to the 1700s and are still readable" (LB to JM, Brown Collections). Edgerton flew himself to Oxford in a plane he had recently bought and took Brown's wife and children on short flights, though a "freak storm" prevented Brown from going up and the two men "had to literally hold the airplane down in order to get the tie-down lines tied. . . . We were laughing while we worked." But Brown's reading at the conference was less enjoyable: he explained to Ravenel on 3 August, "Well the bad karma I had going for the reading at the Faulkner Conference was correct. Some dilbert-head didn't think I'd need a PA system to throw my voice out to people sitting over 100 feet away, a couple of hundred of them. So I had to kind of quietly scream my reading. I cut it short. I had to. People couldn't hear me" (Algonquin Files).

Brown's promotional efforts, combined with those of Algonquin's Ravenel and Jhanke, paid off, and the collection was widely reviewed. According to Keith Perry, much of *Facing the Music*'s success resulted from the press's emphasis on Brown's career as a fireman, but two other significant factors also contributed to the literary world's interest in the volume: first, Brown was clearly a self-made writer in an era when most beginning writers are products of collegiate writing programs; second, Brown wrote realistically and sympathetically about lower-class life in a way that appealed to a reading audience comprised mainly of members of the middle class. Because Brown saw his characters as authentic human beings, worth writing about because of their humanity, his writing seems genuine.

Facing the Music introduced Brown's concern with working-class residents of North Mississippi. Brown's male characters—as well as some of his women—thrive on alcohol, cigarettes, bars, and sex. These men drive their pickup trucks, usually equipped with coolers of cold beer or schnapps, through the backwoods, particularly during the early evening. Brown referred to this time as the "gloam," borrowing James Street's term for the time after the sun has gone down "and left about an hour of light before dark. It's the very best time to ride around and listen to some music" (*OF* 25). In the words of Susan Ketchin, "Brown introduces us to people who seem to be paralyzed by calamity, and who eventually must learn, often with only the slightest glimmer of understanding, how to deal with it—through resignation, denial, or a wan faith" ("Larry" 101). Brown believed that "there is just no way for some lives to have a happy ending" (Weinraub F4). But according to Robert Beuka, Brown possessed a "sense of empathy toward his characters [that] allows Brown's stories to transcend the merely banal or brutal" (59). Brown described his characters as "very much like the people that I know best. All I really do is just kind of watch the people around me, watch what goes on. That's where all my characters come from" (Wein-raub F4). On another occasion, Brown explained, "I build my stories, and I try to be authentic in them. The events have to be authentic, too, no matter how painful the endings might be. I sometimes get accused of being brutal and having a dark vision. . . . Tragedy is inevitable in my stories because of the circumstances people live in" (Bonetti et al. 244). Those "circumstances"—particularly poverty, a lack of family or social connections, and the inability to find a positive sense of self—often lead to conflict and violence, and the resolutions are not always positive.

In one of the first published reviews of *Facing the Music*, which appeared in the *Columbia (South Carolina) State* on 11 September 1988, William Starr declared, "There are small private moments here which Brown dissects with the precision of a neurosurgeon, peeling back layers to expose the heart of darkness within." Other reviewers, including Paul Kaplan, noted the stories' resemblances to the work of Raymond Carver. Wrote Jana Harris in the *Seattle Post-Intelligencer*, "Brown has cut to the heart of deadbeat America, portraying a frighteningly misogynistic world as only someone who has been there could do. Nobody's even thinking of working things out—they just order another beer" (L7). According to the *Atlanta Journal-Constitution*'s Joyce Slater, "You probably wouldn't want to meet many of [Brown's characters], and I feel fairly certain that you wouldn't want to be any of them. Still, their stories manage to touch us in surprisingly potent ways" (K10). A few reviewers criticized the stories for their sameness, and Betsy Leighton of the *Winston-Salem (North Carolina) Journal* wrote that comparisons with Faulkner were premature, but she also noted that Brown "knows the lingo, the country, deep-South dialect, the culture, the heartbreak and the limitations that plague those of whom he writes. He pulls no punches. These stories are not for the fainthearted" (H4).

Brown's stories take a variety of approaches. He had written to Ravenel in October 1987, "I *like* working in new forms. I like inventing a different way to tell a story because if it works I've done something nobody else has" (Algonquin Files). The stories' most prominent theme is the difficulty of maintaining permanent love after the physical thrills of youth and raising children have passed: dreams must be abandoned in the face of aging.

The collection opens with the title story, the idea for which came to Brown while he was sitting at a red light in Oxford and "saw a man and a woman in a bedroom watching TV, and I knew something was seriously wrong between them" (Watkins, "Hot" 1D). Brown turned the situation into the tale of a working-class couple (the husband is a fireman) trying to cope with the wife's breast cancer and mastectomy, a subject that although now commonly discussed was, according to Ravenel, "forbidden territory" at the time. But Brown "just wades right in and deals with it with frankness and tenderness" (Sid Scott 7F). The man and the woman, both in their fifties, have apparently enjoyed a satisfying sexual relationship until the removal of the woman's breast. The wife desperately wants that relationship to continue, but the husband cannot endure the sight of her maimed body and has begun an affair with another woman. According to Jerome Klinkowitz, "The tone is at once conversational and intimate; indeed, by his second paragraph Brown's storyteller has established that he feels cozier with the reader than with his wife" (72).

The story begins with the troubled couple watching Ray Milland in *The Lost Weekend* while lying side by side in bed. Both are drinking to deaden the pain of their loss, but both know that this encounter will end like all the others since her surgery—in darkness both literal and spiritual. Brown told Susan Ketchin, "People think that story is autobiographical. I get letters all the time about that one from people consoling me and my wife about 'her mastectomy.' But this story is really about pain and loss wherever you find it. . . . I did see it as having a hopeful ending" ("Interview" 128). The ending is ambiguous, with readers able to see the man and woman turning off the light as they begin to have sex as a sign either of continued darkness or of hope. The story powerfully evokes the horrors that arise as people grow older and must face life with greater realism.

In "Kubuku Rides (This Is It)," Brown handles the perspective of a young African American female alcoholic. Assuming this point of view would seem to represent a considerable risk for Brown, but he was immediately confident in this narrator: "Sometimes, you know when you write the first line, you know you've got a voice. And that's the way it was when I wrote the first couple of lines of that story. I knew that the rest of the story had to follow. I knew that I had the dialect and the rest of the story had to follow in that vein and be accurate after the first two lines" (LaRue 45–46). Brown wrote "Kubuku Rides" on "Christmas Eve day in 1986, and I didn't do anything for fourteen hours but write that story. It came in one long shot, and when I finished the story, it was basically just like it is today. Just a gift" (Manley 122). Brown imagined the voice "of a young black girl, a writer telling the story, who had an African name. And this was going to be like the first thing she had done, you know. And it was like a horse coming out of the gate for the first time. And that's just the image that I had of the speaker telling the story. It wasn't Angel telling it; it was somebody else telling it. Not me either" (LaRue 46).

Angel's problems with alcohol result not from her race but from her uncontrollable addiction. She has a loving and supportive husband, Alan, and a young son, Randy, both victims of her inability to control her drinking. After cutting his hand while fighting with Angel over a bottle of wine that she has sneaked into the house, Alan says, "This is it! Can't stand it! Sick of it!" (*FM* 15). In a series of flashbacks, Angel recalls episodes that show how addicted she is and how her drinking leads to catastrophe. She recognizes that neither her heartbroken husband nor her desire to quit can control her problem: "This thing not something you throw off cold. This thing deep, this thing beat more good people than her" (27). The story ends with Angel getting into her car to go buy more wine and watching Alan turn off the porch light, symbolizing the hopelessness of her situation.

Mr. Pellisher, the main character in "The Rich," is a travel agent who spends his workday planning trips for people who, unlike him, can afford exotic vacations. In some ways, this story is as close as Brown ever came to voicing a kind of Marxist anger against the capitalist system. Pellisher tries to give his clients the impression that he is their social and economic equal, but he knows otherwise and suffers from what he perceives as deprivation. The phrase "the rich" is repeated constantly in the story—nine times on the first page alone. This repetition re-inforces Pellisher's obsessive jealousy of those he serves as well as Brown's distinction between the classes.

"Old Frank and Jesus" continues the feeling of frustration that per-meates "The Rich." "Old Frank and Jesus" is the oldest story in the collection, written in 1984. Set in the 1960s, the story deals with the imminent suicide of Marvin Parker, a fifty-eight-year-old Mississippi farmer who has lost all hope. Brown told Gary Pettus, "That frame of time, during the Vietnam War, . . . when . . . the kids were rebelling and the parents didn't like it, that's just the time frame that hit me for the story. . . . I would identify more with the kids who were rebelling, because, you know, from [Parker's] point of view, the whole thing was just senseless. Whereas from their point of view, my point of view, in the sixties, hearing the Beatles and Jimi Hendrix, I thought it was great" ("Interview" 14). Having killed his favorite dog, Frank, because Parker's wife fears that the animal will bring rabies into their home, Parker lies on the living room sofa, a borrowed pistol concealed be-neath it. On this, the last morning of his life, Parker reviews his trou-bled existence and decides that death is preferable to struggling with dying farm animals, falling fences, unmanageable debts, irate neigh-bors, a wife too concerned with material possessions, and children whose enthusiasm for popular culture has sapped their work ethic. Brown told Susan Ketchin, "For a long time, I've been trying to under-stand suicide, and I do see how it is not a sin for some people in some cases. The story 'Old Frank and Jesus' is drawn from a man who used to cut my hair. One day, he borrowed a pistol and shot himself through the head. . . . Mr. P. in the story was concerned with two things he couldn't understand: How could anybody be so mean to Jesus? How did he let his wife talk him into shooting his old dog?" ("Interview" 129). Parker has lost his faith in Christianity, looking at a picture of Jesus on the wall and thinking, "There was a time when he could have a little talk with Jesus and everything'd be all right. Four or five years ago he could" (*FM* 50). This loss of faith is one factor in Parker's deci-sion to end his life. The story ends with what Beuka describes as "the blunt observation, 'Mr. Parker, fifty-eight, is reclining on his couch.'

After investing his character with a rounded, idiosyncratic personality through the use of extended interior monologue, Brown leaves his plight unresolved" (59).

Brown deliberately used an experimental form in "Boy and Dog": each sentence has five words. He began crafting the story in his mother-in-law's kitchen; after writing the first page, he thought, "I bet I can do something a little different there and just stack those lines one under the other. And put five words in each sentence and make it look like a poem but really be a short story" (*RS*). Brown also said that he was trying to write in a style that Donald Barthelme had never used (Pettus, "Interview" 14). The strategy initially escaped even his editor: according to Ravenel, when she first started working on the story with him, she "said something in my editorial way like 'Well, Larry, I think you ought to add this word to the 19th sentence in the story,' and he said, 'Well, if I do that, it'll be six words long, that sentence.' And I said, 'So . . . ,' and he said 'Well, all the sentences in that story are five words long'" (Gross).

Brown found the story's subject particularly interesting: he loved dogs and had many killed on the highway "because they don't have sense enough to get out of the road." He recalled that on one occasion, he watched as a dog came "walking out of the ditch and there was this Mustang coming down the road about sixty and the dog never looked around, just walked straight into the car—of course it killed him instantly—and I just got the idea" (Manley 123).

The story itself is bildungsroman: the young protagonist witnesses the death of his pet and then reacts dangerously when he sees the car returning to the scene to recover a hubcap. "The kid" hurls a brick at the driver of the car, with catastrophic results: the driver ends up a charred corpse. At the end of the story, "the kid" suggests that he has learned how to get what he wants: "But fathers must be cautious. / Kids are violent these days. / Especially where pets are concerned" (*FM* 69).

"Julie: A Memory" is another experimental story. The central narrator has impregnated his girlfriend, Julie, and apparently has watched both as she had an abortion and as she was raped in a parked car. The story is at times confusing, since other voices sporadically seem to take over narration. According to Barry Walters, "'Julie: A Memory' presents a young man's impression of how a gang beat him, raped his girlfriend, and left him with a confusion of memories that refuse to be recalled logically" (57). When Ravenel first read the story, she remembered, "It just blew me away. . . . I wrote to him, 'I think it's amazing,' and he said, 'I'm so surprised. That's one of those that I just sat down and wrote and then I . . . cut it up and mix[ed] it up. I just did it so fast that I didn't think anybody would ever like it.'" The story clearly shows the influence of Faulkner. The central narrator is reminiscent of Quentin in *The Sound and the Fury* but is a less intellectual, far more physical young man. Brown avoided such distorted narration in his later work, apparently realizing that he, unlike Faulkner, could not handle the nuances of stream-of-consciousness narration.

"Samaritans," a title that probably alludes to Jesus' parable of the Good Samaritan, introduces down-and-out characters in desperate need of physical salvation. The story evolved from Brown's experiences at an Oxford bar, Opal's: "I wrote it probably about 1985. [I thought,] what if a kid walked into a bar one day, wanted to buy cigarettes, and wasn't old enough. That's where the whole thing started. . . . It just went on from there. And I just lifted the whole place in my mind" (*RS*).

The story's protagonist, Frank, sits in a Mississippi bar, drinking beer to deaden the pain caused by his wife's desertion of him for another man. In spite of his self-pity, he becomes an unwitting Samaritan when a ragged woman, her mother, and her four children, wandering from Alabama to Louisiana, stop at the bar. After the mother sends her underage son into the bar to buy cigarettes, Frank befriends the family, buying the woman beer and cigarettes and ultimately giving her thirty dollars although he realizes that she and her mother will just use the money to get drunk. When the oldest boy calls Frank "a dumb sumbitch" for giving the woman the money, Frank has to agree (*FM* 100). In the story, Brown "wanted to say a lot of things, some contradictory. Like, it's about the futility of helping people who do nothing to help themselves, the outcasts of society. But it's also about that it's a good thing to try. That's what Jesus would have done. It's an ironic title" (Ketchin, "Interview" 129–30). The plural form of the title thus suggests that the true Samaritans may be the members of the ragtag family, who remove Frank from his obsession with himself.

The final three stories in the collection, like "Facing the Music," deal with failed heterosexual relationships. In "Night Life," the protagonist is Gary, an unappealing loser who has been in jail and has returned to live with his mother. Looking to pick up any available woman for sex, he goes to a bar and meets Connie, who is married to a successful contractor but is trying to break away from him and her middle-class life. Although she is reluctant, Gary persuades her to go to a hotel with him; he then learns that she has been leaving her young children at home alone when she goes to bars. Outraged and disgusted, he slaps her, using his open hand because he doesn't "want to scare the little girls with blood. They would be frightened, and might remember it for the rest of their lives" (*FM* 127). The irony here is heavy: it is permissible to hit a woman, but children must be protected at all costs.

"Leaving Town" is written from the alternating perspectives of the two central characters, Richard, a young bricklayer and handyman, and Myra, a middle-aged woman recently divorced from her husband. In a final act of vengeance, Myra's husband has broken the doors of the house where she continues to live, and she calls Richard to fix them. Richard lives with Betty, a slovenly woman who has borne another man's child out of wedlock. Richard loves the little girl, Tracey, but not her mother. Myra and Richard nearly fall into a relationship based on her sexual need and his desire to talk about the no-win situation in which he finds himself with Betty. Though Myra and Richard do not sleep together, their interaction gives him the strength to take Tracey and leave for Florida, with Myra's number still in his pocket.

In "The End of Romance," the final story in the volume, another couple, the unnamed narrator and a woman named Miss Sheila, are "riding around" toward the end of their affair. He is a would-be writer whose friends include "poets, artists, actors, English professors out at Ole Miss" (*FM* 162); Miss Sheila has become tired of their drunken shenanigans. As the narrator and Miss Sheila are about to break up, they stop at a convenience store for beer but end up caught in a shoot-out between two black men. When the cops arrive, the narrator points to Miss Sheila and says, "She did it" (*FM* 167), a comic resolution to a less-than-comic situation. Walters wrote of the story, "Brown's specialty is examining at close range the creepy little things that make his characters tick, while he remains emotionally distant. There's nothing he won't do to achieve the right queasy effect. When you notice that he's using a dying black stickup man, oozing guts and gore to symbolize 'The End of Romance' in his final story, you realize that country folks are just as morbid as we are" (57).

With his well-received volume of short stories winning him acclaim and recognition, Brown returned his attention to his first novel, which he had started writing even before Ravenel read "Facing the Music." In the late summer of 1989, Algonquin released that novel, *Dirty Work*.

CHAPTER FIVE

Dirty Work

A Vietnam Novel, 1989–1990

Larry Brown got the idea for *Dirty Work* in the early 1980s, after his uncle's death. "My mother said my aunt was so sad that all she did was to pray to die every night. I got to thinking about that, and I thought, my god, there's a story in that somewhere. So I began it with a lady who was like that and had this son who stayed in his room. I went ahead and wrote the novel" (Ross 90). The idea "festered," and Brown "just had to get it down. It turned out that I had to write it five different times and throw out six hundred pages. It went through five complete revisions" (Bonetti et al. 250). Brown later identified *Dirty Work* as the most difficult of his books to write: "I had to work the store we had in Tula and the fire department. The store had to be open six in the morning to six in the evening every day. I would have about four hours between the two jobs to sleep and write" (Steven Campbell, "Larry Brown Interview" 8). After he finished the third draft, he showed it to his editor, Shannon Ravenel, who told him, "'Your story starts on page one sixty.' So I had to do two more complete drafts from that point. I ended up working on the novel for two and a half years. . . . That was a rough time" (8).

When Ravenel first read the manuscript in March 1988, she was impressed, but she also believed that it needed more work. On 4 April, she wrote to Brown,

> The story you have to tell is a great big one—powerful, and very
> important. And there are sections in this novel that surpass even your

finest stories. There are ten pages in here where the writing is as good as anything I have EVER read. This is a novel that deserves all the work you have done on it so far—and a lot more.

You say "Be gentle with me." That poses a problem. I don't think I ought to be gentle with you about this book, Larry. It's too important that you get it done and get it done right. It's too important that the power it has the potential to embody not be lost, not be wasted. . . .

You have a frustrating (for the editor) way of dealing with criticism. Probably, you've developed it because you've worked alone for so long, because you have enormous stores of creative energy and not nearly enough time, and because you are proud. . . .

Well, in the case of DIRTY WORK, the only route is revision. You sure as hell don't want to throw this one away. And surely, you don't want it to see the light of day (it won't anyway) the way it is. It has to be revised. And I think I know pretty well how to go about fixing it so that what you want it to do happens. Just say the word. I'm sitting here dying to get to work on it. What about you?" (Algonquin Files)

Brown agreed to make the revisions, and Ravenel ultimately provided him with six legal-sized sheets of recommendations as well as notes on the manuscript itself. She told him, "Whenever Walter is speaking in his own voice the novel lives. When he is not speaking, the narrative often dies. It just goes down and goes flat." She also warned Larry about making Walter a writer: "Doing that is the same as waving a red flag at your reader that says, 'I'm new at this and I do this so I can imagine myself in all these circumstances.'" She also suggested that he balance Walter's story with that of Braiden Chaney since "they are stories of equal thematic weight" (Algonquin Files). At times, Brown "thought I would never deliver what she wanted" (Sid Scott 7F),

By early July, Ravenel had received and read Brown's revised manuscript and pronounced it "GREAT. The description of Beth's death is perfect—and perfectly beautiful. The very last pages are also perfect. You have finished one hell of a good novel, Larry Brown. I congratulate you" (Algonquin Files). On 19 July, he submitted the final version to Ravenel, thanking her for her editorial help: "You sure have spent a lot, lot of time on this. . . . And what you got about the story was so right on target, two people reaching across to each other, two strangers, really. I can hardly believe I wrote all that needless shit to begin with. I'm no great writer, but you're a great editor" (Algonquin Files). In March 1989, Ravenel decided that the novel was ready for publication, offering Brown a contract for the novel with Algonquin/Workman. He would receive ten thousand dollars on signing the contract and another twenty-five hundred dollars when the novel was published on 25 August 1989 (Brown Collections). Brown asked his friend Glennray Tutor, an artist, to create a painting for the novel's front cover. After reading the manuscript, Tutor "called him up and told him I'd be honored" (Ravenel, "Two" 5). According to Tutor, Brown's "original idea for a jacket image was of an African warrior holding a spear silhouetted against the rising sun. I didn't think that image encompassed the breadth of the story. I wanted to preserve the emotion that it engendered. That's why the African spear supports the flag in my painting" (5).

The revision process had not been easy. At one point, Mary Annie Brown remembered that Larry threatened to burn the manuscript, and the two had "one of our worst fights over [the book]. I saved it." But reading *Dirty Work* also caused Mary Annie to realize just how "smart" her husband was. Larry recognized that the revision process had been hard not only for him but also for his wife, telling Ravenel, "I think Mary Annie's breathed a sigh of relief now that this draft is over. I can be not a nice guy to live with when I've got work in progress and things start going wrong" (Algonquin Files). But the work had paid off: Brown later described *Dirty Work* as his "personal favorite" among his novels (Robinson).

Brown wanted to use the novel "to say something about the people who make those sacrifices for us, the veterans—the guys whom we honor every Memorial Day—Sometimes what happens to them" (Bonetti et al. 251). According to Chris Goodrich, Brown also "wanted to write about the after-effects of the war . . . largely because his father was deeply damaged by his four years in the infantry" during World War II (32). Brown thought that Walter James's father in the novel resembles Knox Brown in "little ways," but "my father never killed anybody and went to the penitentiary or anything. I make up all my characters out of little bits and pieces of real life" (Bonetti et al. 239). While serving in the marines in Philadelphia, Brown met wounded veterans who also influenced his creation of Braiden and Walter: "One of them, he didn't even have any legs. Both of his had been machine-gunned off at the groin. But he had a pair of artificial legs and he would just buckle his pants around his waist and come in on a pair of crutches. But all the rest of them were in wheel chairs. We had five or six steps leading up to our club, and we'd pull them up those stairs at night in their chairs and then roll them down at night. I got to know a lot of them really well and got to listen to the stories that they told" (Sullivan 3). Another veteran Brown met "had the kind of injury that Walter has. He had been shot all the way through the base of his skull. To look at him, he didn't have any kind of disfiguring wound. . . . But he had blackouts, seizures" (Bonetti et al. 238). In creating the novel in general and Walter in particular, Brown also borrowed from the experiences of an Oxford man who served in Southeast Asia but "never could get used to his life after Vietnam, and a couple of years ago he wound up shooting his wife through the hip with a shotgun, and he shot at his little boy, missed him, and . . . he finally shot and killed himself. But that guy used to tune my motorcycle for me, and sometimes he was okay, but then sometimes he would go off, and he was dangerous to be around. He would get high and drunk, and he just wasn't a safe person to be around. You know, Vietnam did that to him" (Sullivan 3).

Algonquin provided a twenty-five-thousand-dollar advertising budget for *Dirty Work*, which had a first printing of twenty-five thousand copies (Goodrich 32). The promotional campaign began on 12 June 1989, when Ravenel wrote to a series of book review editors and announced both the publication of *Dirty Work* and the awards that *Facing the Music* had received, including the Mississippi Institute of Arts and Letters award and the inclusion of "Kubuku Rides (This Is It)" in the 1989 edition of *Best American Short Stories* (Perry 135). Other press releases and advance copies followed. In addition, the Workman office in New York would launch a phone campaign to major newspapers and magazines, including the *New York Times*, the *Los Angeles Times*, *Time*, *Newsweek*, *People*, the *Washington Post*, and the *Chicago Tribune* (SR to LB, Algonquin Files).

Because he was still working at the Oxford Fire Department and because he was leery both of his new fame and of flying, Brown was reluctant to promote *Dirty Work*. Algonquin wanted him to go to Dallas, New Orleans, and St. Louis, but his work schedule prohibited the trip. In August, he made appearances closer to home, at Lemuria Books in Jackson and at Square Books in Oxford, where he "signed over 50 [copies], stayed about 3 hours. I read to [the audience] but told them first how much I appreciated their support" (Edgerton Papers). Late in the month, Larry and Mary Annie Brown flew to Atlanta for the Southeastern Booksellers Association convention, where he read from the book.

Brown dedicated *Dirty Work* to Knox Brown: "For Daddy, who knew what war does to men." He presented the first copy he received to his mother, inscribing it "And for Mamma who got me to read" (*RS*). Leona Barlow Brown "didn't know I had dedicated it to Daddy. She was very moved and cried after I left, I found out" (Edgerton Papers).

Dirty Work received favorable notice. By 12 November 1989, the book had sold fourteen thousand copies and been reviewed by Rick Bass in the *New York Times Book Review* (Sid Scott 6F). Bass wrote, "The men (and the women) in 'Dirty Work' somehow manage to stay ahead of their many horrors, never yielding to them, and so the grisliness of the novel is kept at bay. There are no willing victims here, not even the limbless Braiden, despite the decision he reaches at the novel's conclusion. Instead, the vitality and humor of the characters' voices rise above the echoes of the battlefield" ("In" 15). Writing in the *New York Times*, Herbert Mitgang asserted that *Dirty Work* was the best antiwar novel since Dalton Trumbo's *Johnny Got His Gun*, published fifty years earlier. The *Atlanta Journal-Constitution's* Greg Johnson opined that *Dirty Work* "unquestionably puts [Brown] into the front ranks of the South's contemporary writers " ("Stirring" L10). Many reviewers applauded Brown's willingness to let his two central characters speak authentically for themselves. According to Chauncey Mabe, "No white writer has surpassed Brown in capturing a black voice with sympathy and authenticity" (2F).

Brown's power impressed even those reviewers who criticized the novel. Sam Hodges believed that the plot of *Dirty Work* was contrived and that Brown had sacrificed realism to his concern with theme; nevertheless, Hodges declared, "Brown has written one of the best contrived novels I've read" ("These" n.p.). Guy Mannes-Abbott found the narrative compelling but Brown "no stylist. This has all the flawlessness of a creative-writing programme, with none of the airy restraint of, say, a Carver" (46). Several reviewers also commented on the obvious influence of other writers on *Dirty Work*, but Mabe defended Brown: "One of the most disarming attributes of the book is its direct acknowledgment of its debts to other books. The two men discuss similar situations in *The Young Lions* by Irwin Shaw, Dalton Trumbo's *Johnny Got His Gun* and *One Flew over the Cuckoo's Nest* by Ken Kesey. Brown's novel is patently derivative of these sources, but the way they are frankly invoked deflects any criticism" (2F). Vietnam veteran and writer Michael Peterson told Brown that he had read the book on a late-night flight "where the lights were low and nobody could see him crying" (Sullivan 3).

At the end of September, Brown made his second visit to New York City. This time, he was slated to appear on the *Today* show. He initially balked at appearing on television, "but the producer finally called me the other day, and I just couldn't say no to her. It's $1 million worth of free advertising, and I know realistically that I'd be a fool to turn it down. . . . [I]t might create enough publicity so that *Dirty Work* will take off and sell enough to where I can write full time. So even if it's painful for a little bit, it's probably better in the long run" (LB to JM, Brown Collections). Back in Oxford on 2 October, Brown wrote to Clyde Edgerton, "Well I made it up there and back in one piece and I guess I'm no worse for the wear. It was a real good experience and I'm terrifically happy now that I did it. I know it made Shannon happy and I know it made everybody at Workman happy. The whole thing went real smooth. [Jane Pauley] was just as sweet as she could be and she had read quite a bit of *Dirty Work* and that made it a lot easier for me. She kept me talking and you know we had a good time. I think that it probably came across that I was enjoying myself. I was glad that it happened as well as it did" (Edgerton Papers).

While in New York, Brown met Michael Halpern from *American Playhouse*, a PBS anthology series: Halpern was "just crazy about *Dirty*

Work and he thinks that it will work well as a stage play." Larry also did a reading for National Public Radio and an interview with CBS Radio and had a "photography session with . . . *Newsweek*. They will be running their review week after next with a color picture." Less than twenty-four hours after his arrival in New York, Brown was back home (Edgerton Papers).

During the next few weeks, Brown formalized a contract with Halpern: "They want to find a theatre company and crew they like in New York, stage it live and film it, then show it on PBS. There's no big money involved, I don't think, but I'm not worried about it. As this point I'd almost do it for nothing, now that I know they're committed to the project" (LB to JM, Brown Collections). Although Brown continued to work on a script and to confer with Halpern over the next few years, the project came to nothing.

The New York trip altered Brown's life dramatically: as he explained in *On Fire*, "That television show has changed something, the shape and order and regularity my world once had. People know where I am now" (178). But the change was not immediately apparent: two nights later, he was "tearing down a ceiling in Murphy's Marine, a bait shop/grocery store/gas station in Oxford, looking for pockets of fire" (178). Brown was quite taken with Pauley, to the point that he began a new novel in which she was a featured character, though Ravenel found the work unworthy of publication. For her part, Pauley liked Brown and early the following year asked him to be one of her first guests on a new show she was about to begin hosting, although the interview ultimately fell through (Aumen 3).

In October, Brown did another reading in Jackson as well as one in Albany, Georgia, and another in Blytheville, Arkansas. He also read from *Dirty Work* in Nashville at the Southern Festival of Books. He took advantage of his stay in Nashville to hear some music: "Three piece band, one acoustic guitar, one bass fiddle, and one steel guitar. No singing at all. Just playing like I never heard. It was another religious experience. Nothing to say for guys like that but incredible" (Edgerton Papers).

Back in Oxford later in the fall, he read for Lisa Howorth's art appreciation class at Ole Miss and made an appearance at Lafayette County

High School to "talk to some drama students about being on TV. As if I know anything about it " (LB to SR, Algonquin Files). He gave interviews to radio stations from Roanoke, Virginia; Greenville, Raleigh, and Chapel Hill, North Carolina; and Chattanooga, Tennessee, as well as to the Voice of America. The Atlanta-based cable television network CNN also prepared a piece on Brown, taping his readings in Albany, Georgia, and Meridian, Mississippi, before coming to Oxford to interview him: "They all came out here and got me Thursday afternoon and took me up to Mr. Faulkner's house and we did some taping walking around his yard, then inside where they opened up the rooms to us. . . . Then we came back out here and they got the kids in on it, us walking around the yard with Sam [the dog] and all. When Mary Annie walked in the door they had the camera right on her" (LB to SR, Algonquin Files). CNN also interviewed Barry Hannah and Ellen Douglas for the show, which was slated to run on Thanksgiving weekend.

Dirty Work is a tour de force in the tradition of William Faulkner's *As I Lay Dying*, although Brown uses only two perspectives rather than Faulkner's fifteen and the central issue in Brown's novel is far more circumscribed. Brown's novel also bears similarities to Faulkner's *The Unvanquished*, which explores what happens to John Sartoris as the result of his participation in the violence of the Civil War. Sartoris is not maimed physically but has suffered a moral and spiritual decline that accounts for his continuing taste for violence. *Dirty Work* tells the story of two victims of war, Braiden Chaney, an African American, and Walter James, a white man. While in Vietnam, Walter had his face blown away and his brain permanently damaged, and the novel opens with Walter awakening after an epileptic seizure and finding himself in a veterans hospital. He immediately notices that his roommate is "a bro" who has only "nubs" for arms and legs (*Dirty Work* 14). Both are from North Mississippi and had been "cottonpicking cotton chopper[s]" (14), and both have physical problems as a result of the war in Vietnam. Though Walter is an obvious member of the lower class, the group most stereotypically associated with intense racial prejudice, he is immediately concerned for Braiden, a concern based on humanity, mutual suffering, and despair. In Mitgang's words, "The reader comes to realize that these two Mississippians share a brotherhood of understanding that crosses racial lines" (A13). Suzanne Jones identifies this "bonding" as a contemporary version of the relationship Faulkner created between the white Bayard Sartoris and the African American Ringo in *The Unvanquished*. Faulkner's friendships end when his young men mature; in *Dirty Work*, the two adult men develop a friendship based on their similar "war experiences, but more immediately on coping with their debilitating injuries and their frustrated desires for more normal lives" (Jones 108). After each man learns how desperate the other is, Braiden asks Walter to help him commit suicide. After twenty-two years in a veterans' hospital, Braiden is ready to die but cannot even kill himself. Brown later described Braiden as no longer thinking that suicide is wrong: "He believes in it. By that I mean, he believes God is merciful, and that he's suffered enough; he can't stand any more. He longs for death. It's not a sin in his case" (Ketchin, "Interview" 128). Once the two veterans begin to talk, Braiden's ability as a storyteller "convinces Walter that assisted suicide, in Braiden's case, is not only a valid choice but a moral imperative. Before Walter is discharged from the hospital, he fulfills Braiden's wish and helps him die" (Jones 109). Walter's act is totally motivated by empathetic human concern; however, Robert Donahoo notes, the death itself does not appear in the novel: "The outcome of this closing is never revealed; the novel, in short, ends. Any killing, murder or mercy that subsequently transpires does so outside the novel and only in the mind of the reader. If Walter kills Braiden, it is because the reader writes it, forces it to happen, not because either the novel or its author does so" (19).

Though *Dirty Work* is not a directly Christian novel, it does contain elements of Christian morality. Brown told interviewer Susan Ketchin that "any literature, if it's going to be any good, has to be about right and wrong, good and bad, good versus evil" ("Interview" 135). Both Braiden and Walter believe in God and possess Christian values, although their faith has been skewed by their time in Vietnam. Early in the novel, Braiden thinks, "Whole world's a puzzle to me. . . . Why it's got to be the way it is. I don't think the Lord meant for it to be like this originally. I think things just got out of hand" (*Dirty Work* 12). In his dreams, he receives visits from Jesus and talks with him about the morality of suicide. Peter Prescott wrote that such visits constitute "an immensely difficult business for an author to bring off without falling into sentimentality. Brown succeeds because this Jesus is Braiden's invention, no more of a divinity than this dreaming man can grasp" (81). Brown commented, "Some people get upset about that scene. They want to know whether the scene is actually occurring. Is Jesus actually there, or is it a vision, or something in Braiden's mind? To tell you the truth, I don't know" (Ketchin, "Interview" 128). Jesus is struggling under the evil of the world and cannot condone Braiden's desire for suicide, but he also does not condemn Braiden for thinking about killing himself. Brown asserted that in Braiden's situation, "It is not a sin to seek suicide. The ministers I've talked to about this story agree with me. God wouldn't punish Braiden; God would pity him. Braiden has a strong unwavering faith in God. He seeks release and peace" (Ketchin, "Interview" 135). Reviewing the novel in *Theology Today*, William H. Becker praised Brown: "The spirituality of these *Dirty Work* vets is mature, self-critical, tempered by continuing struggle, purified by tears of compassion. It evidences that rare gift, the courage to face the full truth about life and love (what James Baldwin called life's 'terrible laws') in spite of the ever-present temptations of culture and religion to ignore such truth" (215). The novel also prompted a seventeen-year-old British girl, Kathryn Hollingsworth, to write to Brown about her hope of ridding the world of war. Brown replied,

> Kathryn, I don't believe the human race has evolved far enough for all men to live in peace and harmony in this world, and if it ever does happen, it will be a long time coming. . . . Our world is not perfect and we live imperfectly in it. We do the best we can. Our governments, mine and yours, are based on freedom and democracy. Many other countries in the world are not like that. . . . I feel nearly powerless to supply you some answers, but I'm encouraged to know there is a 17-year-old girl in England who is worried enough about the state of her fellow man to write a letter to an obscure novelist in Mississippi. There is nothing wrong with hoping you can change the world. (Algonquin Files)

Other readers also responded positively to the themes of *Dirty Work*—Brown's antiwar stance, humane outlook on race relations, and concern with the meaning of genuine Christianity. Seven major publishers bid for paperback rights to the novel, with Vintage Contemporary emerging as the winner (Mabe 1F). In the wake of the novel's success, Brown was eager to become a full-time writer. He was working on another novel as well as writing more short stories, some of which had been solicited by the *Chattahoochee Review, Carolina Quarterly*, and other journals, although Brown still yearned to be published in the *New Yorker* (O'Brient, "Blazing" L10). Brown was moving toward achieving his goal of becoming a literary writer.

CHAPTER SIX

Full-Time Writer

Big Bad Love, 1990

In late 1989, encouraged by the success of *Dirty Work* and the possibility that it would become a dramatic presentation on *American Playhouse*, Brown decided to leave the Oxford Fire Department. Money was coming in from sales of the hardcover versions of *Dirty Work* and *Facing the Music*, contracts for paperback editions of both books, and the advance for the adaptation of *Dirty Work*. Brown calculated that he needed only about twenty thousand dollars to support his family in the immediate future. He owed nothing on his house and truck, and although he had just borrowed the money to buy his wife, Mary Annie, a new car, he felt that with the help of "a publisher who believes in my work and a good paperback house," he could achieve independent financial security (Weinraub F4). He was planning to spend time in New York City to assist with the production of *Dirty Work* and hoped to "break into writing for stage" (Aumen 3).

On 9 December, Brown wrote to Clyde Edgerton, "I've decided to take the big leap, Clyde, quit the fire department. I probably won't be there past the 15th of January. I'm just waiting for my vacation time to get accrued on the 1st, and then I've got to give them 2 weeks' notice. Hell, they've been expecting it, so it's not going to be any surprise. All the lieutenants are bloodthirsty for my job anyway" (Edgerton Papers). On 15 December, Brown told Jake Mills, "I've got my resignation all neatly typed up right here beside me, ready to give to the chief when I go pick up my paycheck after while. I notified him of my intentions yesterday, but I've got to have it in writing to make it official. I could have left sooner, and wanted to, but I'll miss drawing over a month's pay if I leave before Jan. 1" (Brown Collections). Brown was already at work on his next book, another collection of short stories that he was calling *92 Days* or *Big Bad Love*, and had received an advance on it from Algonquin. "It would have been nearly impossible to meet all the obligations my writing has set up for me and still work at the fire department. They had me down for three different schools in the fire academy and the chief had cancelled all leaves on some weeks that I had readings set up in other states. So I thought it best to just end all the conflict, and devote myself to what I've already devoted my life to." Quitting meant that "there won't be any more hassle about traveling when I need to. I already know I'm going to have to stay in New York for an undetermined amount of time once the play gets under way. And that project alone is paying me more than I make in several years at work for the fire department" (Brown Collections). Brown had also grown tired of being called the "writing fireman": "That was an angle everybody liked to use for a while. It probably helped me early on, but I wanted to be known just as a writer" (Koeppel, "Author"). According to Keith Perry, however, Brown never fully escaped that label: it appeared in many of his obituaries.

Brown's decision to leave the fire department was front-page news in the 4 January 1990 edition of the *Oxford Eagle* (David Smith, "Fireman" 1A). Two days later, Mary Annie was in tears as she photographed him in uniform on the morning of his last shift. Brown "told her I should be the one crying" (Aumen 3). He "hated to leave. When you're in a firehouse with a bunch of guys and have three meals together and sleep together, it's like having another family. But it was just something I felt I had to do" (Weinraub F7). The evening after his last shift, he hosted a celebratory party for his former colleagues (F4).

His publisher was not fully supportive of his decision to leave the Oxford Fire Department, even though it would free Brown to write more and to travel more to promote his books. Brown wrote to Mills, "Nobody at Algonquin wanted me to do it. They seemed to think they knew better than I did what I wanted to do with my life, and I got a little aggravated about it, since they always wanted me to go where they wanted, when they wanted. But all that shit's water over the bridge now anyway" (Brown Collections). According to Shannon Ravenel, she feared that without a regular work schedule, Brown would increase his drinking. She was right.

For most of the rest of his life, Brown supported his family without a regular paycheck, living on advances from Algonquin. The system meant that he constantly faced pressure to write. After the success of *Dirty Work*, the advances became larger, but sales of his books were never substantial enough to help him achieve full economic security.

Larry and Mary Annie Brown sought financial advice but nevertheless spent their money freely on new cars for themselves and their children, on Larry's guitars and CDS, and on other forms of entertainment. The health problems experienced by their daughter, LeAnne, also continued to drain their coffers. His agent, Liz Darhansoff, "knew when he was hurting [financially] and tried to help but I would never have asked him where the money went." Brown often wrote to his friends about his financial problems, including trouble with the Internal Revenue Service over late tax payments. Financial tensions at times were evident in the family, but his son, Billy Ray, remembered that "the one thing we never talked about was money. I don't know how much he made, and I don't know where it went, [but] he bought me a brand-new pickup when I was sixteen." Brown sought to avoid spoiling his children by insisting, for example, that Billy Ray pay for gas and insurance, but when Billy Ray wrecked the truck, his father bought him another: "We were well taken care of . . . when he got to where he was making money. [But] he was not about money. He wanted to have enough to pay the bills and have a little cushion there. That was it." Mary Annie oversaw the family finances, giving her husband what Billy Ray described as "an allowance almost."

In early 1990, Brown bought about six acres of land near Tula, just a few miles from his home in Yocona. Brown had mentioned the idea of purchasing land to Ravenel nearly three years earlier, explaining that he wanted to buy land behind the store in Tula to build himself a little house where he could write, though he added, "That's just dream talk." When he learned that the tract was for sale, he took his friend, Glennray Tutor, out to look at the property. When he asked Tutor, "Do you think I ought to buy this piece of property? They want eight thousand dollars for it." Tutor responded, "'I'll tell you what, Larry: if you don't buy it, I'm going to buy it.' So the next thing I know, he'd bought it. It was a good piece of property, perfect for Larry." In May 1990 he wrote to Mills, "I've bought me a nice little place I wish you could see. A little house, and seven acres, and a little fish pond behind it loaded with crappies, which I haven't been able to get a bite yet. . . . I bought it mainly to work in. The house needs work, but the place is pretty. Mecca. I've wanted it for a long time. It's where I was raised. I fished there lots when I was a boy" (Brown Collections). Six weeks later, he told Mills, "It feels like home already" (Brown Collections).

Brown's retreat at Tula provided him with a link to his heritage, a quiet oasis from the stresses of his writing career, an outlet for his physical energy, a place to meditate and write, and a place to entertain friends. In 1995, Brown reflected,

> I can remember fishing in this pond when I was fourteen, all those years back. And this is the place where I feel my roots are. . . . This is where my family's from. The cemetery up here is where all my kinfolks are buried, all the Barlows, everybody else is up here. They've been here 100 years I guess—a long, long time. . . . It's so peaceful and quiet. It means a lot to have a place like that. To a kid like me in Memphis, I felt like I was kind of imprisoned in that huge city for so long. There wasn't anything I could do about it. I was just a child. But I felt like this was my home, and finally I've got some land. . . . I'm back where I ought to be after all this time. (Rankin, "On" 95, 101)

Tom Rankin, a photographer, filmmaker, and folklorist and long-time friend of Brown's, believes that "having that pond was [proof] that he had achieved something he wanted to achieve, which is to have a kind of independence where you own your own pond. You can fish in your own pond—it's the kind of Old South notion, [proving] that you're not a sharecropper, you're not a tenant. Larry's not a farmer, at this point; he owns his own place." Billy Ray recalled that his father's "happiest times" were at Tula, "sitting on the dock, feeding his fish. . . . I've spent many a day with him on that pond out there. It's not a huge pond, but we'd get in that boat, go out to the middle, ice down a six pack of Budweiser, have us a bucket of minnows, and we'd catch fish, have a good time. He loved his place. He did. He sure did." But equipment needed to improve the Tula property also further strained the Browns' precarious finances.

Brown experienced other life changes during this period. The Brown family dynamics shifted as he, Mary Annie, and their children adjusted to having him at home all the time. Billy Ray was now a teenager, with his first girlfriend, and Larry reflected to Edgerton, "He's getting away from me too fast, is becoming so independent and can do everything by himself now. I try to give him all the freedom I can" (Edgerton Papers). Eleven-year-old Shane was showing an interest in reading and "he's got himself a little reading nest fixed up in the dinner room. He put three chairs together and stretched two afghans over them, pulled his beanbag out and a lamp under there with him. He'll lay over there and read for hours and never make a sound" (Edgerton Papers). LeAnne, youngest, was developing an interest in sports and friends that distanced her a bit from her father. Brown, nearing forty, was also dealing with the illness and death of some of his older relatives. Mary Annie's grandmother, Pat, who had lived with her daughter across the lane from the Browns, was in failing health. Brown told Edgerton, "She's just old. What's going to happen to all of us if we live long enough. Only way to miss it's to die young, I guess. That's the whole scope of life, and something to write about one of these days" (Edgerton Papers). Moreover, two of Larry's maternal uncles died during the summer of 1990.

In addition to writing the script for the stage version of *Dirty Work*, Brown was planning a collection of eight short stories and a twenty-seven-thousand-word novella. Two of Brown's stories, "And Another Thing" and "The Crying," appeared in Barry Hannah's 1990 anthology, *Reb Fiction '90*. When *Southern Living* asked various southern writers to list their favorite works, Brown selected Cormac McCarthy's *Suttree* as well as Jack Butler's *Jujitsu for Christ*, William Faulkner's "The Bear," Flannery O'Connor's "A Good Man Is Hard to Find," Harry Crews's *A Feast of Snakes*, McCarthy's *Child of God*, Barry Hannah's *Airships*, Clyde Edgerton's *The Floatplane Notebooks*, Lewis Nordan's "A Hank of Hair, a Piece of Bone," and Eudora Welty's "The Wide Net" (Peat and Young 92). Brown described *Suttree* as "McCarthy's most moving and rewarding work . . . by any standard one of the greatest novels in American Literature" (Brown Collections). Brown had also begun to write "A Roadside Resurrection," a story that he later often read in public. In March 1990, he wrote to Edgerton, "I finished a new, long story, 12,000 words, my contribution to Southern Grotesque. . . . It's about a healer who can really heal getting thrown in a basement with a large drooling hairy idiot man, and a woman whose husband is dying beside her trying to find the healer before her husband dies. It's one of the darkest things I've ever written. . . . It's the first thing I've written in a long time that made me uneasy" (Edgerton Papers). When Jill McCorkle read the story, she thought, "Flannery [O'Connor] has got nothing on this Larry Brown!" McCorkle found herself "laughing out loud in the midst of what was this horrifying scene, of this big idiot child about to either rape or kill the healer" ("Writers"). Brown submitted the story to the *New Yorker*, but it was ultimately published in the Fall 1991 issue of the *Paris Review*, a journal to which he had sent fiction for several years.

"A Roadside Resurrection" is the most directly religious—and disconcerting—of Brown's fictional writings, depicting the extreme but sincere religiosity of southern characters and recalling O'Connor's declaration that the South remains "Christ-haunted" (*Mystery* 44). Brown later said, "People seem to be spellbound by it. It's the idiot, I think. In fact, I'm spellbound by it. It's a wild story. The writing of it was a process of discovery, one of these things that just started telling itself. The first draft took a week—it was really cooking, burning to be finished. The rhythm of the words developed a life of its own; it assumed its own way of being told. I revised it at least six times to take out stuff and tighten my control on the language. The story just came—it was if I were just a transmitter" (Ketchin, "Interview" 134). The faith healer seems remarkably believable, partly because he expresses doubts about his calling. Brown sought to portray a man "caught up in a dilemma. What is he going to do? Has God turned his face on him?" (134).

Set in the early 1990s in North Mississippi, "A Roadside Resurrection" deals with the South's sometimes extreme religious fanaticism.

Like O'Connor, Brown uses humor to draw readers into the narrative. Brown's use of the grotesque also echoes that of O'Connor, who saw it as a fitting image for humanity's fallen nature. "A Roadside Resurrection" also concerns the redemptive power of absolute faith: though outwardly somewhat skeptical, the characters cling to their fervent belief. As with much of O'Connor's fiction, Brown's combination of telling description and broad humor compels readers both to keep reading and to extract the ultimate Christian meaning in the story. In some episodes in the story—particularly the final creature so in need of healing—Brown treads a thin line between sensationalism and symbolic representation. Dragged to a remote farmhouse, the healer confronts a subhuman being whose behavior has been so antisocial that his parents must keep him in chains. The parents nonetheless love their monstrous offspring—the result of their incestuous relationship—and believe that the healer can transform him. Brown describes the son with a deliberately horrifying realism: "A large, naked, drooling hairy man sits playing with a ball of his own shit in the center of the room, his splayed feet and fuzzy toes black with dirt and his sloped forehead furrowed in concentration" (27).

Facing this repulsive being, the healer doubts his abilities, but the parents' faith remains solid. Using a pistol to show force but simultaneously reminding him of worse cases over which he has triumphed, the parents lock the healer in the basement with the monster; through the door, the farmer calls, "Jesus would heal him if He were here!" (36). Left alone with an insurmountable task, the healer gains spiritual strength, identifying this hideous being with the rest of humanity, limited and suffering, and reaches out. Brown thus asserts that faith in God can heal and redeem even the most physically and morally depraved. Brown ends his story with three gaudy crosses planted in the Mississippi landscape in what he described as an attempt to impose "a startling image of faith on the consciousness" of both passing drivers and readers (Ketchin, "Interview" 135).

In early 1990, Brown was also working on a detective novel, "Bullets Are Cheaper," which he envisioned publishing under a pseudonym, Barry Lane. Because the story was totally different from anything else he had submitted to Algonquin, he had a cousin send the manuscript to the press. Ravenel did not like the farce "about a boxing match on television where a guy is killed in the ring" (Edgerton Papers) enough to consider publishing it.

Although writing had enabled Brown to leave the fire department and to better his family's circumstances, it also brought him a celebrity that he at times found burdensome. He told Jean Ross, "I get a lot of demands on me now. I get invited to a lot of colleges to give readings and I get invited to participate in a lot of stuff. That's one of the main changes, all the traveling I do and talking to people and promoting my work. Of course that's part of publicity and some of it's necessary to do. I just try to keep a handle on it instead of letting it get control of me" (91). Brown "had to change his home telephone number to an unlisted one when calls began coming in from people all over the country at all hours, many of them asking for advice or wanting him to help them write their life stories. One man who called became so upset and told such a nightmarish tale of being persecuted that Brown became a little afraid for his own safety" (Aumen 3). Brown was also bothered when crowds numbering as many as one hundred people turned up at book signings, with each person expecting "to be dealt with on a personal level" (Scott 7F). In general, he confessed to Berkeley Hudson, "It's tough for me to meet all these people I don't know. Go out to dinner. Carry on conversations. Just being afraid, you know, of embarrassing myself or looking bad on something. Maybe it's my background." The people at Algonquin "want me to get out and push myself harder. It's what I ought to do. I have my wife nagging on me to do it. Everybody here in Oxford thinks I ought to do it" (7).

Brown also faced increasing demands from his hometown, where many residents wanted to be able to say they knew the famous author. Brown began to spend more time socializing and less time with his family. He was guest speaker at the February 1990 meeting of the Women's Forum of Oxford. The next month, he attended an American Civil Liberties Union fund-raiser at the home of William Faulkner's niece, Dean Faulkner Wells. Guests at that event included country musician Tom T. Hall, whom Brown had met previously, and he very much enjoyed sitting and listening to Hall "play and sing for nearly an hour.

He had a small guitar, and the way he played it was something to see. He told the whole room how much he liked my work, took me on his bus and mixed me a drink, kissed Mary Annie on the cheek. It was a wonderful night" (Edgerton Papers).

At the end of March, Brown traveled to Florence for the University of North Alabama's annual writers' conference. In addition to participating in a panel discussion with several other writers, he read from the manuscript of "Bullets Are Cheaper" and wrote to Edgerton, "I never had people laugh that much. They loved it" (Edgerton Papers). Early in May, Brown presented a trophy to the winner of a writing contest sponsored by the University of Mississippi. Just over a week later, Brown headlined the Jubilee Jam Literary Lunch in Jackson, where he read from *Dirty Work*. At that point, he told the *Jackson Clarion-Ledger*'s Gary Pettus that although he enjoyed giving readings, "I'm about ready to give it a rest" ("Literary" 1E).

Brown was also traveling farther afield, returning to New York in the spring of 1990 to consult with Peter Workman as well as taking trips to Chicago and to Las Vegas, where the American Booksellers Association held its annual meeting in early June. Brown had a "great time" in Las Vegas (Edgerton Papers); he described the city as "real hot, but [with] lots of cool dark places to hide out." He and Edgerton "stayed out . . . until daybreak one night but we didn't lose too much [money]. I went expecting to lose, but it was fun" (LB to JM, Brown Collections). After learning that Larry Wells, an Oxford publisher, had visited Cormac McCarthy while in Las Vegas, Brown told Mills, "I wished I'd known he was going. I'd have tried to go with him" (Brown Collections).

Also in the spring of 1990, Richard Ford nominated Larry for a fellowship at the Bread Loaf Writer's Conference at Vermont's Middlebury College. In June, Brown learned that he had been selected as one of twenty fellows for the conference, and he was "really looking forward to it" (LB to JM, Brown Collections). Brown spent ten days in August in Vermont, the longest time that he and Mary Annie had been separated since their marriage. She cried when he left (Edgerton Papers). He took with him "a thick camo field jacket . . . the flashlight, the umbrella, and all that crap they said bring" (Edgerton Papers). He also took two short stories, "Waiting for the Ladies" and "A Roadside Resurrection," and forty-five pages from a novel in progress, *Joe*.

At Bread Loaf, Brown settled into a house with "a couple of other guys" and immediately began to wonder whether "this crowd can handle 'Waiting for the Ladies.'" He also soon realized that he was not "known too well in Vermont. I don't think they know my work. I don't know what to do about that but try and deliver a hell of a reading" (Edgerton Papers). Brown made enough of an impression that he was invited back as an associate faculty member for the next three summers, and in 1994 he served as a full member of the faculty.

In June, Ravenel began the publicity campaign for *Big Bad Love*, slated to be released in the fall. Her letter to prospective reviewers included a comment from writer Pat Conroy: "Everything [Brown] writes seems lived-in, authentic, and on the money" (Algonquin Files). For the first time, as Keith Perry asserts, Brown was being seen as a writer, not as just as a fireman who wrote.

The collection was officially published on 30 September 1990. Once again, Brown had Tutor create a painting to serve as the front cover. Even before the book's release, Brown began what would become a four-month odyssey of promotional events. Richard Howorth at Square Books hosted a book signing on 8 September, advertising the collection in the 7 September *Daily Mississippian* as "not for the weak of heart, easily shocked, nor any other variety of intellectual, spiritual or moral WIMP." Brown subsequently traveled to South Carolina, where he did an event at the Happy Bookseller in Columbia and a reading at Newberry College. From there, it was on to Orlando, Florida, before returning to Mississippi for appearances at Jackson's Millsaps College and Lemuria Books. While in Jackson, he had dinner and drinks with Eudora Welty (who asked him to call her by her first name) "and then read for her and a lot of other people the next night. . . . Eudora had her a couple of stiff belts of bourbon the other night. We all did. We loved it. Whiskey with Welty" (LB to SR, Algonquin Files).

After a four-day respite, Brown traveled to Tulsa, Oklahoma, and Wichita, Kansas, in early October. He did a reading at the Mississippi University for Women in Columbus before moving on to Nashville for the Southern Literary Festival on 12–14 October. Next up were Memphis; New York City; Washington, D.C.; Seattle, Washington; Portland, Oregon; and Brentwood, Oakland, Emeryville, and Menlo Park, California. Back in Mississippi at the beginning of November, Brown spoke in Jackson at the Mississippi Library Association and made another appearance at Lemuria. His book tour ended with a reading in Mobile on 24 January 1991.

While in Washington, D.C., Brown gave six interviews (among them a session with CBS's *Nightwatch* and one with the *Washington Post*'s Judith Weinraub) and did one bookstore reading. However, he also managed to find time to visit the Vietnam Veterans Memorial, which he found "awful. Religious. Overpowering. Deeply saddening. Imbittering. All those boys dead. I wanted to cry" (Edgerton Papers). In Portland, he got "a big fat joint" from an interviewer; in Los Angeles, he was annoyed because his hosts booked him into "a swanky hotel on the *gay* side of town" (Edgerton Papers). Overall, Brown did not like the West Coast: "I'm really scared of this place. It's so alien to my sheltered little life in Mississippi. So many cars, streets, and houses. Everything overlooking everything else here. To me it is bleak" (Edgerton Papers).

Brown also took a break from readings to join Edgerton, Lee Smith, and Reynolds Price at a 19 October fund-raiser for Harvey Gantt's campaign for the U.S. Senate seat held by Jesse Helms. The usually apolitical Brown had applied for a twenty-thousand-dollar grant from the National Endowment for the Arts and felt that defeating the incumbent North Carolinian would improve his chances and those of other writers (LB to JM, Brown Collections). Ravenel invited Brown to stay with her during his visit to North Carolina, "but I hate to put up with her stop-smoking-listen-to-me jazz, hate to smoke in her house. . . . [I]t's getting to where I'd almost rather stay in a hotel than offend somebody in their house with my habit. You know how it is. We went down to Jackson the other night to spend a little time with Miss Welty and do a reading for her, and me and Mary Annie were the only ones in the house who smoked, so she refrained and I went outside" (LB to JM, Brown Collections). Brown ultimately stayed with Mills during the trip to North Carolina and later wrote to thank his host and to apologize because "I just didn't have much appetite after all the beer I drank the night before. Nobody's fault but mine, although it's true I'm nervous at any kind of gathering like that and tend to drink more in order to handle it" (Brown Collections).

Big Bad Love received more mixed reviews than either of Brown's earlier works. The *Virginia Quarterly Review*, for example, declared, "His minimalist techniques lead to a superficial treatment of intense emotions, a pandering to prurient interests. The stories do not entertain or enlighten; they disappoint" (94). A more positive assessment appeared in the *Washington Post*, where Clancey Sigal praised *Big Bad Love* but pointed out that Brown was "the beneficiary of an uneasy feeling among critics and editors that attenuating middle-class angst, the keynote of so much recent fiction, is simply not enough" (n.p.). Sigal and other reviewers identified the collection's central theme as the despair felt by underclass male characters when love goes wrong. Don O'Brient wrote in the *Atlanta Journal-Constitution* that Brown's men "have been looking for love in all the wrong places and don't know what to do with it once they find it" ("Love" N8). But perhaps the most meaningful review to Brown was one penned by another of his idols, Harry Crews, and published in the *Los Angeles Times Book Review*. Crews had loved *Facing the Music*, revealing, "In 25 years of writing, it was the first time I picked up the phone and tried to call the author" (3). Though he never reached Brown, Crews remained an enthusiastic reader of the Mississippian's fiction, and he saw the stories in *Big Bad Love* as "rather like some perfect object one has come across in a wilderness like a perfectly shaped stone. Or a piece of hard wood that over the years has been weathered to a natural and unique state" (3). Crews concluded with the hope that Brown "will be one of the most prolific writers we have . . . because whatever he writes, I will read" (8).

Big Bad Love also features a new and obviously autobiographical theme: members of the working class who aspire to become writers find greater fulfillment than those who have nothing to which to cling, no Holy Grail to pursue. Brown's characters seek to add meaning to their lives through drinking, carousing, and womanizing but find little satisfaction. Only those who turn to storytelling and writing, as Brown did, achieve a more complete existence (see Cash, "Saving").

Big Bad Love's ten stories are grouped in three sections: part 1 contains eight stories; part 2 includes a satirical, dramatic dialogue, "Discipline"; and part 3 comprises the novella, "92 Days." All eight stories in part 1 feature male narrators, most of whom are involved in troubled or troubling relationships with women or have no such relationships at all. The men are Brown's typical representatives of the working class: heavy drinkers obsessed with sex and in serious need of more focus in their lives. Brown gave many of the narrators names that evoke his name or initials: Lonnie is the nonwriting husband in "The Apprentice"; Leroy is the narrator of "Big Bad Love"; Leo is the young veteran in "Old Soldiers"; Louis is the elderly man with the troubled wife in "Sleep"; Mr. Lawrence is the defendant in "Discipline"; and Leon Barlow (whose name comes from that of Brown's mother, who was born Leona Barlow) is the struggling writer in "92 Days." Brown explained the characters' names as "something I did for fun, I guess. So many of those stories in *Big Bad Love* have . . . however large or small . . . autobiographical elements" (51).

The eight stories in part 1 vary somewhat in their content and focus. "Falling Out of Love" and "Wild Thing" feature malcontented young men, while "Sleep" and "Old Soldiers" involve older characters with different problems. Despite such differences, the narrative voices used in the stories often seem intensely personal. The most pointedly autobiographical of the stories involve writers and writing; in addition, "Old Soldiers" is based on Brown's experiences hearing war stories while growing up in Tula and later as a store owner there. All the stories except "Discipline" are set in the rural northwestern corner of Mississippi, the region Brown knew best and loved, and involve the types of people Brown knew intimately.

"Falling Out of Love," the first story in *Big Bad Love*, features the same male character as "The End of Romance," the penultimate story in *Facing the Music*. He has "gotten rid" of Miss Sheila and taken up with "Sheena Baby," but that relationship is failing too: she "didn't hurt for me like I did for her. I knew it. I'd thought about shooting her first and me second, but that wouldn't have done either one of us any good" (*BBL* 3). The narrator's failure to form a permanent relationship results from his inability to be much more than he is—a sex-starved, drunken aficionado of classic rock and roll just barely ahead of the law. As Thomas J. Richardson writes, "Love with Sheena-Baby has come to two flat tires on an empty road" (62). Like all of *Big Bad Love*'s stories involving heterosexual relationships, "Falling Out of Love" has a desperate but funny ending, since "Brown uses humor to explore . . . the troubled side of romantic relationships" (Beuka 61).

"The Apprentice," like its companion stories in part 1 of *Big Bad Love*, features a male narrator, but Lonnie is the would-be sensitive husband of a wife so obsessed with publishing her fiction that she no longer has a life outside her imagination. Lonnie begins the story in frustration: he had married Judy expecting her to be an average lower-middle-class wife; instead, she does nothing but "Writewritewrite-writewrite" (*BBL* 15). She will have sex with him only after he praises her latest writings. In many respects, Judy is a female version of the unpublished but increasingly obsessed Larry Brown: she turns their shared bedroom into a writing room, writes a novel about a man-eating grizzly bear in Yellowstone National Park (a detail about his first novel that Brown later said he "kind of stuck . . . in there on purpose" [Gross]), and submits story after story to magazines but receives only rejection letters. Judy eventually improves enough that her stories are occasionally published, but Lonnie sees unwelcome changes in their marriage as a consequence of her drive to express herself—Brown's implicit admission that his obsession with writing caused problems in his marriage. With this story, Brown illustrates what happens to a working-class family when one of its members sets out to break its cultural bindings by aspiring to a life of art. For the writer, the creation of that art becomes fundamental to existence, a means to a fulfillment available through no other outlet, but a price must be paid, not only by the writer but also by the writer's loved ones.

Another unsatisfied male narrates "Wild Thing," the third story in the collection. At its center is the working-class bar where the narrator and a young woman first meet. The narrator is married and has children, but his marriage is unfulfilling: "I'd been out of things for a while.

I was having trouble with my wife. One of the things that was wrong was that I was spending too many nights away from home, and it was causing fights that were hard for me to win. It's hard to win when you don't have right on your side. It's hard to win when you know that your own fucking up is causing the problem" (*BBL* 31–32). Despite such self-awareness, the narrator continues to frequent bars, drink heavily, and look for a woman who will pay him more attention than does his wife. He finds a young married women with sex and intrigue on her mind who turns out to be more than he can handle. Despite problems with both her husband and the law, the narrator cannot stay away from her; parked with her in an isolated rural area, he knows "it wouldn't be but a little bit before those headlights, somebody's, would ease around the curve" (*BBL* 45). The unhappy young narrator is proof again of how little meaning rampant sexuality adds to the life of Brown's undereducated working men. Without a transcendent escape, the character is doomed to endless and meaningless repetition.

The fourth story, "Big Bad Love," begins with a dead dog, a motif Brown often used in his writing, both fiction and nonfiction. Subconsciously at least, the narrator, Leroy, sees the dog as a metaphor for his dead marriage; he finds it difficult to bury either. His wife, Mildred, is "sexually frustrated because of her overlarge organ and it just wore me out trying to apply enough friction to that thing for her to achieve internal orgasm" (*BBL* 52). Leroy, like Brown's other unsatisfied males, drinks, drives, and avoids both his dog's corpse and that of his marriage. He says, "I did not know what I was going to do with Mildred or how I was ever going to be able to come to a life of harmonious tranquility where matrimonial happiness was a constant joy" (59). Leroy's situation reaches an ironic denouement when he discovers that his wife has found a lover big enough to satisfy her needs and has left him. Truly realizing his loss, Leroy says, "Right about then I started missing her, and the loneliness I have been speaking of really started to set in" (61). In Brown's view, then, people enter relationships with the hope that "matrimonial happiness" will compensate for other failures, but the result is often the absence of "harmonious tranquility," let alone "constant joy." Life must have more meaning than a conventional marriage can provide.

The narrator of "Gold Nuggets," the collection's fifth story, is more degenerate and more pathetic than the narrators who precede him. In the midst of a trip to the Mississippi Gulf Coast to pick up shrimp, he confides that he does not "even like" the wealthier acquaintances who send him there (*BBL* 67). One of them, Ed, is "a son of a bitch" who took a similar trip but did not offer to bring back any shrimp for the narrator; another man, Ted, has never invited the narrator to his private lake "when they were jerking those ten-pound lunkers out of there" (68–69). The narrator abandons his mission in favor of tawdry excitement, visiting a strip joint. He falls victim to women who make their living by fleecing naive male customers and ends up beaten and robbed of much of his shrimp money. But he remains clueless, with little concern for the loss of either the money or his fundamental dignity: "I knew all this was just a temporary setback. It didn't mean that I couldn't ever be saved from my life, or that I'd never find the boat I was looking for. Somewhere, somewhere there, was a connection I could make, and I knew that all I had to do was stay out there until I found it" (77). Brown implies that even though alcohol and class envy have blinded his narrator to his culpability, few "gold nuggets" will reward such hapless seeking.

"Waiting for the Ladies" features another narrator who is a middle-aged loser. This time he has left his long-term job and now has too little to occupy his time. When his wife tells him that a man has exposed himself to her at the local dump (a situation inspired when the wife of one of his fellow firefighters "went to take the garbage off [*sic*] and some guy pulled his pants down in front of her" [Brown Collections]), he sets out to track down the offender, casting himself as a grudging knight in not-so-shining armor. At the same time, because he suspects that his wife is having an affair with her boss, the husband identifies to some extent with the flasher, since both men are seeking sexual gratification outside socially acceptable avenues. The narrator feels that tracking down and punishing this public nuisance will somehow restore his lost masculinity, a quest whose outright silliness soon becomes apparent. When the narrator visits the sheriff, he learns that local officers are well aware of the man's existence but have declared him less harmless than other public menaces. Assuming the role of a lone avenger, the narrator pursues the flasher on a long chase that ends at the man's home. But what happens next reveals the avenger's vulnerability:

> The door was open, and the knob turned under my hand. The barrel of the gun slanted down from under my arm, and I tracked their mud on their floor. He didn't have his cap on, and his hair wasn't what I'd imagined. It was gray, but neatly combed, and his mother was sobbing silently on the couch and feeding a pillow into her mouth.
>
> He said one thing, quietly: "Are you fixing to kill us?"
>
> Their eyes got me.
>
> I sat down, asking first if I could. That's when I started to tell both of them what my life then was like. (*BBL* 89)

More than revenge, the narrator needs someone to listen to the story of his increasingly woeful life. His storytelling becomes his release. With "Waiting for the Ladies," Brown begins moving toward his ultimate conclusion that narrative art can offer hard-to-find fulfillment—can save such a man from what otherwise had been his life. This revelation is significant; many of the earlier narrators in the collection not only fail to understand it but do not even begin to consider it.

Joy Farmer compares the narrator of "Waiting for the Ladies" with all three Compson brothers in Faulkner's *The Sound and the Fury*. According to Farmer, Brown's protagonist most resembles Jason in his pursuit of his niece, Quentin, and her underclassed lover. Both Jason and Brown's narrator are sexually intrigued with the object of their search, and both are obsessed with maintaining family honor. Brown's protagonist is like Benjy in his lack of articulation.

"Old Soldiers" and "Sleep," the final two stories in part 1 of *Big Bad Love*, stand apart from the drinking/driving/womanizing sagas of the earlier stories. "Old Soldiers" is narrated by young Leo, a military veteran who straddles the chasm between the story's older veterans and its nonvets, many of whom differ little from the bar-hopping narrators Brown has presented previously. "Old Soldiers" resulted directly from the many hours Brown spent listening to veterans tell war stories, both as a child and later in his life. Although Leo hangs out in bars, Brown has granted him qualities more sympathetic than those of many of the author's other protagonists. Leo describes himself as "between women" and looking (*BBL* 96) for comfort in bars: "I always think I'm going to find something when I go out at night, I don't know why. I always think that, and I never do. I always think I'll find a woman. But if you go out in sadness, that's all you're going to find" (*BBL* 98–99). However, he does find a basic humanity that surpasses his sexual needs. Leo's interactions with veterans of World War I, World War II, and the Korean War demonstrate war's costs to the men who fight. Aaron and Squirrel are so physically and psychologically impaired that they have never married. They seem to have known that they, like Leo's father, would have failed as both husbands and fathers. These veterans depend only on each other, but Leo's time in the service makes him empathize with their suffering and internalize the war stories they tell him, including the tale of a soldier looking on helplessly as fifty of his fellows are "cut . . . all to pieces with machine guns" (*BBL* 101) and the story of a man who spent three weeks on the front lines and then lay down and cried "all night long" (102). Storytelling thus becomes a focus in "Old Soldiers"; as Leo retells the older men's stories, he gives permanence to their often tragic content.

Brown creates a clever link between the end of "Old Soldiers" and the next story in the volume, "Sleep": the story ends with Leo offering an elegy to Aaron, "So long, old buddy. God Bless you and keep you. Me, I need some sleep myself" (*BBL* 104). Originally published in the *Carolina Quarterly* in 1989, "Sleep" is an anomaly in the collection, a story whose narrator does not share Brown's age, social status, or search for fulfillment through storytelling. The narrator, Louis, is married to a woman who repeatedly hears noises in the night and fearfully and pointlessly demands that he get out of bed to reassure her of their harmlessness. Brown contrasts the warmth Louis feels under the covers with the cold outside. Despite his growing frustration with these nightly expeditions, he remains firmly tied to the joys of physical existence: he recalls other times when he has been freezing and appreciates the warmth of his home and the good food and coffee that he will enjoy when morning comes. Brown does not analyze the wife's unnatural fear, leaving readers to ponder that question on their own.

Is hers an existential fear based on the nothingness that lies at the core of existence? Is she afraid of death, and is that fear growing as she ages? Is she suffering from some sort of dementia? Is this a way for her to gain control from a husband who has dominated her existence throughout their marriage?

The stories in parts 2 and 3 of *Big Bad Love* return to the theme of "The Apprentice," aspiring writers from working-class backgrounds. "Discipline," a satirical colloquy, features an unskillful plagiarist, while "92 Days" tells the story of a writer on the edge of success. All three are clearly autobiographical, with both self-satire and self-satisfied swagger. All three also further the collection's focus on characters who try to save themselves from dead-end lives by telling stories. More significantly, they also provide the lesson—never learned by the narrators of "Waiting for the Ladies" and "Old Soldiers"—that telling stories is one skill, but getting them published is another matter entirely, fraught with complications.

In 1994, Brown said of "Discipline," "I don't know if you could call it a story. It's more of an exercise, an experiment in form" (Manley 128). He conceived it as "an idea that hadn't been tried on before, so I just invented all this stuff" (127). The story's main character is Doyle Huey Lawrence, an obvious play not only on Brown's name but also that of D. H. Lawrence. Brown's character is a plagiarist serving a five-year prison term. During the parole hearing that constitutes the story's action, Lawrence argues that he has faced cruel and unusual punishment—being forced to have sex with tattooed, toothless, obese women—and should consequently serve only four years of his sentence. His captors disagree, arguing that he has not even begun to reform, as is evidenced by the fact that he has recently been caught "copying Faulkner, at *night*, under the covers, with a flashlight" (131). The story thus combines the obscene, the phantasmagoric, and, of course, the comic. Trying to force Lawrence to testify against a fellow inmate accused of plagiarizing Flannery O'Connor and Cormac McCarthy, the prosecutor demands, "You don't think it's bad to steal from a dead woman? Pilfer words from a sick, dying writer, who barely had the strength to work three hours a day? Who had more guts and talent in one little finger than you and your buddy Varrick have in your whole bodies?" (*BBL* 123). The questioning eventually causes Lawrence to break down and confess his crimes. When he is forced to read some of "his" most recent work to the court, he begins unwillingly, moving from "unbelievable horror" to "bitter resignation" (136). But after Lawrence reads a page of what sounds like Faulkner at his most florid, the prosecutor is unable to cut Lawrence off, and bailiffs finally have to restrain him. He stops only when "Discipline" does: his final words are "Wait! There's more! Do you hear me? Just listen!" (138). "Discipline" thus shows a writer struggling not only to deal with overzealous fans—the tattooed, toothless, obese woman is a member of a book club and poetry society who has been told that Lawrence is a famous writer—but also to have his most recent work read, even when he knows it is patently derivative.

Reviewer Neely Tucker described "Discipline" as "oddly hip and snide in an otherwise themed collection of simple dirt-scratchin' real stories" ("Weaving" 7G). Brown had attempted to find a magazine that would publish the story but "it wasn't received worth shit. Nobody would take that story, and it was one of the ones I'd sent out so much I finally gave up on it" (Manley 128). When he was compiling *Big Bad Love*, he showed "Discipline" to Ravenel, who said, "Oh, we've got to publish this" (128).

"92 Days" is the most autobiographical work of fiction that Brown ever wrote. Mary Annie Brown declared that narrator Leon Barlow's marriage was "close" to that of the Browns, which "was pretty negative at times." Larry Brown confirmed that other aspects of the novella were drawn from his own life: "There's more than a little autobiography in that story, mainly a lot of frustration that I felt, not so much in the early days . . . [b]ut later when they were admitting at magazines that yes, this story is good, but we're not going to touch it" ("Larry Brown").

Leon Barlow has reached the point where, as Brown said, "even after . . . you were writing publishable work . . . there could still be obstacles in your way to keep you from getting published" (LaRue 50–51). Whereas "The Apprentice" depicts the beginning writer's struggle as semicomic, "92 Days" highlights the abject depression, alcoholic misery, and all around self-destructiveness that can accompany continued failure. Barlow has sacrificed his wife, his children, and his job to his drive to write yet receives in return only grief from friends and family and rejection letters from editors. Reflecting Brown's experience, one editor tells Barlow that a novel in which he has invested two years "is hilarious in many places and extremely well-written with a good plot, real characters, refreshing dialogue, beautiful descriptions," but the market "is not amenable to novels about drunk pulpwood haulers and rednecks and deer hunting" (*BBL* 143). Barlow finds the situation more trying even than the impatient threats made by his wife's lawyer and the two jail sentences he serves for public intoxication:

> I tried to write all I could. I tried to put balls and heart and blood into it like a good writer had once told me to do. Sometimes it wasted me, just laid me out. I knew that at least some of what I was writing was good, but I just hadn't found anybody to share my vision yet. Nobody with any power. Nobody who could say yes or no to publication. I knew about the pecking order, and jealousy, and interdepartmental office memos and the little notes that were jotted with a quick hand. They didn't know about the careers they were advancing or retarding with their little papers the number of us who lived and died with a stroke of their pens. They didn't have any idea of the power they wielded." (192–93).

"It seemed almost hopeless sometimes," Leon concludes, "but I knew I had to keep going on. I had chosen my own path. Nothing could turn me from it" (193).

Thus, "92 Days" is also a story of hope and determination. Leon has his lows, at one point seeing himself as almost as desperate as Breece D'J Pancake and John Kennedy Toole and at another saying he "wanted to go out into the forest and live like a madman with leaves for clothes and live in a hole in the ground and throw rocks at anyone who came near" (*BBL* 211). But hope arrives in the form of letters from Betti DeLoreo, an editor who rejects his work but nonetheless offers encouragement: one letter closes, "Please keep writing. Don't let this be disappointing to you. You have great talent, and with material like this you will need great stamina" (156), while another ends, "You're

too good a writer to remain unknown forever. . . . Please don't give up"
(220–21). Leon's stamina and perseverance, not the realization of his
long-held dream of seeing his work in print, ultimately becomes the
subject of the novella; when it concludes, he still has not published a
single word. But he heeds DeLoreo's advice.

Like the character he created, Brown, too, kept writing. With his
promotional tour on behalf of *Big Bad Love* behind him, Brown was
ready to settle in at Yocona to complete work on his next novel, *Joe*.

CHAPTER SEVEN

Joe

A Major Novel, 1991

Larry Brown recalled that he started writing *Joe* "around 1984 or 1985, after I had already written five bad novels and thrown them all away. . . . The image of that family came before Joe came. Later on I invented my protagonist. But the opening shot that I wanted was that family, walking down that hot blacktop through a deserted landscape in the middle of the summer, with no place to go" (Bonetti et al. 243). Brown laid the manuscript aside in the late 1980s, while he was writing the stories that became *Facing the Music* and *Dirty Work*. In the fall of 1989, as he was working on the stories for *Big Bad Love*, he wrote to Jake Mills, "All I'm really doing is killing time by writing stories until I decide to turn my full attention back to the novel I started so long ago called *Joe*. I'm just putting off strapping it back on again full time because I'll be in for the long haul then, just like I was on *Dirty Work*. . . . I don't like to do anything else when I'm working on a novel . . . [w]hat I call hibernation, long days, long nights, the discipline it takes" (Brown Collections). Brown showed a version of *Joe* to Shannon Ravenel late in 1987, but she found its "narrative tone . . . cockeyed and uncertain. The reader can't get a grip on the narrative stance" (Algonquin Files).

In the spring of 1990, Brown showed the manuscript of *Joe* to Houghton Mifflin's Seymour Lawrence, and Brown subsequently wrote to Ravenel that Lawrence was "lightly sniffing for a taste of the novel you read" (Algonquin Files). Lawrence immediately offered Brown a fifty-thousand-dollar advance if he agreed to switch to Houghton Mifflin. Lawrence was Barry Hannah's publisher, and Brown had met

Lawrence on his earlier visits to Oxford. Moreover, Brown's relationship with Algonquin had become testy a few months earlier when the press refused to accept Glennray Tutor's original cover art for *Big Bad Love*; Lawrence, in contrast, was a collector of Tutor's paintings.

At the beginning of April, Brown made a list of pros and cons of remaining with Algonquin. The points in favor of the switch included the increased money and exposure that a "big New York publisher" would bring to Brown as well as the fact that Houghton Mifflin had expressed an interest in Brown's detective novel, *Bullets Are Cheaper*, which Ravenel had rejected. On Algonquin's side of the ledger were his loyalty to his agent, Liz Darhansoff, and to the people with whom he had developed relationships at Algonquin/Workman, plus the possibility that if he took the novel elsewhere, Algonquin might become "so mad they might not publish me again" (Tutor Papers). Darhansoff weighed in with a 22 April letter to Brown, reinforcing the idea that if he took *Joe* to another publisher, Algonquin might sever its relationship with him and warning him of the dangers of overexposure: "Adding an additional primary publisher would inevitably breed a climate of suspicion, distrust, doubt & confusion—not only at Algonquin/Workman (who, I am certain, would not want to continue to publish you under those circumstances), but in a marketplace which will not know what to make of a new Larry Brown title every season. Reviewers like to find writers to get behind, but they won't pay the kind of attention you've been getting every six months; they tend to become skeptical about writers who write too much—or, at least, publish too frequently" (Brown Collections).

Brown's calculations apparently came down on the side of Houghton Mifflin, because in early May, he wrote to Mills that he might "be moving to a major publisher. We're dealing. Algonquin's probably going to call me an ungrateful little son of a bitch" (Brown Collections). On 9 May, however, Brown reported, "Houghton Mifflin made an offer, $50,000, I took it, called my agent, she flipped, she called Shannon, she really flipped, now everybody's called everybody else, I've been talked to like a dog and don't know what to do. Algonquin's holding a gun on me nearly, saying they'll never publish me again if I make this move and offering the same or more money. I've been drunk for two nights straight and I've got to stop. They laid a bunch of guilt on me, you know, what all they've done for me, my career, my future, all that. I haven't been this upset for a long time. I can hardly sit still" (Brown Collections). Later that day, Brown had a telephone conversation with Ravenel and the two smoothed over the situation: "She said things would be the same. . . . I really got myself in a mess this time. I hope I don't mess around and wind up without any publisher at all" (LB to JM, Brown Collections). In late June, Brown signed a contract calling for Algonquin to publish the novel and pay him a twenty-five-thousand-dollar advance (Peter Workman to Liz Darhansoff, Algonquin Files; LB to JM, Brown Collections).

Lawrence later told Ravenel that Brown had approached Houghton Mifflin because "he felt his books would get wider distribution and more effective promotion with another publisher" (Algonquin Files). From that time forward, however, both Ravenel and Brown remained wary of Lawrence.

With his publishing problems behind him, Brown returned to writing. By late May 1990, he was "working a good bit on *Joe*. I'm going to write for a while and then go back and revise for a while. I figure I'm still a couple of hundred pages away from a first draft" (LB to SR, Algonquin Files). The writing process was not easy for Brown, and on 20 June, he told Mills, "I hope *Joe* will be everything I want it to be. It's been very hard to write. I hope that shows, too. I've never gotten in any hurry on it but they want a finished ms. By Dec 31st this year. I signed the contract and I'll take the first money but I don't know if it will be ready by then. I hate a damn deadline" (Brown Collections).

He did not miss the 31 December deadline by much, submitting the finished manuscript to Ravenel on 10 January 1991. His accompanying note told Ravenel, "I'm glad to have it out of my hands and into yours. I worried over the ending for a long time and wrote it 4 or 5 times, then did it again today and decided to go on and send it, that I'd done about all I could to it at this point on my own" (Algonquin Files). Ravenel responded enthusiastically just over a week later: "I can't say it enough times! WOW! WOW! WOW! It's great. I feel like I ought to sit down and write a tribute to this novel, to the majesty of its major themes, to the brilliance of its characterizations, to its tension and movement and action, to the extraordinary ending" (Algonquin Files). On 22 January, she wrote to him suggesting only "really very minor" changes to the manuscript; she even suggested that he would not have to retype but could fix the problems "right here on THIS manuscript" (Algonquin Files). When Brown was subsequently asked about how much he cut or edited his works, he answered that he had to cut all of his novels except *Joe*, which was "pretty much published . . . the way I turned it in" (Blanchard 17).

In *Joe*, Brown "was trying to tell a story in a way I had not done before. I was trying to make the landscape—the areas where I live—an integral part of the story" (Summer 46). Though he intended the main focus of the story to be the Jones family, he created Joe "as a way to try to save Gary from what his fate would have ordinarily been—probably something bad on down the road somewhere. The kid had never really been given a chance, and his father's not good. I wanted him to have a chance at a relationship with—not another father, but somebody who could take care of him for a little while. Joe was invented to do that. In the course of working on the story about him, I began to find that his story was important, too" (Bonetti et al. 243). Joe was based at least partly on a man whom Brown knew: "I got to talking the other night when I was drunk about the guy Joe is modeled after. . . . I've got a copy of *Joe* that I'm keeping in my truck all the time, waiting to run up on the guy it's all about so I can give it to him and sign it for him, not that he'll ever read it, but just because I owe it to him. Because I respect him. Because he's one of the baddest motherfuckers I know. And a friend. He let me stay with him one time for four days, once when I left Mary Annie. I didn't have any place to go and he let me stay with him. I worked for him for several years. Me and a bunch of black guys. Those were bad days back then." Brown also said that the knowledge that Cormac McCarthy had also used autobiographical material, particularly in *The Orchard Keeper*, "makes me feel better about using so much stuff from my own life" (LB to JM, Brown Collections).

John Coleman's store, where Joe and his crew buy their lunches and where Gary Jones buys groceries for his family, is also based on a real-life establishment run by Norman Clark while Brown was growing up in Tula (Rankin, "On" 96). According to Brown, Clark "came out of the war just about the same time my father did and he never went anywhere after that. At one point he had a brand-new four-door 1962 Chevrolet Impala. The car sat right across the road and rotted into the ground. There was a period of twelve years when he never left Tula, and Tula's only a few hundred yards long. He stayed in that store every day for thirty-something years" (Bonetti et al. 239). Like the novel's Coleman, Clark had plenty of money: recalled Brown, "Somebody would bring a check in and say, 'Can you cash this check for me, Norman?' He'd say, 'Yes.' They'd say, 'Well, that's a pretty big check now. Sure you can cash it?' He'd say, 'Yeah.' It didn't matter how big the check was, he could cash it. He had the money in there. And he had that pistol, too. Everybody knew it. He kept his Budweiser in the candy case, too. He didn't mind drinking it hot" (239).

Perhaps because Brown had threatened to leave Algonquin/Workman or perhaps because, as Ravenel contended, the novel merited such efforts, the publisher launched a massive promotional campaign for *Joe*. Ina Stern, who had met Brown during his first visit to New York and had subsequently become Algonquin's marketing director, recalled that the novel really had to be sold three times: to sales representatives for book companies, to wholesalers, and to booksellers ("Go, Little Book" 48). One promotional idea that Stern discarded would have had Brown barnstorm "through America via pick-up truck" ("Go, Little Book" 49).

On 12 March 1991, Louis Rubin solicited an essay from Cleanth Brooks in support of the novel. Convincing Brooks to write the essay was a real coup, as Brown recognized: on 7 May, he wrote to Clyde Edgerton, "Check this. You know Cleanth Brooks. Know who I'm talking about? That old man with white hair, little baby-talking guy, real small and mild-mannered, the most renowned Faulkner scholar in the world who was at Chattanooga when we were there? Well, he's read *Joe* and has written an essay on it that Shannon's supposed to send me. That blows my mind" (Edgerton Papers). Edgerton pronounced the news "one of the best things in the world that could happen" (Brown Collections).

Algonquin/Workman printed Brooks's essay as a prepublication brochure, *An Affair of Honor, Larry Brown's Joe*. Brooks described

Brown's writing as not "imitation Faulkner." Rather, Brown writes in a "rather simple and straightforward [style]. His descriptions are exact" (1). Brown draws readers into the action by describing "simple and habitual actions" in "minute detail" (1). Ultimately, Brooks wrote, "*Joe* is a very fine piece of fiction. For all its seriousness, Larry Brown's novel is thoroughly readable, not because it has a good measure of sex and blood and thunder in it, but because the author knows how to write, has a real story to tell, and knows how to tell it" (2).

Algonquin/Workman's marketing plan for *Joe* also included full-page ads in the *New York Times Book Review* and *Publishers Weekly* ("Go, Little Book" 49). Moreover, at the May 1991 American Booksellers Association conference in Washington, D.C., Algonquin/Workman featured *Joe* as the top work of fiction on the company's list, using a photo of Brown "enlarged [to] ten times life size . . . as a backdrop" for the Algonquin booth ("Go, Little Book" 49). Brown's friend, Oxford bookseller Richard Howorth, recalled that the "blow-up of Larry Brown's face . . . was so huge that all over the convention hall, you could see the top of Larry Brown's forehead. When I first got to the convention, I was hundreds of feet away from the Algonquin booth and I saw Larry Brown's forehead and recognized it. . . . It was a sort of landmark for the whole convention" ("Go, Little Book" 5). Conference attendees also were offered not only advance reading copies but also a "specially prepared booklet containing, among more than fifty excerpts from reviews of Brown's first three books, four profiles each reproduced in its entirety, complete with photos" (Perry 142).

At the beginning of April, Brown "spoke passionately . . . about his life and his writing" to a class at the University of Mississippi (Sullivan 3). In June, he, John Grisham, and several other writers helped inaugurate Ole Miss's High Cotton Writers' Conference. These events as well as Brown's teaching at the Bread Loaf conference at Middlebury College in Vermont marked his increasing involvement in academia, a trend that would intensify over the next few years.

On 9 July 1991, Brown celebrated his fortieth birthday, an occasion commemorated by a surprise birthday party planned by his wife, Mary Annie, and friends and hosted by Mary Hartwell and Beckett Howorth. Edgerton and his family flew to Oxford to join in the celebration, and their presence both pleased and touched Brown. He wrote to thank Edgerton for coming and told him, "I treasure your friendship. I'm almost ashamed that you went to all that trouble and expense for me, but not quite" (Edgerton Papers).

Soon thereafter, Brown wrote a humorous short story, "A Birthday Party," which, he told Edgerton, "has a fistfight and a knifefight and some stuff about my daddy being in the war and I'm using Leon Barlow as the character telling it, only now he's married, but I don't know if it's too maudlin and nasty or not. I've got to tinker with it some more. I ain't wanting to publish it. What I'm wanting to do is get it right and then give a copy of it to everybody who was at the surprise party at Mary Hartwell's house, so I hope it works out. Maybe it wouldn't matter if it *is* too maudlin and nasty. It's just a way of saying thanks to everybody for being so good to me anyway" (Edgerton Papers). Brown eventually decided that the story should be published, and it appeared in the autumn 1992 issue of the *Southern Review*.

Algonquin's sales representatives continued to push *Joe* throughout the summer of 1991. Well before publication, the book "began to receive extraordinary prepublication reviews in the trade journals," and the publisher "launched a separate telemarketing campaign to supplement the [sales] reps' efforts, encouraging stores that they had ordered too conservatively." Stern also sent reading copies to "development specialists at 325 of the largest library systems in the country" ("Go, Little Book" 50). The novel soon received more than a hundred reviews in national and regional publications, including *Mirabella*, *Vanity Fair*, *Time*, *Newsweek*, the *Wall Street Journal*, the *New York Review of Books*, the *New York Times Book Review*, and the *Washington Post* (50).

Most of these reviews were positive, and according to Stern, "at the end of 1991, *Joe* held a place on virtually every reviewer's list of the best books of the year. The American Library Association selected it as one of the twelve best books of 1991. The Southern Book Critics' Circle honored Larry with their 1991 award for fiction. *Publishers Weekly* . . . not only ran an interview with Larry, but gave the book a starred review, selected it as one of the best books of the year and even ran two pieces about Larry in their gossip column called 'Talk of the Trade'" ("Go, Little Book" 50). *Joe* was "one of the final ten nominees for the

National Book Award. . . . JOE was right up there until the very end—
it was next to the last book cut to make the final five nominees" (SR to
LB, Algonquin Files).

Brian E. Crowley of the *New York Times* called *Joe* Brown's "finest
work to date" (n.p.). According to the *Memphis Commercial Appeal's*
Fredric Koeppel, the book made Brown "a major writer" ("Art" n.p.).
Daniel Woodrell declared in the *Washington Post*, "In *Joe*, this brilliant
novel of downhome grit, tragedy, and redemption, Larry Brown has
slapped his own fresh tattoo on the big right arm of Southern Lit"
(9). In the opinion of Robert F. Geary, Brown had recorded "superbly
the sights, sounds, and smells of the rural environment, capturing the
local idiom, and most of all, seeing a stern dignity in the lives of the
most unpromising of ordinary people" (417). The book demonstrated
"none of the fashionable contempt for" lower-class characters; indeed, "Brown genuinely respects the hard-drinking, occasionally violent men he sees as forming the backbone of this rural community"
(422). Gene Lyons compared Brown favorably with Theodore Dreiser
and John Dos Passos, while Kenneth Holditch wrote that *Joe* brought
"to mind the work of Erskine Caldwell" (4). Glenda Winders called the
novel "a tale of man's inhumanity to man so grisly and cruel it might
have made even Mark Twain, the master of that theme, flinch and
turn away" (n.p.).

David L. Ulin dubbed the title character "an icon of the new South
caught on the uncertain ground between the past and the future, a
loner who realizes that the money he throws around so loosely can do
nothing to assuage the emptiness inside him, who misses his family
yet understands it's his own fault that they left him. In his distant,
undemonstrative fashion, Joe provides Gary with things that the boy
sorely needs—a job for one, and some confidence and self-esteem.
Through taking on Gary, Joe fills the emptiness within himself and
enhances his chances for redemption in spite of the violent, anti-social
life he has led" (18). Geary agreed that Joe has a basic understanding
of evil and that "in the end, he is willing to pay the price of his freedom
to buy a chance for Gary and the boy's abused sister and to block in
some way the evil being spread by Wade. Joe, however flawed, is a man
of honor" (423).

Three weeks before the book's official publication date, 1 October, Brown did a reading and signing at Oxford's Square Books. The event was an unqualified success: Howorth wrote to Ravenel that Brown "was splendid, it killed us. . . . Here at the store for Larry's reading we had without question the largest crowd ever for a reading, I'd say about 200 people, and we locked the door, unplugged the phones, and turned off all the lights except one lamp for Larry to read by. He read the part where Wade gets mistreated by the local cops out on the Square, and as he read you could hear outside the store pick-up mufflers and the occasional shriek of a redneck youth, so the effect was 3-D, sensurround, and everyone loved it. People here really love Larry; really, really love the fact he's standing on his own hind legs and casting a shadow" (Algonquin Files).

Much like the promotional tour for *Big Bad Love*, the effort on behalf of *Joe* was a whirlwind affair that took Brown across the country. He began with a reading in New York on 24 October, then traveled the next day to Washington, D.C., where he taped several radio and TV interviews and did a reading. From there, he flew to the West Coast for readings in Seattle and Portland before visiting Los Angeles to appear on a local television show and do three readings and signings. At the end of October, he was in San Francisco for more events.

Joe is in some respects a classic study of good and evil. Joe Ransom functions as both an unlikely Samaritan and an instrument of divine retribution as he obliterates the evil that blackens his world and spoils his attempts to save his young protégé, Gary Jones. Though Joe has lived a rebellious life, he is an appealing human being with a strong set of human values, including adherence to what Brown saw as an almost puritanical work ethic: "He believes a man ought to get up and go to work every morning" (Bonetti et al. 241). Critic Erik Bledsoe sees Joe as another in the long line of American rebels whose behavior often runs afoul of the law but whose ethical values are generally superior to the society to which they do not conform (76).

If Joe stands as the avatar of good in Brown's novel, Wade Jones, an unsavory patriarch of a disintegrating family, is patently evil. Jones will do anything for the money he needs to satisfy his lust for alcohol. Brown intended for Joe to combat the power of absolute evil represented by Wade Jones: Joe "must do what he does . . . as a moral imperative. . . . Joe knows that evil is real not some abstraction. Whatever good is in this world has to have teeth in it if evil is to be dealt with" (Ketchin, "Interview" 135). Jones's fifteen-year-old son, Gary, has transcended his bleak heritage. Like Joe, the boy is a hard worker, strongly devoted to his family. Joe gives Gary a job, "sells" him an old pickup, and introduces him to the pleasures of beer and women. In so doing, as Martha Phifer asserts, Joe is giving Gary a better life "than anything he has ever known" (12). More ambiguously, in Woodrell's view, "By the end of the novel Joe has passed on to Gary his virtues and his vices and though, in some ways he has freed the boy and made him stronger, in others he has poisoned him, much like he would an unwanted tree on company land" (9).

The novel also explores the theme of the ruin of the agrarian South, which William Faulkner prophesied in *Go Down, Moses*. In much of Faulkner's narrative, part of the North Mississippi landscape remains untouched by human corruption. *Joe* takes up where *Go Down, Moses* leaves off, showing the remnants of the wilderness in a much different light, bearing the marks of human degradation and rampant commercialism. Brown told Kay Bonetti that writing *Joe* gave him "a great opportunity to show the landscape, and to set my characters against it. And to have this larger thing, even larger than the lives that are going on, which is the land. The ground is so ancient. It's the oldest thing we've got. I like to have people picture what it looks like—that distant watershed where all the lines of trees fade into this little blue line that's the end of the horizon. That's what I love. This is my country, and I love this place. I try to re-create it on the page" (Bonetti et al. 243). On another occasion, Brown stated that he "was trying to tell a story in a way I had not done before. I was trying to make the landscape—the areas where I live—an integral part of the story" (Summer 46).

Joe Ransom works for a timber company that hires men to kill off all of the forest's native vegetation so that more profitable pines can be planted, an endeavor in which Brown had engaged earlier in his life and which he regretted: "I used to do that for a part-time living. I'm not proud of what I did. I did it simply for the money, to feed my family. . . . It's brutal work" (Bonetti et al. 242). Although Joe needs the money, he has regrets, standing "in the bladed road with his hands on his hips" and watching the work crew. "He surveyed his domain and the dominion he held over them not lightly, his eyes half-lidded and sleepy under the dying forest. He didn't feel good about being the one to kill it. He guessed it never occurred to any of them what they were doing. But it had occurred to him" (*Joe* 202–3). The members of Joe's crew demonstrate their alienation from nature when they encounter a huge snake. Like Popeye in Faulkner's *Sanctuary*, the workers are terrified by the snake's sudden appearance and can react only with the primitive desire to save themselves, chopping and stamping the creature to death. Brown presents people who are primarily creatures of their senses. Any notion of solace from nature is completely alien: his postmodern people are creatures of the moment, inhabiting the natural world without the reverence that both Faulkner and Brown knew that it deserved.

Although Brown's writings have generally received little scholarly attention, two articles have examined the wilderness theme in *Joe*. Paul Lyons argues that the novel "depicts the poor, rural life of contemporary Mississippi and shows that nostalgia must not just be for a simpler, purer society but can be a blue-collar attachment to individual freedom without illusions about the past" (106). According to Lyons, "The 'hero' in *Joe* no longer hunts bear for sport in the forest; rather, he hunts the forest itself in the least sportsmanlike manner, for profit, without any sustaining connection to the land. . . . In part through his complicity in such inversions, Joe becomes representative of a generation that participates uneasily in cutting itself off from crucial aspects of an identity that imagines itself nonetheless connected to a 'first settler,' rebel mentality" (109). Nevertheless, Joe evidences a connection with this frontier mentality (293). Finally, the lower-class inhabitants of Brown's world lack knowledge of the South's pre–Civil War values: "Lacking cultural memory, this South cannot feel nostalgia, or feel that there is any former dignity to be upheld. Lacking a sense of place-history, they lack a sense of future direction" (112).

Jay Watson asserts that "all too often the rootedness of the poor only underscores their vulnerability. [Brown's characters] still ache with longing, a longing utterly conditioned by the unrelieved poverty of the characters. We see once again how economic exigencies work to shape Southern responses to the environment" ("Economics" 513). Gary Jones, "marginalized and isolated elsewhere," finds an almost spiritual "intimacy, even a kind of recognition in the woods" (499). But after "having the deadening work explained to him," Gary "instantly and uncritically accepts the older man's offer to hire on with the crew. . . . His desire to escape or ameliorate the human violence that surrounds him makes violence against the woods seem acceptable" (503, 504). Watson also compares the poisoning of the forest and the "human damage wreaked by alcohol. . . . We might say that alcohol leaves the novel's human landscape as poisoned and deadened as Joe's chemicals leave the forest landscape" (506). In Koeppel's view, Brown's male characters "drink seriously to assuage a thirst deeper than the body knows and, in drunkenness, take monumental offense and fight and cut and shoot and kill each other over exaggerated notions of honor and family name, or act simply out of a drunken impulsive stupidity that sweeps them into prison or death" ("Art" n.p.). Because of Wade Jones's addiction, Gary's situation is no better in the end than it is when we meet him and his family walking down that desolate road: despite "Gary's brief forays up the class ladder in earlier chapters," "the family's situation seems more precarious than ever" as the novel closes (Watson, "Economics" 512).

Having completed *Joe* with considerable difficulty, Brown must have been relieved by its success. The novel certainly helped validate his stature as a literary novelist. Brown remained fascinated with the members of the Jones family: not only did he return to them with *Fay*, published nearly ten years later, but he even considered writing a third volume, *Gary*. However, his other interests prevented him from immediately continuing work on his proposed trilogy; instead, he proceeded with a plan to publish a book of nonfiction.

CHAPTER EIGHT

"Fire Notes" becomes
On Fire, 1991–1994

After his promotional efforts for *Joe* had ended, Larry Brown settled into a routine that he followed for the next few years. He alternated among traveling in support of his books, writing at home in Yocona and Tula, and teaching assignments, which included a return to Bread Loaf at Vermont's Middlebury College every summer from 1991 through 1994.

Brown always felt somewhat dubious about his ability to teach, telling Billy Watkins, "Once you have books published, you're qualified to teach—they think" ("Hot" 2D). He also hesitated to criticize student writing, since "you're messing with something that has come out of somebody's heart and soul. I tell them if it doesn't work this time, they've got to keep trying and believing in themselves" (Summer 46). At the 1991 Bread Loaf conference, Brown's first as an associate instructor, there were "16 students and I've got half of them. So I've got to read 8 manuscripts & meet with 8 people for an hour a piece, plus go to everything, plus eat, plus party, plus constantly talk to all the people who want to talk to me, plus get ready for my own reading next Monday at 4:30. They think I'm a wild man up here. . . . We had one keg party already down by the pond, about 100 people around a campfire, guitars all that" (Tutor Papers).

Orman Day, a 1991 participant at Bread Loaf, recalled Brown as "quite approachable and while he sat on the steps of the barn, he could converse with us about just about everything." Day found Brown particularly sympathetic to students, like Day, "who had to fit our literary efforts into our job schedules. He preached a strong work ethic and toughened us against rejection." Brown's workshops were popular and thus quite crowded, and Brown was much less formal in the classroom than were some of the other teachers: "Larry was his folksy self, critiquing student work and discussing his theory of writing, which is that you weigh a character down with a problem and then you add another problem. I remember that he made us laugh and with his own example, inspired us." When Day asked Brown to read an excerpt from a novel Day was writing, however, Brown "begged off": according to Day, "because of his lack of academic training, he didn't feel qualified to discuss my piece's merits." Nevertheless, Brown did not regret his lack of academic credentials and "prided himself on honing his craft on his own . . . on being a self-made man." Dorie LaRue confirms Day's assessment of Brown at Bread Loaf, describing him as "a popular teacher, accessible, funny, totally committed to his students. He was known to leave functions early or refuse late socializing so that he could mark short stories" (39). Writer Pinckney Benedict, who was with Brown at Bread Loaf from 1992 to 1994, objected to what he saw as the snobby selfishness that characterized some of the other participants; Brown, however, "was very different from that paradigm. It was like meeting someone from home in a foreign country where the natives don't like you very much." During the summer of 1993, the two men shared lodgings "back in the woods, about a mile from the main campus. I think they put us there because we were both rednecks and were not alarmed by the bugs and snakes and mice that lived in the cabin, or the remoteness. . . . We both liked the cabin a lot. It could have been a cabin in the woods anywhere." Benedict agreed with Day and LaRue that Brown was a real asset at Bread Loaf:

> He took his students very seriously. He was (compared to a lot of the faculty) new to writing himself, and so he knew what they were facing, how they felt, the people who wanted to publish. It wasn't blasé to him. He talked to students as though they were his colleagues rather than his acolytes. I learned a lot from him that way.
>
> I liked Larry a lot. He was very kind to me, personally and professionally. I was also envious of him, to my shame, as many people were.

He was extremely talented, charismatic, humble, capable, gentle: an extremely attractive sort of person to be. . . . He was a generous teacher who took everybody seriously—good writers, poor writers, people who were trying to imitate him, people whose styles and backgrounds were nothing like his.

Graham Lewis, a poet and fiction writer who described himself as in awe of Brown, met his idol at Bread Loaf in 1993: "I felt a nudge on my arm, turned to my right, and there he was, sitting cross-legged not a foot away. He raised a half-dead fifth of tequila. 'You look like you could use a hit of this, bro,' he said. I took the bottle, bubbled it a couple times, and said, 'You're Larry Brown.' . . . He grinned, extended his hand, and we shook. 'That's what I hear,' he said, almost in a whisper. 'But don't let it get around.' His self-effacing manner and gentle humor wrapped in his warm Mississippi drawl put me at ease, and before I knew it we were jawing away about fishing, music, and dogs" ("Letters"). For Lewis, the real value of Bread Loaf and other conferences "lay not in workshops and lectures, but in talking to the writers on a personal basis, seeing that they're human, drinking with them, and listening to their opinions unfiltered over the course of several hours. Larry was determined to give me that opportunity, and it was obvious he enjoyed the role of benefactor" ("Letters").

In the fall of 1991, Brown became involved in a film about one of his idols, Harry Crews, that Gary Hawkins was making for North Carolina Public Television. Though Hawkins mainly sought to gather material for *The Rough South of Harry Crews*, he and Brown also talked about his history as a writer, his family life, and his love for rural Mississippi. The film won an Emmy award in 1992; more important for Brown, it helped establish a friendship with Hawkins that would result ten years later in a movie about Brown's life, *The Rough South of Larry Brown*.

Brown spent the next spring in Ohio, where he had accepted a position as writer-in-residence and teacher in the master's of fine arts program at Bowling Green State University. Brown had serious reservations about taking the offer, both because of his lack of formal higher education and because "when I said yes I . . . wanted and needed the money" (Edgerton Papers). Brown did not like the cold weather and snow of Ohio's winter, but he nevertheless saw beauty in his surroundings: "It may be the blackest dirt I've ever seen. There's lots of farm country just a few miles outside town. Huge fields, hundreds and hundreds of acres. I wish I'd had my camera with me. I could've gotten some good shots as the sun was going down. I want some shots of these huge barns up here, too. Up here when they build a barn, they put their name on it, along with the year it was built. I saw one a while ago, in real good shape, it said MIKE REYNOLDS 1921" (Tutor Papers). Ohioans were "real nice," but he was amazed that the underground water was undrinkable because of seepage from oil wells, and he noticed that the area had few blacks: "I haven't seen one outside the campus. Not one. It seems strange" (Tutor Papers). After attending a dinner party with some of the faculty, he wrote to his friend, Glennray Tutor, "I doubt I'll be hanging out with them much. I mostly stay [in] and work on students' stuff or read" (Tutor Papers). Brown also socialized with his students, writing to his editor, Shannon Ravenel, "Some of these kids keep me company here sometimes. Sometimes too much. They don't seem to have manners, though. I'll invite the whole gang over here and buy all the beer and the chips and dip and everything, and they'll leave about 20 empty cans on the coffee table, stuff like that" (Algonquin Files).

Brown found the separation from his wife, Mary Annie, and his children particularly difficult. Early in February 1992, Brown wrote to Edgerton, "She's been like a baby, man, calling and crying every night. She's not handling it well at all. I can't do nothing about it but buy her a plane ticket. I knew it would be tough on her but I didn't think it would be this bad" (Edgerton Papers). She came for a weekend visit a few weeks later, but "it just didn't last long enough" (Tutor Papers).

In January 1992, Brown began a journal in which he recorded his experiences at Bowling Green and some of his other thoughts. Perhaps his first extended absence from Mississippi since his military service caused him to reflect on his early life and on his father's death:

I remember Mama frying chicken in the kitchen, rolling out dough for biscuits cut with a beer bottle and how she would sprinkle the flour on the side table before she put the dough on it. I remember the smell of the Stag in the icebox, how powerful and pervading that scent was. It brings back bad memories of terrible times and the childhood of the lost days in Memphis, the family of us struggling to hold together until finally there was nothing to hold to.

I remember the World War II mementoes, the rifleman's badge, the patches from the infantry divisions, the silver German cigarette cases, the silver bright with a skull on it, the Solingen switchblade, the .50 caliber bullet, the rock from Hitler's fireplace, pink granite, chopped from the hearth with my father's bayonet.

I remember the long line of cars wrecked and burned, and my mother pulling money from the cleft of her brassiere to buy a car we were sitting in that the drunken man sitting beside us swore was the best car in Memphis.

I, too, remember the lipstick-stained cigarette butts left in the ashtray of that same car, and my mother did not smoke.

The days go by so fast when you are young. What there is of the world you learn from your parents. If they tell you to hate black people, you hate them. If you see them smoking and drinking, you tend to smoke and drink. But love lasts.

Of all the hard days and miserable nights we endured, from all the headlong flights in our pajamas in the dead of night from his wrath, one sweet memory rises swimming up, and that is the last night I was allowed to share with him, on the front porch in Mississippi, where he smoked one of the last cigarettes that would kill him, and told me of catfish in the rivers below us, and of beavers my brother had seen. I would have clung to him tighter if I had known [what would happen] the next morning, but it grew late, and he advised me to go to bed, and I would like to say that I kissed him, though I probably did not. Sixteen year old boys lose that affinity for their daddies, and later, wish they could call it back.

Next morning he was dead.

. . . . I remember the linoleum, and the cinders in the back yard, and the turkey my uncle brought over for Christmas. I wish that things could have gone differently, but now it seems they did not go badly.

I love you, Father, wherever you are, and I wish you were here with me now. (Brown Collections)

Brown also used the journal to vent some of his more prosaic feelings: he hated being at Bowling Green and was disgusted with the bad writing of some of his thirteen students. On 15 February, he wrote, "Teaching writing is the most humbling and embarrassing experience a writer can go through. I've already decided that when I finish Bread Loaf this year I'm through with that. I want my own world, one where I stay home and write my words" (Brown Collections). Brown also realized that teaching allowed him little time to write. He had begun to prepare a nonfiction work, "Fire Notes," in 1991, but between his arrival in Ohio and 5 March, he wrote only "about 3 pages" (LB to SR, Algonquin Files).

Despite his frustration, Brown took considerable pride in the success of the most promising of his students, including Andrew McDonald and Anne Panning. In 1994, Brown told Michael Manley, "Anne is really good and she's working on a novel, she's written a nonfiction book. She really didn't need anything from me except a pat on the back. She had been writing all her life" (126). Brown's prediction of Panning's success proved correct: her *Super America: Stories and a Novella*, won the University of Georgia Press's 2006 Flannery O'Connor Award for Short Fiction. For her part, Panning recalled Brown as having treated her "like a fellow writer instead of a student. He was always so honest and didn't worry about 'playing favorites,' of which I was clearly one. I was somewhat shy and his support of my work gave me confidence in my abilities. I also had a hard time believing it when he'd say my work was ready to go. He wasn't afraid to say in a workshop, 'This is publishable,' nor was he afraid to say, 'This is not working at all and you need to start over.'" Panning thinks that Brown felt a particular affinity for her because she was "a trailer court kid from a non educated family. I think he could relate." According to Panning, Brown had students "over to his apartment a lot for drinks and talk. He had a pretty crappy kind of basement apartment that was furnished with chunky old plaid furniture and milk crates full of books, and I got the feeling that he had never really moved in and settled. He was not afraid to swear, sing, and smoke and drink freely with the . . . students. I remember him being very kind, very tenderhearted about his family, who he spoke of often. He loved music and would play old blues, rock.

. . . We also had him over to our apartment for parties, and he seemed to love that, seemed to thrive in that environment." In contrast, Panning remembered, "an unspoken tension" sometimes existed as students vied for his attention in the classroom. Brown gave her the impression that "he felt a bit like an imposter in his university professor role." When a student brought a one-act play rather than a story to class, Brown "just about blew a gasket. He refused to comment on it, saying that the person was wasting his time and our time." He was also completely honest with students about the viability of their work, an approach that "went over well if you were the writer of the piece (I often was), but left others feeling sort of disenfranchised as writers and as critics, I think." Moreover, Brown's frequent practice of reading aloud from published stories bothered some students, who thought it "an odd way to spend workshop time" and "a waste of time."

While in Ohio, Brown became involved in an affair with one of his students. Mary Annie learned of the relationship, and tensions rose so high in their marriage that Larry found it difficult to return to their household at the end of the semester. In June, he wrote to Edgerton, "It's hard to get any work done around here. Lots of days, [Mary Annie] comes in with a look on her face that makes my heart sink. . . . Me and [Mary Annie] can go off and have a wonderful time and then five minutes later get into a terrible fight that fucks up everything for several days. I don't know what the answer is. And probably stopped caring long ago if there was one" (Edgerton Papers). He soon moved to an Oxford hotel and later rented a room in a house in town. The room was intended to be an office for writing, but his landlady supplied him with a bed. Brown told Edgerton that he had come "close to splitting with my family for good. . . . One of the things that hurt me most was that Mary Annie told me she had learned how to live without me during those 3½ months I was gone. We had some bitter, crying talks. I even stopped drinking for a while" (Edgerton Papers).

During that summer, Brown met Tom Rankin, who moved to Oxford to become an associate professor of art and southern studies at the University of Mississippi and who would become another of Brown's close friends. As Rankin was moving into his house, he saw his tenant "sitting there talking to this other guy who I recognized as

Larry. I think I had heard him read once . . . and I had read *Facing the Music*. One of the things in the back of my truck was an old stove made in Oxford, actually. So he walks up and he starts talking about this stove. He didn't want to talk about anything but this stove. . . . Later, maybe after a half hour after we started talking, we sort of formally introduced ourselves and I told him I liked his work. . . . I met Larry, really, as a guy in the backyard talking about a load in the back of a pickup truck."

The two men shared interests in writing and in the outdoors as well as in hanging out at the City Grocery bar, though both had strong ties to their families. This close relationship with Brown, both emotionally and geographically, gave Rankin a front-row seat from which to observe Brown's drinking problem, which became most acute during the mid-1990s. According to Rankin, "There were periods when Larry was out night after night. I might be with him one night in a two week stretch. I don't know where he was the other nights. After the bars closed, it was always somebody's house; he never wanted to go home. It was four or five before he went home. He wanted to go play music [with] these younger college types." Rankin believes that many Oxford residents wanted to be able to brag that they had gone drinking or smoked pot with the famous Larry Brown and consequently took advantage of him. Rankin was also able to see the importance that Brown placed on his writing: "He wanted his books to last. He wanted his voice to be recognized, his literary voice, [but] he never was comfortable . . . being the spokesperson for the voice of Larry Brown, though he did . . . like the attention; he wanted people to read his stuff and he wanted to get good reviews. . . . He did like the whole idea of fans, but he was much more comfortable sitting at the end of the bar in the corner talking to two people than having to read to an audience. There was this real shy part of Larry." In 1993, the *Oxford American* published some of Rankin's photographs of animals being butchered for food in rural Mississippi. Brown wrote a foreword to the photographs, drawing on his childhood experiences: "I remember my mother and aunt killing chickens in the back yard on a Saturday, and frosty mornings at daylight when hogs hung their heels steaming in the cold air, and the deer gambreled on a singletree swaying gently in the shadowy hall of the barn on a November afternoon. I helped at hog-killing time, and learned to skin the animals I brought down with my gun and delivered to my mother's capable hands and seasoned black skillets. I learned old and established rituals that were passed down to me through time and blood kin and my own sons know them now" (27).

In July 1992, Brown was offered and soon accepted the position of Thornton Writer-in-Residence at Virginia's Lynchburg College for the fall semester. Brown was much happier at Lynchburg than he had been in Bowling Green, writing to Tutor on 6 October, "I'm up here . . . in my palatial Virginia estate, and what an estate it is. Place [offers a] wonderful house furnished free, lots of good food to eat at no cost to me. And I'm working like hell, halfway through [*Fire Notes*], and only meeting one class a week. Best gig I ever had, bro. . . . We got free movies, free chili, ice cream, and the faculty thinks I'm a rare bird. The rarest of birds: somebody who makes a living by writing. . . . It's a nice little very rich school, only about 1700 students. . . . I even got free paper to write on, much better than the Xerox shit I usually use" (Tutor Papers). In addition to teaching fifteen students, Brown gave public readings, visited other classes, and held private conferences with students and faculty writers.

In October, despite their continuing marital problems, Mary Annie joined Larry in Nashville for the Southern Festival of Books, where he accepted the Southern Book Critics Circle Award for *Joe*. Later in the month, Brown traveled to Knoxville, Tennessee, where he introduced William Kennedy at "An Evening with the Novelist" at the Tennessee Theater (Don Williams B1). He was paid one thousand dollars for his three days there and accepted the offer because his "gigs have been few and far between" (Edgerton Papers).

Larry returned to Oxford at the beginning of November, apparently because of the ongoing problems in his marriage. On 7 December, he wrote to Ravenel, "I'm okay. I'm working, and I got my students' stories from Lynchburg, and I'm working hard on them, trying to finish up their critiques by Friday and turn in grades by the 18th. I'm grateful for that, that they didn't get pissed off and not give me the chance to at least fulfill my obligation long distance. I really hate I left the way I did, but you'd have to know my life to know why I did that" (Algonquin

Files). Brown also told Ravenel that although he "never meant all this to happen," he did not think that he would be returning to his family: "It don't feel like my home any more. . . . I was unhappy a long time before this. I had decided a long time ago that the right thing to do was to just keep living the way I was, in order to make the rest of them happy. But even that was impossible a lot of the time. . . . This is not just about this girl in Ohio. It *is* about her, because I think I could be happy with her, but what I'm saying is all this other had [been] building for a long time. Even Mary Annie will tell you that she doesn't know how I stood it as long as I did. It was because I came from a broken home, and always swore I'd never put mine through it. Now I've done it" (Algonquin Files).

Brown continued his affair, traveling to Ohio after Christmas. On 13 January, Brown again wrote to Ravenel that he was "doing okay." He had "seen Mary Annie and Shane and LeAnne, but not Billy Ray. Things are up and down sometimes, and I still don't know what will happen. I had a bad phone conversation with her Sunday night and then a civil meeting with her Monday night. Sunday night she said she wanted me out of Mississippi and Monday night she said she didn't want a divorce. That's how it goes. But don't worry about me because I'm writing every day and reading every day, having a few drinks in the evening, then working and reading until bedtime which is always late. Riding my bike some, trying to keep my blood pressure down" (Algonquin Files). By April, when Ravenel visited the Browns, they had reconciled; thereafter, Larry remained solidly committed to Mary Annie and his children.

In late 1991, in the midst of their marital turmoil, the Browns met twenty-one-year-old Jonathan Miles, an aspiring writer and blues guitarist who had moved to Oxford to attend Ole Miss and to further his music career. After dropping out of the university so that he would have more time to devote to music, he supported himself with a series of odd jobs that included writing for several local papers, including the *Oxford Eagle*. After Miles had published a short story in another local publication, Brown approached him and said, "I liked your story." Larry and Mary Annie invited Miles to join them for dinner at City Grocery. In the middle of the dinner, Brown excused himself from the table, went over to a table occupied by two well-dressed older couples whom Brown knew, and "stepped onto the corner of a chair, onto the table, onto their food." Then he "started doing the twist in their food. Mary Annie [was really upset]. The whole restaurant was absolutely frozen. Larry finished the song—three minutes, just doing the twist. Then he stepped down, came right back to his pork chop. I remember thinking, 'I gotta hang out with this guy.'" Miles never discovered exactly why Brown chose to dance on the other diners' table.

Because Miles was somewhat alienated from his parents, the Browns began to invite him to spend holidays with them, and he gradually became part of the family. He remembered, "Mary Annie really adopted me. I think she felt sorry for me. They take in strays." LeAnne Brown recalled that her father and Miles "would sit and talk and have beers and play their instruments."

In 2008, Miles published his first novel, *Dear American Airlines*. In subsequent interviews, he credited Brown with serving as his mentor, though Miles dislikes the term. Miles could not have asked "for a better education than driving around Mississippi, drinking beer and talking about books and writing with Larry" (Zane). Miles told another interviewer that he and Brown talked "about writing the way other guys talk about football. It was an astonishing education. Some people go to the Iowa Writers' Workshop. I had Larry" (Minzesheimer, "Reluctant"). Miles described Brown's "discipline and determination" as "breathtaking. Look, writing is difficult, it's an act of endurance—every writer experiences those moments of self-doubt and frustration when the prudent course seems to be to quit, when everything seems tilted against you. . . . But Larry's example rendered those kinds of thoughts moot. With him around, there was no way *not* to press on—because how could you justify quitting to *him*? And, oddly, that feeling only intensified after he died. . . . Even now I hear his voice: *Keep going. Write it*" (Miles, interview).

Again living with his family in the summer of 1993, Brown found himself occupied largely with mundane domestic matters, including a flea infestation and the birth of a litter of beagles. He was also drinking heavily, however, and while driving drunk one night, he rolled his pickup truck, totaling the vehicle. He wrote to Jake Mills, "I was drunk, and didn't hit anybody, and just luckily caught a ride home a few minutes after." Fortunately, "I had my seat belt on and came out of it with just a few scars. I had to go to the jail Saturday morning and talk to the state trooper, but they couldn't prove anything, and I got out of it with a $47 ticket for not reporting an accident." The penalties could have been much worse: "If I hadn't walked away from it, it would've been $1500, a night in jail, much embarrassment, and the loss of my license for a year. If somebody else had been involved I'd've stayed and faced the music. But it was just me and myself and my car." The incident "taught me a lesson. I was lucky to walk away" (Brown Collections). According to Tutor, Brown's habit of drinking and driving led to "a lot of close calls through the years."

Brown was also having problems with the Internal Revenue Service, apparently because he had failed to file adequate returns. He later told Mills, "I've had a lot of trouble with the IRS is the main thing. The little fuckup that I pulled a few years back probably cost me about $25,000 I couldn't afford to lose" (Brown Collections).

Brown was also serving as an evaluator for National Endowment for the Arts fiction award, a position that absorbed much of his attention during the summer of 1993 since it required that he read three hundred manuscripts, each about thirty pages long. He told Mills that he was reading about two hundred pages a day, and "it's just bad when it's all bad, as it sometimes is. I found two really fine stories this afternoon, though, both by the same writer. . . . I try to read 7 a day, sometimes more. I have to recommend 12 and 2 alternates out of the 300, then defend my choices when I get to Washington in October. That's a hoot, me working for the federal government. But somebody's got to pick that cotton" (Brown Collections).

In early September 1993, the Browns took a three-day family vacation to Gulf Shores, Alabama. He wrote to Ravenel, "We took the kids down for the weekend and just swam in the surf and ate seafood. It was really nice and we all got blistered except for LeAnne. . . . The hotel was right on the beach and they had a Jacuzzi and a pool as well. We swam all the time" (Algonquin Files). The Browns subsequently visited Gulf Shores on many other occasions.

All the while, Brown steadily worked on the manuscript that would become *On Fire*. The project had its genesis in a journal he began keeping in 1989, just after he "finished reading Rick Bass's *Oil Notes*, and I liked it a whole lot and enjoyed the style that he used, autobiographical" (LaRue 44). Brown elaborated to Michael Manley that *On Fire*

> came from not being able to sleep at the fire station, kind of late in my career there. Because we'd have so many runs at night, you'd get to sleep for a couple of hours, but than you'd have to get back up. Then you'd go back, sleep a couple more hours, then go make another run. It totally wrecked my sleep. . . .
>
> So one night I got tired of that. I just decided instead of tossing and turning there all night, I was going to get up and make some coffee and write down everything that had happened that day. And that's when it started. . . .
>
> It just became—not exactly a diary, but I began to write about some of the other events that occurred over the years. I started finding out there was a whole lot of material there that might be worth enough to try to make a book out of it. So when I finally got up to about a hundred and twenty pages, I sent all those pages to [Ravenel] and said, "What do you think about this? Think we could make a book out of it?" And she said yeah. So that's when I started working on it in earnest. It took me about four years to complete. (121)

To write nonfiction, Brown sought "to just put it down effectively and concentrate on telling the story in my own voice and as honestly as I could" (Steven Campbell, "Larry Brown Interview" 8).

Brown sent the first sections of "Fire Notes" to Ravenel in late December 1990. Her initial reactions were mixed: she worried about his constant references to Bass, telling Brown, "I love everything in these pages here except one thing. The thing I don't like is the self-consciousness about being a writer and knowing writers and having cards and letters around you from writers (and editors—even though it gave me a thrill to read that you have 'about a hundred' from me)" (Algonquin Files). To Algonquin cofounder Louis Rubin and his son, Robert, who was working at the press, Ravenel described the 120 pages that Brown had submitted as "filled with vivid stories from his experiences as a fireman, stories of death and of robbing death, of funerals, of dogs who died, kittens who didn't die, of a mouse who battled Larry valiantly to a noble death, of stalking and killing and dressing a deer in the woods. There are a few slips . . . but once he's into the swing of the thing (at about page 16), Larry writes here as he's rarely written before. I believe the final piece in this manuscript is one of his most beautiful passages" (Algonquin Files). Both men had minor reservations about the manuscript, but Robert Rubin wrote, "Larry is a craftsman, and his voice is calculated. The man knows what he's doing. When this book is published, it must be, very clearly, a crafted work of non fiction, with a shape, with a progression" (Algonquin Files).

Brown continued to work on the manuscript and in January 1993 sent Ravenel what he hoped was the final version. Algonquin gave him a fifty-thousand-dollar advance for the work (Algonquin Files). At the end of the month, Ravenel returned the manuscript to him with detailed recommendations, urging him to finish incorporating them by 22 February. In her opinion, the second half of the book, which concerned his firefighting experiences, was stronger than the earlier essays on Brown as a writer. She also insisted that the title had to be changed so that it less closely resembled Bass's *Oil Notes* and suggested *On Fire* as alternative. Brown returned the revised manuscript on 4 March. Ravenel approved of his changes and cuts: "I've just finished reading it—it's wonderful. You've met and dealt with every single problem. The book is, in my opinion, much much much stronger. The progression is there. The answer is there. It says all you want it to, I think. The writing in this book is as good as anything of yours I've ever seen. It's spare and yet it speaks, as the old saying goes, 'volumes.' You are the best writer writing today" (Algonquin Files). *On Fire: A Personal Account of Life and Death and Choices* would officially be published in February 1994, with copies shipped to bookstores the preceding month (Algonquin Files).

Some of the material included in *On Fire* was initially published in two articles, a strategy intended to promote interest in the book. Brown deliberately chose incidents that would draw readers in by both entertaining them and offering them insight into how humans deal with the tragedies of life. The first article, "Fire Notes," appeared in the inaugural issue of the *Oxford American*. Brown provides background on the Oxford Fire Department before giving anecdotes about a runaway fire truck, the rescue of a boy trapped in a wrecked automobile, and the funeral of a fellow firefighter at a rural black church. Brown also reflects on the "weird callousness" sometimes exhibited by the firemen, as when they continued to play poker even when a man whose two children had just been killed in a fire came into the station: "We couldn't let it get too close because we didn't want to be touched by it. You never heard anybody talk about it later" ("Fire" 21).

Parts of *On Fire* also appeared in "A Fireman's Sketches" in the *North American Review*. Some of the material was the same as what Brown published in the *Oxford American*, but he added other vignettes: a "training fire" (some decaying houses deliberately set ablaze so that firefighters could practice) during which his fellow firefighters turned a 250-gallon-a-minute hose on him as a prank; an occasion when drunken residents became so hostile after the fire department extinguished a house fire that Brown, as captain, hesitated to go back to retrieve a piece of equipment the firemen had left behind; and an alcoholic man who was twice rescued from his burning house but was not so lucky the third time. Brown also tells of a man "who lives in a nice house in a nice neighborhood in Oxford" (43) and who repeatedly gets drunk and then sleeps while his house catches fire. Twice he is rescued and his house rebuilt; the third time, however, he burns to death. On such days, according to Brown, "all of us are taken to our limits" ("Fireman's" 43). Brown also lists the "dumbass" (43) things that always seem to happen in the middle of the night: dumpster fires; fires started by people trying to thaw frozen pipes with propane lighters; fires caused by people who put pennies behind fuses; fires caused by people—drunk or sober—who forget about food they are cooking or smoke in bed; cars and houses deliberately set on fire for insurance money; gasoline that is flushed out of service station storage tanks and into sewers, where it then catches fire.

In June 1993, Brown received the Algonquin catalog containing *On Fire*, his first look at the volume's cover: he liked it; however, he groused to Mills, "they printed that I had a 10 city tour and they haven't even talked about it with me. They'll fuck with me too much one of these days and then they won't have me anymore." His idea of a promotional tour would not involve plane rides—"maybe just a driving tour of the South with me and [Mary Annie] in our T-Bird." If he refused a more extensive tour, he wondered, "Hell, what can they do, shoot me? Send somebody down here to break my arms?" (Brown Collections).

While *On Fire* was in production, Brown participated in several events near his home. In April 1993, he joined literary luminaries George Plimpton, William Styron, Willie Morris, Barry Hannah, and Kaye Gibbons in reading at the first Oxford Conference for the Book, hosted by Ole Miss's Center for the Study of Southern Culture. On 5 June, he Hannah, and John Grisham read and signed books at Oxford's City Hall as part of the Living South Festival.

In the fall of 1993, Brown returned to work on a stage version of *Dirty Work*. Four years of attempts to produce a script for Michael Halpern and PBS's *American Playhouse* had failed, but in 1989, a young filmmaker, Rick Corley, wrote to Brown about adapting the novel for the theater. Corley staged dramatic readings of "Samaritans," "Leaving Town," and "Kubuku Rides" in New York City in 1990 and 1991 and produced "Kubuku Rides" again in late May or early June 1991. Ravenel watched a rehearsal and described it to Brown as "the greatest dramatic experience of my life. Whoever Rick Corley is, Larry, he's got his finger right slam on your pulse. What he got out of the actors was incredible (and, as far as I could tell, he didn't change or cut a single word from the story). When it was over, I tried to tell them how great it was and burst into tears" (Algonquin Files). For two years beginning in 1991, Corley and Brown worked intermittently on a script for *Dirty Work*, and Arena Stage in Washington, D.C., accepted it for production during the 1993–94 season. The play ran from 21 January to 30 January 1994 at the Arena complex's Old Vat Theater. Brown spent the month in Washington, helping to craft the script and to direct the production. He was nervous about the experience: "I'm facing my play with more than a little trepidation. I don't know if I can sit there for a month every day and watch them rehearse those lines. I'm afraid it's going to bore me out of my head after a while and make me wish

Leona Barlow
Brown, ca. 1940.
Courtesy of
Leona B. Brown

Knox Brown Sr., ca. 1940.
Courtesy of Glennray Tutor

Larry on his first birthday,
9 July 1952. Courtesy of
Leona B. Brown

The Brown family in Memphis, mid-1950s: (left to right) Knox Jr., Larry, Leona, Joy, Knox Sr., (front) Darrell. Courtesy of Leona B. Brown

Brown family in Memphis at Galloway Methodist Church, ca. 1960: (left to right) Knox Jr.; Leona, Joy, Larry, Darrell (front). Courtesy of Leona B. Brown

Larry, early 1960s.
Courtesy of Tom Rankin

Larry, 1971. Courtesy of
Leona B. Brown

Larry, mid-1970s.
Courtesy of Leona B.
Brown

Shannon Ravenel.
Courtesy of Dale Purves

Larry, ca. 1989. Courtesy of Glennray Tutor

Larry and friends, ca. 1989: (left to right) Glennray Tutor, Bill Beckwith, Richard Howorth, Barry Hannah, Larry Brown. Courtesy of Glennray Tutor

Glennray Tutor and Larry, ca. 1989. Courtesy of Glennray Tutor

Larry and Clyde Edgerton, ca. 1990.
Courtesy of Clyde Edgerton

Larry in his cool pad, ca. 1990. Courtesy
of Clyde Edgerton

Larry and Richard
Howorth, ca. 1990.
Courtesy of Clyde
Edgerton

Larry and Andrea
Hollander Budy, Bread
Loaf, 1991. Courtesy of
Andrea Hollander Budy

Larry and David Bain,
Bread Loaf, 1991.
Courtesy of Andrea
Hollander Budy

Larry, mid-1990s.
Courtesy of Tom Rankin

Larry with one of his many dogs, mid-1990s. Courtesy of Tom Rankin

Larry signing books at Lyon College, Batesville, Arkansas, May 1995. Courtesy of Andrea Hollander Budy

The Brown family, 1996: (left to right) Joy, Darrell, Larry, Leona, Knox Jr. Courtesy of Leona Brown

Larry teaching at Ole Miss, 1998. Courtesy of Brand Photography Services and Archives and Special Collections, University of Mississippi

Larry and Mary Annie at City Grocery, 1998. Courtesy of LeAnne Brown Corbin

The Brown family, fall 1998: (left to right) Larry, Mary Annie, Shane (standing), Billy Ray, LeAnne. Courtesy of Mary Annie Brown

Larry recording with Clyde Edgerton, ca. 2000. Courtesy of Clyde Edgerton

Larry and Barry Hannah, 2000.
Photo by Nancy N. Jacobs;
courtesy of Nancy N. Jacobs,
http://mswritersandmusicians
.com

Gary Hawkins and Larry, ca.
2000. Courtesy of Gary Hawkins

Larry and the fake dog used in
the filming of "Boy and Dog,"
ca. 2000. Courtesy of Clyde
Edgerton

Larry reading at Thacker Mountain Radio, 2002.
Courtesy of Thacker Mountain Radio

Larry at the first showing of *The Rough South
of Larry Brown*, 2002. Courtesy of the *Durham
Independent Weekly*

Larry and Tom Rankin, 2002. Courtesy of the *Durham Independent Weekly*

Larry and Silas House, August 2004. Courtesy of Silas House

The pond at Tula, 2005

Larry's writing cabin at Tula, 2005

Larry's gravestone at Tula, 2005

Jean W. Cash, at Tula, 2008. Courtesy of Robert McDonald

Billy Ray and family celebrating the opening of the Brown Family Dairy, June 2009: (left to right) Molly, Sarah, Paula (carrying Harris), Billy Ray. Courtesy of Mary Annie Brown

I was back home writing another novel or some stories" (LB to JM, Brown Collections). Many of Brown's friends came to see the play, including Jake Mills and his wife, Rachel, and Richard and Lisa Howorth and George Kehoe from Oxford. According to Kehoe, the set involved two beds, with variations in lighting used to indicate movement into the past. Brown showed Kehoe around the theater and was on "cloud nine" about the whole production.

Richard Howorth pronounced the production "excellent," but not all performances went as well as the one the Howorths attended: Brown told Mills that one show was "horrible . . . people missing their cues, forgetting lines, and the first act ran an hour and 16 minutes. Rick [Corley] got up and walked out of it and I went home to a bottle of Wild Turkey and wound up calling Harry Crews twice at 6 AM. And lo and behold if he didn't call about 7 and cheer me up with a 30 minute pep talk. He'd read the new book and talked good about it. We had a great show that night and everything was all right again" (Brown Collections). On the whole, Brown was pleased to finally see a dramatization of one of his works despite the effort that had been involved: "I did a lot of hard work up there, writing mostly, but it was a great experience. I hope to do some more stage work. The cast really enjoyed what they were doing" (LB to JM, Brown Collections). Other theaters subsequently expressed interest in producing *Dirty Work* (LB to JM, Brown Collections).

While in Washington, Brown reluctantly did a reading from his works at the Folger Theater: he told Mills that he "damn sure didn't have anything to do with [scheduling the event]; it was set up by Algonquin. I guess I'll go along with it but I just probably won't be comfortable with it. I never read in no theatre before and maybe nobody'll even show up. I've got no idea why they would" (Brown Collections).

Brown's stay in Washington also coincided with official release of *On Fire*. The first printing, with firefighting equipment on the cover, consisted of twenty-five thousand copies. The inside flap featured a quotation from the *Jackson (Mississippi) Clarion-Ledger*'s review of the book: "Larry Brown writing is like Mozart setting open-heart surgery to music." Among the blurbs on the back cover is one written by

Grisham. Brown dedicated the book to his dog, Sam, a "faithful friend, loyal companion." Anecdotes about Sam's life and death constitute a significant portion of the book.

Before returning to Mississippi, Brown went to Indianapolis for a reading at Butler University. He then gave a reading and signed copies of the book at Square Books on 4 February before departing on the ten-city tour about which he had complained to Mills. He started out at Lemuria Books in Jackson in early February before moving on to Manteo and Raleigh/Durham, North Carolina, and then Athens, Georgia. In addition to the appearances at North Carolina bookstores, Algonquin's publicity staff arranged for Brown to do an "interview with *The Independent* and it looks like they've set me up to talk to old Wayne Pond [of North Carolina Public Television] again at the studio. I didn't know until last night that I was doing the extra stuff" (LB to JM, Brown Collections). After Georgia, he would be going to Alabama, where he was booked "on some damn TV show in Birmingham at 7:30 in the morning and I was hoping to drink some whiskey with Shelby Foote the night before, but at least I'll have Mary Annie with me to drag me out of bed in the mornings" (LB to JM, Brown Collections). In North Carolina, Brown enjoyed seeing Tim McLaurin but was bothered by the "crush of people. . . . I didn't think I'd ever get through signing books. And some guy approached me with all the facts about those people who died in that chicken plant fire a few years ago. Some kind of fanatic, I saw quickly. He never said what his stake in it was but he wants me to do something, I can tell. Probably wants me to write a book. I'm just going to tell him no and hope he leaves me alone. I feel bad about the people who lost their lives but I'm not *60 Minutes* either. . . . That's the only thing I hate about this stuff, running into people like that or getting short stories shoved at me" (LB to JM, Brown Collections).

Another promotional effort involved Brown's appearance in an advertisement for Absolut vodka in a 1993 issue of *Southern Accents*, for which he received a thousand dollars. The full-page ad features a stylized image of a group of firemen facing a fire with the words *Absolut Brown*. The facing page features background information on Brown and an announcement of the appearance of *On Fire*, along with a photograph of the book's dust jacket. Brown later put a poster of the advertisement on the wall of his writing room (Day). The first printing of *On Fire* quickly sold out, and Algonquin ordered five thousand additional copies.

Booklist published one of the first reviews of the book in November 1993; reviewer John Mort objected to what he saw as the disjunction between the firefighting stories and the lower-key descriptions of Brown's time away from the firehouse. Conversely, the writer for the *Kirkus Review* approved of the combined content: "This episodic memoir of his life as a firefighter is also a testament of family, courage, and hard work, and Brown isn't afraid to risk being sappy, albeit in a manly way" (n.p.). Writing in the *New York Times Book Review*, Madison Smartt Bell praised Brown's use of "artful understatement" to deal with the subjects of danger and death in the lives of both humans and animals, asking, "Does one laugh or weep?" (38). Bell continued, "'On Fire' shows itself to be constructed like a spider web; one may touch one filament to discover the delicate interdependence of the whole. In this context, fragility and beauty are twinned. Mr. Brown is never romantic about danger, but the presence of real danger does illuminate the preciousness of life, and in this book Mr. Brown goes through his life with the same meticulous attention with which Thoreau circled the woods around Walden Pond" (38). Michael Pearson read the book as a tract "about how to live one's life. 'You have to do something in your life that is honorable and not cowardly if you are able to live in peace with yourself, and for the firefighter it is fire'" (E8).

Brown wrote *On Fire* to detail his progression from skilled firefighter through novice writer to accomplished author, explaining to readers that he trained himself to write with the same tenacity that he brought to firefighting. His mastery of his first career enabled him to make the transition to the second.

Much of *On Fire* is taken up with incidents that reflect Brown's feeling for animals. Shortly after the book's publication, the author told interviewer Chico Harris, "I do have a love and respect for living things. That's just the way I feel about things. I've reconsidered a lot of things as I've gotten older. Reading literature and writing has probably helped that along" (3). In addition to the stories about his beloved

Sam, Brown included the tale of a dog that he and his fellow firefighters rescued and resuscitated: after receiving a jolt of pure oxygen,

> the puppy makes some noise halfway between a bark and a yelp, blows smoke out like he's enjoying a Marlboro, then takes another breath. . . . Pretty soon the puppy's making all kind of yelping noises and trying to raise his head, howling like the oldest ghost in the world, and we figure he's reliving the fire.
>
> You done come back to the world, boy, we tell him. (*OF* 106)

Brown also included several incidents that pointed to his growing inability to kill animals. He attended a pig roast, where his friend, Louie, "hands me a loaded Ruger .22, a nice little semi-automatic pistol. It's heavy in my hand. The pig grunts and walks up to the wire of the pen. He seems friendly. If he were a dog he'd be wagging his tail." Louie finally grabs the pistol and kills the pig, "a little disgusted" with Brown (*OF* 145). Although as a boy he was "slapdab teetotally crazy" about hunting, as he aged, "something came over me. Maybe I got too much of it when I was a kid. I still like to walk in a forest, but I'm not crazy about killing anymore. The killing never was the thing for me, anyway. It was mainly just being out in all that beauty. There are few things prettier to me than an old hardwood forest. We just don't have them around here much anymore. They've all been cut down" (64). He regretted killing a mouse that had invaded his bathroom: when he threw the carcass "out on the carport and looked at him, dead, wanting to live. I could hardly get over it. It made me uneasy for a long time" (33). Similarly, his attempt to raise rabbits to sell for meat failed when he released the animals into their natural environment.

On Fire also contains frequent references to the members of Brown's family. He describes the difficulties of living with Mary Annie's family and the relief he felt when he, Mary Annie, and their children finally built and moved into their own house. "We couldn't live in the house with Mary Annie's mother anymore, because it all came down to my writing, which I couldn't do over there, across the driveway. When her daddy, Preston, or Topknot, as everybody called him, died many years ago, everybody said the right thing to do was move in with her mother and take care of her and *her* mother, Pat, and I listened to the people who said those things and believed them being young and naïve and not knowing that a man and his wife needed to form their own life to-gether, since that's usually the plan, and it took some years and some heartbreak to find out moving in with Mary Annie's mother was not the right thing to do" (*OF* 24). Brown candidly discusses his drinking and carousing and the problems they caused in his marriage as well as the loss of his infant daughter, but he also illuminates the loving relationship that he and Mary Annie shared. In addition, he describes his fears about his children: "You get these babies, these little miracles, and then you do something stupid that nearly kills them. You think, Jesus, kid, you need somebody better than me to take care of you" (26). On one occasion, he was away from Oxford when he learned that Mary Annie and their second child, Shane, had been involved in an au-tomobile accident. Brown sat for many hours, knowing only that they had been taken to the local hospital: "It was a terrible time, that wait-ing, I couldn't drive it out of my mind that one of them or maybe both of them were dead. All those dead in the highways I'd seen, the bodies I'd pulled from cars. I knew that was the wrong thing to think, and I sat there and willed for the phone to ring. It did. It was Richard [Ho-worth]. He gave me the number of the hospital, and I called, and was eventually connected to my brother who was there waiting, and he told me that [Mary Annie] and Shane were bruised up some, but not seriously hurt" (113). And he relates the protectiveness he felt regard-ing his daughter, LeAnne: "Some day some little boy's going to look at her bottom in a pair of blue jeans and come over here to take her out and I'm going to get him down in the kitchen floor and just beat the shit out of him" (28).

On Fire opens with an "Author's Note" in which Brown describes his journey to becoming a writer and explains, "This book is an attempt to explore what I felt about my years in the fire service and what it was like to live through those years, and the way two totally different careers had to mesh and make room for each other until one of them finished first" (*OF* ix). After Brown left the Oxford Fire Department, he and Glennray Tutor came upon an automobile accident. The fire-fighter in Brown felt drawn to help, but he was now only a spectator, and he experienced a sense of regret: "I see how things are now. I step to the other side of the road" (180).

After the end of the dreaded ten-city promotional tour, Brown read in late March at the Tennessee Williams/New Orleans Literary Festival, where he joined Dorothy Allison on a panel titled "Grit Lit: Poor White Southerners." He was back home in time for the Oxford Conference for the Book, participating along with Barry Hannah in an 8 April feature-writing workshop. In July, Brown entertained Clyde Edgerton and Susan Ketchin, who had come to Oxford to promote her newly published book, *The Christ-Haunted Landscape*, which contained Brown's "A Roadside Resurrection." Brown took the visitors out to Tula, where he "let [Edgerton] run my brush cutter and fed them shrimp over here one night and catfish at [the nearby town of] Taylor the next " (Brown Collections).

In August, Brown returned for his final stint at Bread Loaf. At the end of September, he went to Florida, where he read as part of the Writers on the Bay Series at the Biscayne Bay campus of the Florida International University. He was also settling into the process of writing his next novel, *Father and Son*.

CHAPTER NINE

Solid Success

Father and Son, 1994–1996

During the early 1990s, Larry Brown and Clyde Edgerton decided to write a short story together. According to Edgerton, each writer would "do a few paragraphs or so and then send it to the other person. It was lots of fun." The result was the unfinished but hilarious "And How Are You." The manuscript sat for several years until Edgerton "decided to send it out [for publication], and asked [Brown] if I could edit the whole thing to get it ready and he said fine. So I tightened it a bit, and found it hard to remember who wrote what." Although Edgerton sent the piece to at least one journal, it was rejected, and by early February 1995, Brown had the manuscript and was planning "to haul it out and work on it before long I hope. Be nice if we could finish it and publish it" (Edgerton Papers). They never did so.

Brown's main project during the mid-1990s was a new novel, *Father and Son*, on which he began working in early 1994. He sent his editor, Shannon Ravenel, the first fifty pages in May, claiming that he was "rusty and it probably shows, because I've been away from my fiction so long, writing that screenplay and the non-fiction book." He liked the story and characters so far, "but I just haven't written enough of it yet to know them well enough so far. I've got to know more about them and I plan to. I want to explore Bobby Blanchard more, Glen's daddy more, Jewel a lot more, and Glen himself. I know I've got to make them real" (Algonquin Files). Ravenel generally liked what she read, declaring that parts of the manuscript "may be your best ever" (Algonquin Files); however, she thought he had too many driving and drinking scenes reminiscent of those in *Big Bad Love*. Still, she solicited thirty-seven-thousand-dollar advance for the book (Algonquin Files). In mid-June, Brown reported that he had "written some new chapters. . . . I'm happy with them, which probably means they're not right" (Algonquin Files). He had read from the manuscript at the Faulkner Conference on 4 August, and the experience made him "see a lot of things in it that need improving already, so that's a good sign" (LB to JM, Brown Collections).

By March 1995, Brown had written 233 manuscript pages and thought he was about half finished with the novel. He sent a chunk of the book to Ravenel, explaining that he was afraid that the action of the novel was too slow. She disagreed:

> I love it. Really. It took me over completely and I can't wait to see what happens. Boy! You can build suspense and dread, Larry Brown. You can.
>
> The characters are fine—FINE. And the scenes! Well, you've never written any better. . . . There's not a bad or flat scene in these 200 pages. (Algonquin Files)

Not surprisingly, Brown was pleased by Ravenel's response: "Months of toiling alone not knowing if it was good or not now makes perfect sense and I keep relearning the old lessons of discipline and hard work. I'm tremendously heartened to carry on now" (Algonquin Files).

His progress on the novel during late 1994 and early 1995 had been hindered not only by travel—he visited Kentucky and California in the fall of 1994—but also by a local dramatic production of scenes from *Joe*. Tupelo native and Ole Miss graduate Jim Hall, an actor with movie and stage experience in New York and Hollywood, had returned to Oxford, read *Joe*, and then suggested that a new group he had organized, the Performance Workshop for Oxford Writers, work with Brown to put on a dramatic version of parts of the book at the Hoka Theater. The production took place on 18–20 November, with Hall playing Joe. Among the other actors was Brown's classmate from Ole Miss, George Kehoe, who carried the narration in the sequence of scenes. Kehoe believes that "the script was Xeroxed directly from the book," with the scenes tied together by "chapter lead-ins . . . meant to set up a scene but not interrupt it. Once a scene began, I don't recall any narration within the scene. For example the opening narration was from the first page and a half of the book and set up the first scene." Brown frequently attended rehearsals, and he and Hall consulted often. Brown was excited by the prospect of seeing his characters on stage: Kehoe believes that Brown's "strong and genuine attraction to theater was all about seeing characters live and in motion in another dimension; not in his head or on the page, but out there in front of him (and other people) living and breathing and speaking his lines. . . . Seeing new visual possibilities on a stage seemed a natural instinct to Larry. I think he got very comfortable very quickly with the theater."

Brown told the *Oxford Town*, "I have always wanted to be involved in the staging of my work. When we finally, after four years of looking, found a stage for *Dirty Work* at the Arena in D.C. and I had a chance to see first hand one of these things coming together, I was hooked. I feel like if the people show up to see what Jimmy and the cast have put together, they will be hooked too. And that is the way to assure the future of the workshop and the future of theater in Oxford" (Steven Campbell, "Larry Brown's Joe" 4).

According to Kehoe, the Hoka had a full house of about 150 people for each night's performance. Hall had a "penchant for improvisation," which meant that "the show was different every night with varying measures of success and shortcoming. Maybe too varying for Larry—I'm not sure." Brown wrote to Edgerton, "We've had some minor fuck-ups as you will. . . . Had some drunk woman [who] tried to crash it last night. She was in our staging area trying to get in and I shoved a QUIET PLEASE! sign in her face two or three times and she was talking shit . . . and finally I got her by the sleeve and led her out into the lobby and she wanted to know who I was and I told her and she got so nice suddenly, she was an artist, she was a patron, she was a friend of our lead actor, blah, blah. I told her she had no ticket, the play had been running for ten minutes and she was fucking it up, come back tomorrow night, then I told her I had to get back to it and left her" (Edgerton Papers).

Brown also made time during the fall of 1994 to travel to North Carolina, where he went fishing with authors Phil Gerard and Kevin

Canty, whom he had met at Bread Loaf and who were teaching at the University of North Carolina at Wilmington. Brown also met Mark Richard, who was in Oxford as the John and Renee Grisham Writer-in-Residence at Ole Miss. Brown and Richard became immediate friends, and a photograph that appeared in *Oxford Town* in December 1994 shows Brown, Richard, Barry Hannah, and Tim O'Brien at a club, Proud Larry's. Friendship with Richard, a California resident, gave Larry a West Coast connection that became important to him as he traveled to promote his books.

Music also began to consume increasing amounts of Brown's time and energy. In addition to visiting such Oxford venues as Proud Larry's that hosted musical acts, Brown bought himself a left-handed Martin guitar and began to play more and more for his own pleasure. His favorite local bands included the Kudzu Kings, the North Mississippi All-Stars, the Tangents, and Blue Mountain. Brown wrote liner notes for Blue Mountain's second album and for the All-Stars' first release. Tim Lee, a Nashville musician and producer who moved to Oxford early in the 1990s, ran into Brown "sitting in his little truck just off the downtown square, grooving to a cassette. I stopped to speak and he told me about the band he was listening to. . . . I don't remember the name of the combo, but I remember the sparkle in Larry's eyes when he talked about their music" (3). Lee remembered that Brown "treated everybody great, but he treated musicians just at little bit better" (Caligiuri).

On 25 September 1995, Brown sent Ravenel 532 pages of the *Father and Son* manuscript: although it was "not finished and not perfect," he was "ready for some help" (Algonquin Files). In mid-October, she told him, "I think it's great. Huge. And it reads like a streak of lightning," before offering some constructive criticism: the female characters were not complex enough, there were "too many instances of male response to the beauty and peace in nature," "Virgil's sexual magnetism" was hard to accept (Algonquin Files). By 27 November, Brown had made the recommended changes but remained afraid that the new novel would not equal the success of *Joe.*

The same fall, Tom Rankin, a close friend of Brown's, published an interview with him. The article represents one of the first serious attempts to establish Brown as a literary novelist. Brown said that he became attached to his characters and had a hard time letting them go and giving them the right endings:

> Whatever fate you hand them, [if] it's not a good fate, you got to live with it. And you always wonder if you've done the right thing. You can't really do anything but just keep working and working and working until there's nothing else you can possibly do to it. Send it to your editor.
>
> I'm just thinking harder and harder about it now than I have ever before. . . . [T]he writing that has gone before has been relatively easy compared to what I'm going through now. It's hard to describe it. It's kind of like finishing a house, where you got all these little details and you got to make sure that there are no loose ends. ("On" 101)

Brown told Rankin that he had conceived the idea for *Father and Son* in the early 1990s but had put it aside to do other work. Brown set the novel in the Oxford area of the late 1960s, when the town square featured simple stores and restaurants and local truck farmers selling "watermelons and roasting ears and purple hull peas. . . . I saw all that and I knew that [his characters] had driven in one hot Saturday afternoon during my childhood" (*BRF* 2–3). Another character, Virgil Davis, resembles Brown's father, Knox Brown—a veteran of World War II deeply scarred physically and psychologically by participation in war. Mary Blanchard, a genuinely nurturing mother, possesses the qualities of Brown's mother, Leona. The long-suffering Jewel Coleman reflects the work ethic and loyalty of Brown's wife, who was born Mary Annie Coleman. And Brown developed his ideas about relations between fathers and sons "from [my] relationship with my father and his relationship with his father and my relationships with my sons. I've always regretted that they never were able to meet their grandfather. Preston [Coleman] died when Billy Ray was just a baby. . . . And that's been something that's always been missing from their lives that I did have in mine, at least for a short while" (Rankin, "On" 101). Brown even pays tribute to one of the men who taught him to hunt, Ontis Mize, by giving two dogs in the novel the names of Mize's dogs, Nimrod and Naman.

However, Brown also said that the characters are "not really people I know at all. I don't think there's anybody in here who is based on anybody I know. They're fictitious. The places are real, but in some instances the names have been altered. I don't want certain places to reflect real names" (Rankin, "On" 101). As it did in *Joe*, a fictionalized version of Norman Clark's Tula store appears in *Father and Son*, providing Virgil and other men in the community a place to gather to tell stories, to reminisce about the past, and to gossip about current affairs.

The monkey episode in the novel was inspired by one of Knox Brown Sr.'s stories about an animal trainer at the Mid-South Fair whose "damn monkey just snapped one day, and jumped on that trainer and shredded his hand with them damn teeth. . . . Tore his damn hand up" (Dees, "Bard" 14). Brown also incorporated a friend's pet monkey, "the horniest thing I'd ever seen. Humping the cage, and carryin' on with himself. Anyway, he'd get out of his cage and go sit up in a tree and scare people and be a nuisance. Scared the s—— out of me. . . . A damn monkey can be nasty. . . F——in primate sumbitch" (14). And Brown encountered still another monkey owned by the brother-in-law of a fellow firefighter: "I's just terrified of him, man. He would just run crazy all over that fire station. He'd just come in and they'd turn him loose and I'd squeeze up in my damn chair. I was scared of him" (14).

One of the most horrifying episodes in *Father and Son*, Glen's accidental killing of his brother, Theron, also had a factual basis:

> The whole germ of that story was something that a friend of mine told me probably 20 years ago. About an old man who had just died. But when he was a boy, his parents would catch him up on the roof of the barn trying to jump off and have to make him climb down. He had gone into the kitchen one morning, with this ole shotgun—always hung above the door—always unloaded—and his little brother was eating breakfast.
>
> He didn't know it but his Daddy had got up during the night—something had gotten after his chickens—and he went out there to see about it. Loaded the shotgun. Went out there to see about it; came back in. And that one time, he didn't unload it.

And that was the morning [the boy] took it down, cocked it, and held it up to his brother's head and said, "Go out there and feed them chickens."

And his brother said, "I will when I get done eating." And he said, "Naw, I said go on and feed 'em now." And he said, "I told you I'll go when I finish eating my breakfast."

And he pulled the trigger.

Now he was an old man when he died and this had happened when he was child, so you're talking about a really old, old story, but it always stuck with me. (Dees, "Bard" 14–15)

Brown summarized the plot and particular tensions in *Father and Son* in a June 1995 interview conducted by Kay Bonetti. Both Bobby, the sheriff, and Glen, the young antagonist, are in love with Jewel Coleman, who has given birth to Glen's son, David. The author saw Bobby as "a really good man. He's [the] voice of reason. . . . Glen doesn't really care if he ever has a family or not because he's very estranged from his own family, from his father, from things that have gone before. He has a lot of hatred. He blames a lot of people for the mistakes that he's made. The one thing that he's going to do when he comes home is take care of his enemies. He begins to do that as soon as he gets home" (Bonetti et al. 247). Like many readers of the novel, Brown was troubled by the scene in which Glen rapes Irline Price. In March 1995, he told Ravenel, "there are some things I've written in this novel that are painful for me to read, but I felt they were necessary or I wouldn't have written them. There is one scene in particular that I've worried and worried over, just because it's so brutal to me and involves a young woman. But I've got it revised now and when I read it over it hurts to see it but I think it has to be in there" (Algonquin Files). He later told Susan Larson that the rape scene was the "hardest thing I wrote, . . . but I felt that was the way it would go. I felt so bad for the girl, you know. That's the thing about writing a novel. You make these people and you live with them and you feel for them, and sometimes you wonder what happens to them" ("Keeper" E2).

While Brown continued to polish *Father and Son*, he began writing the essays that would ultimately become *Billy Ray's Farm*: the title essay appeared in the May–June 1995 issue of the *Oxford American*, which also carried an advertisement for Algonquin Books of Chapel Hill illustrated with a photo of Brown. At around the same time, Brown also wrote a promotional blurb for a book of photographs by Maggie Lee Sayre that Rankin edited.

The spring of 1995 also took Brown on a short book tour through the South, after which he was

> glad to be home. Most of the trips I've taken have been reading gigs, always at colleges, only one writers conference and that was in Tampa where I had to eat lettuce with doctors and drink wine, try to make some kind of conversation with them. I hate that shit so bad. But if I hadn't done all that this year I don't know where we'd be right now. Things got really fucked up after I came home and I stayed on a drinking binge for a long time and didn't write shit. I finally snapped out of it . . . and I've been getting the work done ever since then. It was like I lost my writing for a while, got scared of it or something, but hell, I'm scared of it every day, still am. I just have to overcome the fear every morning when I sit down to that blank page. Once I whip it each morning the rest of the day will be okay. (LB to JM, Brown Collections)

One trip had taken him to Lyon College in Batesville, Arkansas, where he read "Billy Ray's Farm." He had met the college's writer-in-residence, Andrea Hollander Budy, at Bread Loaf, and she offered Larry and Mary Annie a weekend at the bed-and-breakfast she ran with her husband. Budy "was amazed at how slowly Larry drove; I had to drive very slowly myself in order not to lose him. Later we talked about that, and he said that because of what he'd seen as a fireman (people maimed or killed in serious car accidents), he took no chances. And I said I understood. But a few moments later I said (in a half-joking tone, although he knew that I meant it) that he evidently hadn't seen the awful deaths that cigarettes cause."

Early in the summer, Brown described his family life as "real good here at home. Mary Annie and I are happy and the kids are almost grown. . . . We're just kind of broke until I get this novel finished" (LB to JM, Brown Collections). To bring in some money, Brown was thinking about applying for a Guggenheim Fellowship, with Louis Rubin, Clyde Edgerton, Thom Jones, and Mark Richard as his sponsors.

Another dramatic presentation of *Dirty Work* took place from 30 March to 2 April 1995 at the Hoka Theater in connection with the 1995 Oxford Conference for the Book and the Southern Literary Festival, sponsored by the University of Mississippi. The play, directed by Scott McCoy of the Ole Miss theater department, featured Michael Cal Stewart from Dallas as Braiden and Christian Stolte from Chicago as Walter, with local actors playing the other roles. The play, directed by Richard Corley, was performed again at the Dallas Theater Center in June. Also during that summer, Marcos Martinez directed a four-week workshop production of *Dirty Work* at the National Theater of Ghana. Perhaps because his involvement with the Oxford production of *Dirty Work* had given him the acting bug, Brown accepted a role in a low-budget film, *100 Proof*, during the fall of 1995. The film was directed by Jeremy Horton, whom Brown had met in Nashville the preceding year. He spent two weeks working on the film. He told Jake Mills that he

> rehearsed for four days, then shot my parts. I play a small-time drug dealer in a little country store. All I had to do for makeup was grow my beard out a little. I basically wore my own clothes. It was fun but long hours and a lot of waiting.
>
> I think the only thing that enabled me to do it without being nervous was working so closely with the actors who've done my play three times. All I figured I had to do was not be nervous, know my lines, and try to be natural. Not to shift around from foot to foot or any of that stuff. They all said I did a good job and was natural. That made me feel good but I don't plan on changing careers. But if *Dirty Work* gets made I'm going to try to get a small role in that. (Brown Collections)

Producer George Maranville sought to exploit Brown's reputation and image in publicizing the film, issuing a promotional release that read, "Larry Brown's influence is unquestionable. . . . *100 Proof* shows the markings of a Larry Brown story. While screenwriter Jeremy Horton wouldn't be so bold as to claim Larry's talents, he shamelessly acknowledges his influence. Like *Joe* and, particularly, *Father and Son*,

100 *Proof* is rooted in Southern culture, with rural working class characters whose sad hopefulness can never seem to outweigh the futility of their surroundings" (Algonquin Files). Brown saw the movie in
1996 and wrote to Edgerton, "It looks okay. Billy Ray said I looked like
a banty rooster cause I was smartmouthing these two tough broads
in my store" (Edgerton Papers). The movie was released in September
1997.

The October 1995 issue of *Glamour* magazine included Brown's one-
page essay, "By the Pond." In the piece, which was illustrated by Glennray Tutor, Brown describes working on his land near Tula: "I spent
the first summer starting to clear it, cutting the matted tangles and
piling them to burn later. I would work until my clothes were drip-
ping with sweat, until my eyes were nearly blinded with it and I was
too tired to keep on, then I'd drive home with a good feeling of having
done a day's work, and come back and to it again the next morning. It
was hard labor, but I didn't mind. It made me sleep well at night" (254).
When he completed a dock on the pond that he had "fished in . . . when
I was a boy," he stocked it with "tiny black crappie, channel catfish and
100 Florida bass" (254). He enjoyed hosting visits from Oxford friends:
"I like to see little boys fishing, learning this sport of patience and discovering the beauty of nature's gifts" (254). He concludes, "No matter
what else is going wrong, I can feel better by just sitting for a while, as
the leaves keep wafting down, as the wind rustles the grass and moves
the water. I may not ever own much else in my life, but this is enough.
Or almost enough. One of these days when I get through cleaning up
. . . , I'm going to start building a little cabin right over there above the
pond, up in the deep part of the shade" (254). When *Billy Ray's Farm*
was published, "By the Pond" was the first essay in the volume.

Brown spent two weeks in January 1996 as writer-in-residence at
Centre College in Danville, Kentucky. During one creative writing
class, a "student asked Brown how writers walk the line between pla-
giarism and homage, when they become so familiar with their heroes'
work. As an answer, Brown recited the entire opening italicized pas-
sage from Cormac McCarthy's *Suttree*. . . . [A]fter his recitation, Brown
explained to the class that the power of such writing just 'gets into
your blood'" (Reeves, "White Trash Gothic" 4). While Brown was in

Kentucky, journalist Rhonda Reeves introduced him to the music of Alejandro Escovedo, who became one of his favorites.

Back home in Oxford, Larry participated in the April 1996 inauguration ceremonies for new University of Mississippi chancellor Robert C. Khayat. Four other "revered authors . . . with strong Mississippi ties" shared the stage—Ellen Douglas, John Grisham, Barry Hannah, and Willie Morris (Miles, "Writers" 1A). Brown told Ravenel that because the authors went in alphabetical order, he "read first and it was my first public appearance in a suit and tie since my wedding in 1974. I was glad I bought one since everybody else had one on, even Willie, even though he hadn't shaved and looked kind of scruffy" (Algonquin Files). Before the reading, Brown was "sweating bullets, trying to find something with not too many cuss words or anything moist and pubic in it"; he settled on "Sleep," from *Big Bad Love*, which was "about the only thing I had that would stand on its own in fifteen minutes. . . . I got up and read my story. I didn't mean to, but I let 'shit on a shingle' slip out. I read it very slowly. I pronounced all my words very carefully, didn't make any slips. Father [Edward] Malloy the president of Notre Dame was sitting out there on the front row, too" (Algonquin Files). Brown presented Khayat with a signed copy of *Dirty Work*.

Through that spring and summer, Brown's connections with the University of Mississippi strengthened. At Richard Howorth's request, Brown introduced Padgett Powell and Cynthia Shearer at the Oxford Conference for the Book in April (LB to SR, Algonquin Files). In June, he participated in the Young Writers Workshop sponsored by the Department of English and the Center for Public Service and Continuing Education. And in July, he sold "a substantial collection of . . . papers" to the university's Department of Archives and Special Collections. The papers included more than one hundred short stories, essays, poems, and drafts as well as a few letters and other papers and the manuscript of one of his early unpublished novels, "Mama's Waiting."

During this period, Algonquin began its promotional efforts for *Father and Son*, scheduled for publication in September. The company's head of promotion, Katharine Walton, budgeted fifty thousand dollars for the effort and planned to have Brown undertake a ten-city tour as well as make an appearance at the American Booksellers Association conference. Algonquin purchased advertisements in the *New York Times Book Review* and the *Oxford American*. When Walton gave Brown a standard questionnaire that asked him to distinguish *Father and Son* from other recent books on the same subject, he was annoyed, replying, "That's not a good question. I would hope that my book, fiction, is not like any other book that has been published before because of the characters I have created and my own special view of the world. I would hope that it says something fresh about Mississippi in the middle 60s" (Algonquin Files).

Several of Brown's writer friends, including Rick Bass, Thom Jones, Kaye Gibbons, and Harry Crews, read advance copies of the novel and sent unsolicited blurbs to Algonquin, which the press used in various publicity materials and on the book's jacket. Other blurbs used were written by Jack Butler, Barry Hannah, Madison Smartt Bell, Bob Shacochis, Willie Morris, Pat Conroy, and John Grisham.

Brown's personal promotion of the novel began at the meeting of the Mid-South Booksellers Association in New Orleans in early September 1996. He ultimately traveled to a total of twenty-four cities in support of the book. In addition to Square Books in Oxford, where he did a reading and signing on 26 September, other stops included Washington, Oregon, California, Iowa, Minnesota, Tennessee, and North Carolina. His wife and younger two children joined him in North Carolina, and "we had a good time and a pretty good crowd, had it packed to the walls, in fact." Tim McLaurin, Clyde Edgerton, Susan Ketchin, Shannon Ravenel, Kaye Gibbons, and "a whole bunch of people from Algonquin" also attended. After an introduction by McLaurin, Brown "read the monkey killing and events leading up to it and then they showed a seven or eight minute clip from the movie I was in, and then everybody just drank for a while while I signed books. (Had a few myself, too)" (LB to JM, Brown Collections).

In Mississippi, Brown also read in Hattiesburg, Starkville, and Bay St. Louis, where, Billy Watkins wrote,

About 15 people sit in folding chairs, staring at Brown, measuring his every word, listening so intently one can almost hear their ears straining. When he finishes the 15-minute reading, there is a unified exhale.

Some shake their heads. Some smile. Susan Daigre, owner of Bookends, puts a hand to her chest as if she's having trouble catching her breath.

"I've done a lot of national stuff with writers, hung out with some big-wigs," Daigre says later. "I'm pretty hardened when it comes to writers, but Larry Brown . . . he's the first one who left me speechless. I was completely tongue-tied when I tried to talk to him." ("Hot" 1D)

After finishing the tour at the Miami Book Fair on 23 November, Brown returned home and wrote to Mills, "I'm pretty far behind in my work now and just got started back today. . . . I'm working on that screenplay for *Dirty Work*, doing a complete rewrite of the second draft, or a polish as the Hollywood types call it, so actually, I'll have written three full drafts of it this year by the time I finish it. . . . I had some good times on the book tour but much hell too. Survived only on whiskey and cigarettes many days and nights which ain't good for a person to do. So rather than complain about it, I'll just say I'm glad the book has sold so well and sure am glad it's over" (Brown Collections).

At its publication, *Father and Son* was the most widely reviewed of Brown's works, with advance notices appearing in *Kirkus Review*, *Publishers Weekly*, and *Booklist* and subsequent reviews in the *New York Times Book Review*, the *New Yorker*, the *Atlanta Journal-Constitution*, the *Boston Globe*, *Southern Living*, and *Men's Journal*, among other publications. Since his previous novel, *Joe*, had been so well received, reviewers were eager to see whether the new novel would measure up. Several reviewers declared *Father and Son* Brown's best work. *Publishers Weekly* declared the "most impressive" feature of the novel to be "Brown's compassionate view of human nature and his understanding of the subtleties of human behavior and the fabric of society, which after tragedy reknits itself anew to reaffirm the essential kinship of a community of souls" (44). The *Atlanta Journal-Constitution*'s Greg Johnson described the novel as "suspenseful, tautly written and deeply imagined" ("Strong" L11). James Hynes's *Washington Post* review warned readers "that this novel is not for the fainthearted: There's a good deal of violent death and rape in the book, graphically rendered" (C2). Rick Bass declared *Father and Son* "another great and durable book from Larry Brown. . . . The oldest themes in literature are illuminated sharply in 'Father and Son.' The poisons of anger and violence and an inability to forgive become the stew of tragedy, and the characters' struggles against these lines of fate become the story" ("Heart" M17). Critics such as Harry Levins also applauded Brown's stylistic finesse: "Brown writes in a sparse, lean and simple declarative English, and his ear for dialogue doesn't miss a note" ("This" C5).

Johnson pointed out the title's allusions to Ivan Turgenev's *Fathers and Sons* and cited John Steinbeck and William Faulkner among Brown's other literary ancestors ("Strong" L11). Walter Kirn of *New York* magazine compared *Father and Son* to Faulkner's *Sanctuary* and Truman Capote's *In Cold Blood*, combining the "highbrow" and the "hard-boiled" (n.p.). The *Spectator*'s Paul Sussman not only described Brown's prose as "Faulkneresque" but saw the story as an antidote to the television show *The Waltons*: "Brown gives the downside of this idyll, the nightmare counterpart to the American dream: a booze-sozzled society underpinned by festering hatreds and familial dysfunction" (31). Lawrence Rungren saw both pop culture and biblical connections: "The novel is filled with the gritty, working-class realism of Bruce Springsteen's darker songs and resonates back to Cain and Abel and Jacob and Esau" (110).

Father and Son covers the last few days in the life of Glen Davis, an angry, misguided young man just released from prison after serving three years for vehicular homicide. Davis is viciously cruel, unrepentant, and unable to accept any responsibility for his evil actions. As Glen's history slowly unfolds, however, readers learn that he is the victim of a ruinous family. Because his parents fail to love each other, they can never give their sons the quality of love essential to normal survival. Because Davis is so desperate, his three-day rampage becomes increasingly violent: he kills his "enemy's" pet monkey, rapes an innocent seventeen-year-old acquaintance, murders his "enemy" and another man, crawls into the window of his faithful girlfriend's bedroom and terrorizes his young son, and behaves abominably to his ailing father, Virgil. Glen's actions at the end are even more hideous, but because Brown has so carefully and consistently created Glen's psychological destruction, the character continues to evoke sympathy. After Glen captures, rapes, and tortures Mary Blanchard, whom his father has long loved, he says, "'I'm sorry,' and she believed him" (*Father and Son* 341). Both his words and her acceptance of them imply the possibility of his salvation. According to Ted Atkinson, as the confrontation between Mary and Glen "unfolds, Brown references New Testament passion to fashion a sublimely perverted version of the *Pieta*, reconfiguring both the positions and meaning of the suffering mother and crucified son." In Greg Johnson's view, the novel offers the "reader a guided tour of hell without neglecting the possibility of redemption" ("Strong" L11).

Brown's characterization of both men and women—and even of animals—contributes most to the novel's success. The richness of the development of the female characters in *Father and Son* foreshadows Brown's use of the female perspective in his next novel, *Fay*. Both Mary Blanchard and Jewel Coleman are fully believable. Max Winter found Jewel particularly appealing: "Jewel is alone in the world with her child; Brown often places her in reflective poses, perhaps making her an emblem of the alienation that criminal behavior leaves in its wake, particularly in the lives of lovers and family members" (n.p.). Mary and Jewel become financially self-supporting when their relationships with men deteriorate, but Brown sympathetically and realistically also presents them as nurturers. Good cooks, they take pride in feeding their families both literally and figuratively.

Though primarily a study of the effects of the lack of love within a working-class family, *Father and Son* also has strong Christian references. Oxford, the novel's North Mississippi setting, is presented as a typical rural Christian community. The women attend church regularly. Non-churchgoer Virgil Davis believes in God and wants to be a better father to his sons, and his relationship with Glen seems almost biblical. Like Bruce Springsteen in "Adam Raised a Cain" (1978), Brown uses biblical allusion to depict the contemporary destruction of the family (see Cash, "Dissolution").

Brown was pleased with *Father and Son*'s success, telling Mills, "I've seen a lot of good reviews and I've been grateful for them. . . . It's sold better than anything else ever, and by a wide margin, and I've got a good new paperback publisher, Holt" (Brown Collections). Nevertheless, Brown was not content to rest on his success. As 1996 drew to a close, Brown celebrated a "good" but hectic Christmas with his family: "Everybody's been at home and it fills the house with noise and it's hard to get anything done around here." Brown was "trying to knuckle back down to work" (LB to Katharine Walton, Algonquin Files). He continued to tinker with the script for *Dirty Work*, to work on essays for *Billy Ray's Farm*, and to write new fiction. He had "three . . . novels in progress, different lengths. I've got more than anything of one called *Wild Child*, which is about the girl Fay, who ran off half-way through *Joe*. Got about 80 pages of another one called *Dog Love*, which is about a writing teacher, and another thing I'm working on set in olden times with mules and sawmills and wagons and wilderness and some mean white folks called *White Devils*. I've got about 200 pages of *Billy Ray's Farm* but I don't know which one I'll finish first. I look for *Wild Child* to wind out long like *Joe* and *Father and Son*." Most important, he was "just glad to be back home and working" (LB to JM, Brown Collections).

CHAPTER TEN

Continued Success

Fay in Progress and a Semester at Ole Miss,
1997–1998

For Larry Brown, the period between 1997 and 2001 was filled with success and total dedication to writing. As usual, he worried about money, telling Billy Watkins in December 1996, "I ain't rich yet. Some people may think I am, but I still have to keep working. I still worry about how I'm gonna get paid next year" ("Hot" 2D). Brown also faced a variety of family issues as his children matured.

Brown had begun to write the novel that would become *Fay* in the summer of 1996, working, as he had from the start of his writing career, on a typewriter, though he had replaced his machine more than a dozen times. In late January 1997, he sent Shannon Ravenel a hundred pages of the novel, explaining, "I always wondered what happened to" his character, Fay, after she left the pages of *Joe*, "and I wanted to find out. I think I know pretty well where I'm going with this, and I look for it to be long, but certainly hope to have a full draft of it before the end of this year. That's what I'm planning, anyway" (Algonquin Files). Ravenel liked what she read but wrote to Brown's agent, Liz Darhansoff, "*Fay is* too holy and LB's view of her is, too. We should give him all the criticism we can at this point. And his $25K [advance]. I think this start is promising" (Algonquin Files). On 10 February, Ravenel took her own advice, writing to Brown, "Fay has got to have a little grit in her craw. After all, she's been messed with bad by her father. That doesn't just roll off a real life girl's back" (Algonquin Files). Brown agreed with her criticism but felt that Fay had to be naive and innocent in the beginning so that she could be changed by her experiences (LB to SR, Algonquin Files).

Also in late January, Brown traveled to Utah for the Sundance Film Festival, where Jeremy Horton was showing *100 Proof*. Algonquin's Katharine Walton lined up publicity events for Brown to do while at the festival, and he was "slightly worried" about being overbooked: "I wouldn't want for things like that to interfere with me attending all of the festival that I want to while I'm there. If you have a schedule ready, could you fax it to me as soon as you can? I'd like to see it before too much more time passes, just to ease my mind" (Algonquin Files). Brown was looking forward to the trip west, but when asked if he was planning to ski, he replied, "Naw, man, I ain't gonna go out there and break a leg. I'm gonna sit by the picture-window and watch them break theirs" (Watkins, "Hot" 2D). More than a year later, Brown recalled the trip in a letter to Jake Mills: "I went there for six frozen days. . . . I mean a person could really freeze to death out there if you got locked out or were drunk and stumbling around or something" (Brown Collections).

Brown made another public appearance on 13 April when he served as the keynote speaker at the opening of the new Oxford–Lafayette County Library. Brown used the occasion to talk about what libraries in general and the Oxford library in particular had meant to him: "I've been a patron of this library for a number of years, going all the way back to when it was located up near the Square, just off Jackson Avenue on top of the hill. When I sat down to write this I realized that I was probably still in high school back then, and I can remember some of the books I was checking out then: the James Bond novels by Ian Fleming, the John D. McDonald novels about a private detective named Travis McGee who always managed to get the girl and keep half the money, too. All my life, the library has always been one of my favorite places to go. When I was a child living in Memphis I used the Memphis Public Library, and when I was in the Marine Corps I used the Navy libraries located on whatever base I was on. Reading, for pleasure and knowledge, has always been, will always be one of my favorite things to do." He continued, "It was in this library that I first found a novel called *Suttree* by a writer named Cormac McCarthy.

I had never heard of this man or any of his work, but one lucky day I saw a pretty book with a nice black spine, and I pulled it from the shelf and opened it up and read a few paragraphs, and that was all I needed to see. . . . On that day I discovered the man that I think now may be our greatest living novelist, and since then I've read everything by him that I've been able to lay my hands on. He's become a great influence on me, and I'll never forget that I found him here."

In July, Brown again participated in the University of Mississippi's annual Faulkner Conference. Brown paid tribute to William Faulkner not only for his genius as a writer but also for his knowledge of the woods and hunting. Brown told conference attendees that reading "The Bear" had led him to other Faulkner works, which ultimately "became tools for learning how to create my own characters and settings. They taught me what to write about and how to say things, how to portray the landscape as a vast background for the action that plays out among characters. They taught me that the little touches are important in fiction, the slash of a cold rain on the face or the warble of a bird sitting on a springtime branch. They taught me determination and perseverance, to keep on writing in the face of constant failure" ("Tribute" 270). Brown touched on Faulkner's isolation as he sat at Rowan Oak, "all alone, unmindful of the world about him when the work was at hand," and was awed "to think about all the books and stories that came out of there" (271). Finally, Brown reminded his audience of some of the points Faulkner had made in his speech accepting the 1949 Nobel Prize for literature: "A young writer starts out knowing nothing and trying to write about it, and it's only after enough time and work that he or she finds out that the condition of the human being is endlessly varied and an inexhaustible source of material for fiction, and that the truths of the human heart are the only things worth writing about" (271).

Through the summer and into the fall, Brown continued work on *Wild Child*, which remained his working title for the next year or so. (In late 1999, he told his former student, John Taylor Moses, "I had to change the title [to *Fay*] because *Wild Child* had already been used by romance novelists 50 or 60 times" ["Take" 16].) On 15 September, Brown reported to Ravenel that he had now written "just a few pages shy of 500 and it's nowhere near finished so brace yourself for it to be the longest thing I've done" (Algonquin Files). Five weeks later, he had 526 pages; however, he was spending considerable time "out on the road" touring in support of the paperback version of *Father and Son*, which Henry Holt had published (LB to SR, Algonquin Files).

On 25 September, Oxford celebrated the centennial of Faulkner's birth with a "statue unveiling, talks by Willie Morris and Shelby Foote, toast to Faulkner at the bookstore, panel at Ole Miss including Evans Harrington, Don Kartiganer (resident Faulkner scholars), Richard Howorth and me" (LB to SR, Algonquin Files). The next day, Brown had a scheduled interview with National Public Radio as well as a signing for *Faulkner's World: The Photographs of Martin J. Dain*, for which Brown had written the foreword. In the piece, Brown compared Faulkner's Oxford of the 1960s to the present-day town: "The stores still line the square and the stones on the courthouse steps are cupped from the feet of people who have passed up and down them for years. But there's more traffic in Oxford now. Friday afternoons are always bad. The old Henry Hotel is gone, the Ritz Theatre is gone, the Lyric, but the streets Faulkner walked still look almost the same" (7). Outside of town, most of the "big timber is gone now," along with the mules, the country stores, and the old houses, "the ones with a breezeway through the middle and rooms on both sides" (8).

On 3 October, Brown traveled to the Southern Festival of Books in Nashville to receive the Southern Book Critics Circle Award for *Father and Son*, the same honor *Joe* had received five years earlier. Later that month, Brown and Barry Hannah read at a fund-raiser for Chico Harris, an Oxford writer who had been seriously injured in an automobile accident. That commitment prevented Brown from watching his daughter, LeAnne, participate in Homecoming activities at Lafayette High School (LB to SR, Algonquin Files).

On 29 October, the University of Mississippi announced Brown's appointment as a creative writing instructor for the spring 1998 semester. He would be teaching courses in short-story writing and in advanced creative writing. Hannah described Brown's appointment as "marvelous. I'm delighted the students will get a new and different voice" (Dees, "UM" 1A). Brown was more skeptical about his abilities as a teacher, describing the experience as "kind of tough haul" (1A). Brown was considering using Cormac McCarthy's *Child of God* in the class: "If it curls their hair that'll be good for 'em" (1A). He also did not believe in having students criticize each other's work or in putting "red marks all over a paper." He told Jim Dees of the *Oxford Eagle*, "I'll probably have each student come in and we'll discuss their work" (1A). He wrote to Ravenel to tell her of his new role, signing his letter "Prof. Brown": "You're talking to the new writer-in-residence at Ole Miss. For the spring semester anyway . . . hopefully just down the hall from where I studied with Ellen Douglas way back in '82. Ain't it weird how it goes around and comes around? I even get an office. Shit, I may move into it, hang out a big sign that sticks out in the hall" (Algonquin Files).

In November 1997, Gary Hawkins traveled to Yocona to begin work on his next film, *The Rough South of Larry Brown*. Hawkins had first met Brown in the late 1980s when the Mississippian came to North Carolina to promote *Dirty Work*. According to Hawkins, the two men ended up "crashing" at his place, where Brown drank Hawkins "under the table" before insisting that he drive Brown to a reading (Hawkins, "Just One More" 138). The two men had subsequently worked together on Hawkins's Emmy-winning 1991 documentary, *The Rough South of Harry Crews*.

For his Brown project, Hawkins had originally envisioned "a hybrid of three short films based on three short stories glued together by author commentary" (Hawkins, "Just One More" 138). He planned to shoot the stories first and then "make one trip to Mississippi to interview Larry, and Larry would tell me on camera everything I needed to hear and more" (138). Ultimately, however, Hawkins traveled to Yocona in 1997, 1998, and 2000, "meeting three different Larry Browns, each afflicted with an outsized need for both companionship and solitude, and each dealing with these paradoxical needs in different ways" (138).

Brown recalled Hawkins's first visit: "I'd known Hawkins for a number of years and we'd become friends. He talked me into letting him and his crew come down here and make a documentary about me and my work, so when the time came, we let him stay here with us, along with most of the cameras and the film. It kind of evolved once the rest of the crew got here and we started shooting. We started with the interviews in the rocking chair, in November, and went to Tula from there."

For the 1997 trip to Yocona, Hawkins drove fourteen hours from North Carolina to Mississippi, where he was surprised to find Brown preparing a supper of fried chicken, mashed potatoes, gravy, green beans, pie, and ice tea. Hawkins had previously "met Road Larry, Book Tour Larry, and I'd heard the stories of Petulant Larry, who once drank an entire mini-bar; Wild Larry, who silenced a group of Yankees in a four-star restaurant by leaping on their table and kicking their entrees in their laps; Heroic Larry, who pulled children from burning houses; and Genius Larry, who stood before an audience at the Bread Loaf Writers' Conference and spoke—that's *spoke*, not read—a twenty page short story, missing but three words" (Hawkins, "Just One More" 138). The Yocona version was a family man who introduced Hawkins to his wife, Mary Annie; son, Billy Ray; and daughter, LeAnne.

The next day, Hawkins and his two-man crew "set up the camera in Larry's pasture for the first interview. Larry poured himself a beer in a clear, blue glass, and we settled in to start" (Hawkins, "Just One More" 140). Hawkins soon returned home to North Carolina, where he shot the three stories dramatized in the film: "Boy and Dog," "Wild Thing," and "Samaritans." Brown played a fire captain in "Boy and Dog" but did not appear in the other dramatizations.

In December, Brown went hunting with Tom Rankin and Jonny Miles in Copiah County, Mississippi. Although Brown had written in *On Fire* that he no longer liked to kill animals, on this trip, he shot "a heavy one, an old scrappy buck that would have boasted a 10-point rack had not the tips of one side of his antler been chipped off in a brawl" (Miles, "Deer" 98). According to Rankin, after the kill, Brown said, "'The pressure's off now, bro. I'll just be cooking and reading the rest of the weekend.' The next morning when the rest of us returned from our deer stands, Larry had a full breakfast waiting, filling the house trailer with the aroma of fresh biscuits, bacon, eggs, and fried venison" ("Putting" 42). Enjoying the camaraderie, Brown told his friends that "it felt good to be out there. When I first started hunting it was about getting something to eat. Now it's about being out in the woods with all that beauty. Appreciating what's left. About going off with your friends, enjoying the world without traffic and noise, having a good time, I guess. It's pretty simple" (Miles, "Deer" 98). Miles's published account of the hunting trip includes a description of the forty-seven-year-old Brown: "Larry Brown is the son of a Mississippi sharecropper and—despite his forays into the rarefied sphere of literary publishing—somehow looks it. He often wears an expression of achy worry, like a farmer staring into a dusty sun, wanting for rain; there is a certain gravitas to his face, to its deep riverine lines" (98).

In spite of the time he spent making the movie and hunting, Brown continued to work on *Fay*. On 16 December, he wrote to Ravenel,

> I'm working. I'm working. I'm working. I was up till 4:30 this morning and wrote 23 new pages. I've been goofing off too much lately going to too many parties and dinners and things. . . . So much has happened in this book and it's gotten so big. I'm trying to close out Book II now but don't know how much longer it will be. I've got all these new characters now and I've got to come to some kind of closure with at least some of them. And I've still got to write Book III. . . . I just want to finish this book. I mean the first draft. Sometimes I think I'll never finish it. There's just so much that's got to take place before I can get to the end of it. I know some of it, some of it I don't, and I usually get surprised every day I'm writing what happens.
>
> Well. One day. (Algonquin Files)

He also told Ravenel, "The time is drawing close when I'll have to start teaching. Less than a month away now, and I know that time is going to close in fast and I won't have my novel finished. And I'm so scared that the teaching will take up most of my time, I'm just trying to write all I can right now, as much as I can, no matter how long I have to stay up" (Algonquin Files).

The spring 1998 semester began at Ole Miss on 7 January. Brown was teaching English 424, an introductory short-story-writing class with twenty-two students. Each student would be required to submit two original stories and had three options for receiving feedback: "a written critique from me; a discussion with me," or a workshop discussion in class in which other students would give their opinions (Brown Collections). The students also read one outside story each week: among the titles Brown assigned were Denis Johnson's "Emergency," Ron Hansen's "Wickedness," Mona Simpson's, "Lawns," Thom Jones's "Cold Snap," Charles Dowdy's "The Cold Truth" and "Cody's Story," and Robert Stone's "Helping." Brown also planned to read aloud to the students from works by James Lee Burke and Cormac McCarthy. For the first class, he planned to "talk a little about what I've done and how the only way I think I can help them is by knowing what they're going through," but he wanted the class members to ask questions "instead of me just sitting up there and talking to them." Their first story assignment was due on 28 January.

Lafe Benson, a student in the class, remembered,

> We met a few times during the semester. We talked about a lot of things and he recommended a lot of authors to me. I remember one time I had a story due in his class. I had started on a pretty lame story about a farmer trying to kill a tomcat and never really saw where the story was going. So I tore the story in pieces and burned [them] on my grill. I told Larry about this and he laughed.
>   "Yeah, I did that once too."
>   "Really?"
>   "Yeah," he paused and asked, "did it make you feel any better?"
>   "Nope."
>   "Yeah, it never does." ("Larry Brown")

According to Benson, Brown "wasn't that excited about teaching" but "would critique our stories with honesty. If he didn't like anything, he would write it down or tell you. But he would always mention something encouraging. I remember that he said that he liked the way I wrote with humor." Brown "was always kind to his students. . . . He always wanted us to know that writing was not . . . easy. His classroom was very laid back. We were in a regular classroom for one session. After that first class, he found us a meeting room in Bishop Hall with a big round table. . . . Whenever it came time for an open forum on our stories, he always tried to make everything end up on an even keel. If our classmates were talking about how terrible a story was, Larry would try to direct people towards the positive points about the story. If our classmates were talking about how great and wonderful a story was, Larry would try to find some points of the story that needed to be worked on." Similarly, another student, John Taylor Moses, recalled Brown as "a very loving guy, and he had a sincere interest in being around young people. I never knew him to spend a lot of time around peers his actual age—being around twenty- and thirty-somethings inspired him to an extent, in my opinion." To Moses, English 424 felt "like sitting around a campfire with a cooler of beer—very relaxed. No rules. We just sat around in a circle and commented on the text we were reading, or the process of writing. It was a very nurturing and intimate class—he made people feel comfortable about just throwing their thoughts out into the room." Moses does not remember Brown "having any intimate friendships with the Ph.D.'s. Larry was not intellectual in the way that academia defines the word, in my opinion, so I think there was a bit of professional separation between him and most English professors."

Brown did connect with his officemate, Randall Kenan, who was spending the semester as the John and Renee Grisham Writer-in-Residence and whom Brown had met several years earlier. Brown told Ravenel that he "really enjoy[ed] talking to" Kenan. "I finally caught him out in a club *one* time dancing and gave him some shit about it. He's been good to share his office with me. We hardly ever use it. I only use it two hours a week to meet with my students. Some of my graduate students come in there sometimes and we raise the window and smoke" (Algonquin Files).

Brown also taught English 521, an advanced graduate course in writing nonfiction. On the first day of class, Brown gave the fourteen students the same basic introduction that he used for his other course but told them that they would "be discussing mostly novels and nonfiction books and essays" and "might veer into screenwriting or maybe even songwriting, depending on who I get to come talk to the class" (Brown Collections). Watching films—including Hawkins's films on Harry Crews and Tim McLaurin—and taped interviews was also a possibility. He told the students that they would mostly be talking to each other and that "we'll cover whatever you want to cover" (Brown Collections). He offered them the same options for critiques that he had offered those enrolled in his other class. He maintained the point of view that "nobody can teach them how to write, but I can give them the benefit of my experience over the last seventeen years. That's the only thing that qualifies me to teach, the fact that I've been where they are now and once sat in a classroom just like this one" (Brown Collections).

Brown had these students read and discuss McCarthy's *Child of God*. He also required them to submit a twenty-page essay and a piece of fiction of between fifteen and thirty pages (Brown Collections). He also planned to share with them the guidance he had received from an editor for *Outdoor Life*: "Write the way you'd write a letter to a friend. . . . That little piece of advice did [me] more good than anything at that point" (Brown Collections).

Brown had initially thought that he would be able to work on *Fay* between classes, but he soon found that teaching consumed all his time (Glendenning, "Booklovers" L6). Brown's close friend, Lisa Howorth, later reflected, "I don't think that teaching was something Larry particularly wanted to do, but it was always a struggle for money and I don't understand why [a more permanent position at Ole Miss] was never an option that was available." Although Brown became close to some of his students and liked talking with them about writing, Lisa Howorth believes that he found teaching "confining" and thought of teaching creative writing classes as "a racket." Richard Howorth concurred: Brown "was initially enchanted with the idea of being a teacher . . . but after he had done it a few times, he realized how much time and energy and attention it required and that detracted from his ability to write, and so I think he got tired of it right away and preferred not to do it."

Brown played a significant part in that spring's Oxford Conference for the Book. He joined Fredric Koeppel and Alane Mason on a panel moderated by Kenan. Mary Annie also participated in a panel, "'It Really Was My Idea': Spouses of Writers Speak Out," with Barry Hannah's wife, Susan, and John Rusher, husband of Elizabeth Spencer. Brown also took time from his teaching and novel writing to pen an article, "Little Big Band," that appeared in the June 1998 issue of *Oxford Town*. In it, Brown urged music lovers to attend an upcoming performance at Proud Larry's by one of his favorite musicians, Alejandro Escovedo: "I like his voice, his writing, his guitar work, and the arrangements. He reminds me a great deal of Leonard Cohen in the way he puts a song together with different instruments to make it more interesting and beautiful. . . . In his writing, he has the voice and the heart and the soul of a poet, but to me he soars much higher than a poet simply because he's able to put his words to music and sing them" (9).

After the semester ended, Brown stopped drinking and got back to work on his novel. By mid-July, he wrote that he had "been on it about 27 months now and I'm trying to end it. I've got over 750 pages right now and hope to keep it under 900 pages. I figure to finish the first draft if everything goes right in five or six weeks. . . . I imagine Shannon's about to shit a brick to get her hands on this thing. They've been real good to leave me alone, though. Already she's scared it's too big. I've worried over it so much and it's been going on for so long" (LB to JM, Brown Collections). In late August, Brown finally submitted the manuscript to Ravenel: "I think this is ready for you to see. It's got a beginning, a middle, and an ending. . . . I've fixed 117 things that were wrong with it, things of logic, things of motivation. I know there are still holes to patch up and characterizations to beef up, and still some scenes need to be changed" (Algonquin Files). After reading the massive novel, Ravenel found it "greatly in need of revision, massive cutting, and much clearer definition of purpose" (Algonquin Files). She particularly objected to Brown's constant references to drinking and smoking and thought that Sam Harris was too much of "an idealized good guy." She also asked, "Can Fay have a little streak of something— like personality—in her besides being so innocent and 'fine'?" She also wrote, "I *think* there's a good story in here someplace. At the heart of it is a girl raised in the 'wilderness' whose instinct for survival is steely and in whose wake many lives are lost" (Algonquin Files).

Ravenel told Brown that the manuscript needed too much work to be put on Algonquin/Workman's fall 1999 list. She urged him to cut at least two hundred pages and to give the novel a stronger focus. Brown was "bewildered" by her criticism and tried to answer her objections and thereby justify what he had done. He balked at the enormous cuts Ravenel had suggested, asserting he had deliberately written a long novel and that his readers would not object. And he disagreed with Ravenel's assessment that the novel overemphasized alcohol: "There is no drinking theme that I see in my novel. Some of them just drink. That's it. I hope it's an accurate representation of their lives, which sometimes are pretty sleazy. I had no drinking theme in mind when I wrote it. It just keeps cropping up. It runs through all my work. It's a handy source for trouble, and people being in trouble is what drives my fiction. That's the only way I know how to explain it. Trouble & conflict: resolution" (Algonquin Files). Finally, Brown was "totally stunned" by the criticism of Sam: "He's in the novel from about page 50 off and on until the very end. His role is to love Fay, lose Fay, try to get her back, and fail, as does Aaron. Neither of them can hold onto her. I tried to show Sam as a basically good man with flaws" (Algonquin Files).

On 8 October, Ravenel replied to Brown, apologizing for her negative comments but saying that her job was to be honest. She reiterated the aspects of the novel that disturbed her and advised him to get another reader's opinion (Algonquin Files). The discouraged Brown penned another defensive response four days later (LB to SR, Algonquin Files) and then decided to take a break from the novel.

That fall, Larry and Mary Annie Brown hosted a gathering at which they fed more than two hundred friends. Continuing a long-standing tradition, Brown took off "a few days . . . to cook up a large cauldron of his mother's famous chicken stew" (Dees, "Writers Series at Library" 1). However, 1998 was the last year that the Browns hosted the cookout. According to Mary Annie Brown, the event had just become too much work for her and had "gotten just way too big." Richard Howorth agreed that "it got out of hand." (See appendix B for Brown's "recipe" for chicken stew.)

The fall of 1998 also saw continued interest in dramatic versions of some of Brown's work. A New York acting company had performed "92 Days" the previous year and now planned to restage the production in Santa Monica, California. Brown was paid very little for the rights and did not go west to see it. Another California woman was staging "A Roadside Resurrection," but Brown did not plan to attend; however, he would go to California if a proposed staging of *Dirty Work* took place in Los Angeles in 1999. In addition, Jeremy Horton, the director of *100 Proof*, had paid Brown five hundred dollars for an option on "A Roadside Resurrection." Brown had become wiser about Hollywood after several years of trying to arrange productions of *Dirty Work, Joe,* and other scripts: "The movie bidness is a strange thing. It's where all the money's at. I don't need to be rich but I'd sure like to stop struggling so hard sometimes" (LB to JM, Brown Collections). Lisa Howorth believes that failing to have one of his novels made into a film was "one thing that was never fully realized for Larry. . . . He knew so much about movies in a huge way, and he really would have liked to do that. [But] it was easy [for him] to get taken in by Hollywood stuff." Larry's Hollywood agent, Lynn Pleshette, explained that "the reason that Hollywood has not been seriously interested in Larry's work is because Southern Gothic stories basically scare Hollywood. These are not an easy genre to sell. It is not horror or high concept comedy or HARRY POTTER or BATMAN. Basically, Larry's brilliant work is drama" (Darhansoff e-mail interview).

Hawkins returned to Yocona in the fall of 1998 to get more material for his movie. When he arrived, "there was no fried chicken dinner waiting for me this time, no happy family. Just cold weather and a very serious writer, obsessed with *Fay*, a novel he had failed to deliver" (Hawkins, "Just One More" 140). Brown lamented the time he had wasted "sitting on a barstool" but refused to give Hawkins more detail about what had gone wrong. Mary Annie Brown, however, angrily told Hawkins, "You think this writing thing is so glamorous. Well let me tell you, it isn't" (141). Mary Annie confirmed that her husband had recently been drinking too much and told Hawkins that Larry had even been jailed after being ticketed for drunk driving. She continued, "When Larry writes, that's when he's the happiest. And when he's not writing, that's when he's so depressed you can't stand to be around him" (*RS*). When Brown showed off his "cool pad," Hawkins saw it as enabling Brown "to live apart from his family while remaining under the same roof" (Hawkins, "Just One More," 141). This idea of "the conflict between this man's calling to write and his duty to his family" became the overriding theme for *The Rough South of Larry Brown* (141).

At around this time, Brown began work on his writing cabin at Tula, which he envisioned as a "little house . . . on the back bank of my pond. It'll sit across from the boat dock, a little off to the left, slightly up in the woods" (LB to JM, Brown Collections). Brown planned every step of the project in meticulous detail: once he started construction, the cabin moved along "pretty fast but I've been building it in my head for a couple of months so it was just a matter of getting the lumber and cutting it and nailing it all together. . . . Part of the floor's cantilevered so that two feet of it just hangs out in space. But I've already decided to build a big deck out on the front of it and build it around two big pines and a cedar that would make me stop short of a big porch and no way would I cut them" (LB to JM, Brown Collections).

The rest of Brown's time that fall was taken up by working to complete *Fay*, building his cabin, and taking care of Mary Annie, who had gall bladder surgery. He entertained Kaye Gibbons, Rick Bass, and other writer friends who came to Oxford to read at Square Books. And he pursued two of his favorite pastimes: one was sitting "in his old dun-colored Dodge pickup 'riding the gloam'—driving around, listening to music, drinking beer or peppermint schnapps—what his mama used to call, with some degree of futility, 'acting ugly.'" The other was taking a boat out on the pond "fishing for bass and bream with either a cane pole or the same bandaged Eagle Claw rod that he'd fished with since he returned from his stint in the Marine Corps" (Miles, "Deer" 98).

At the end of December, Brown's reading of his story, "Merry Christmas, Scotty," aired on the Oxford-based Thacker Mountain Radio show, and the same story appeared in *Oxford Town*. The piece was prefaced by Brown's explanation that he "spent about five nights trying to write a Christmas story. I've got a friend in town that I don't see nearly as much these days as I used to, and he was in my mind while I was writing this story because I needed a good bartender, so I used him. . . . And since I haven't gotten my friend a present, yet, I thought I'd call this story, 'Merry Christmas, Scotty'" (4). Set in an Oxford bar, the story features a narrator, Nick, who has returned to town for Christmas even though he no longer has any family living there. Nick tries to stay at a local motel, but there is literally no room at the inn; the motel's owner supplies Nick with a tent in which to camp. Nearing midnight on Christmas Eve, Nick, under the influence of the Christmas spirit, feels sympathy for an elderly man who he thinks has passed out on the bar; he believes the man to be destitute and homeless. Nick ultimately learns that the old man is the bartender's Uncle Kris, just in from Australia and suffering from jet lag. The story ends happily with Nick attending a party at the bartender's apartment, where he meets "a longlegged brown-haired beauty named Desiree" who is more than willing to share his tent for the night. The story ends, "Merry Christmas, everybody" (7).

CHAPTER ELEVEN

Years of Triumph

Fay, the Wallace Award, and Montana, 1999–2000

At the beginning of 1999, Larry Brown received another honor: a poll conducted by *Oxford Town* named him favorite local writer, and "Merry Christmas, Scotty" tied for favorite signing/reading. In late January or early February, he gave the keynote address for the Perspective Series at the University of Tennessee, Chattanooga (Glendenning, "Mississippi"). His next triumph came in March when he was announced as the winner of the Lila Wallace Readers Digest Award (Herbst 8). Dorothy Fitts, the head librarian at the Oxford–Lafayette County Library, had nominated Brown for the grant, which would pay him thirty-five thousand dollars per year over the next three years. This funding would give him the financial security to concentrate fully on his writing. Brown later said that the award "allowed me to live and write mostly unmolested for three years. Priceless" (Kingsbury). Brown also received ten thousand dollars per year to establish an affiliation with a nonprofit cultural, educational, or community organization. Brown chose the Oxford–Lafayette County Public library and established the Larry Brown Writers' Series, which brought writers to the library to give readings and to hold workshops with aspiring authors: "I thought of bringing in writers that the community might not have had a chance to become familiar with. Having these readings and talks at the public library makes them accessible to more people" (Herbst 8). Most of the writers who participated, including Andre Dubus III, Mark Richard, and Jill McCorkle, were Brown's good friends. Fitts described the workshops as "very relaxed and informal. It has a different atmosphere than a classroom. . . . People usually feel a little more comfortable. Everyone is welcome" (McDermid 8). "This is really for a wide variety of people—from students to 85-year-olds" ("Larry Brown Writer's Series" 5). Fitts publicized the reading series in Memphis and Tupelo newspapers as well as to people who had participated in Ole Miss's Faulkner Conference, and out-of-towners as well as Oxford residents came to the readings.

McCorkle enjoyed her October visit to Oxford, remembering that after she arrived,

> The first thing we did was ride around. Larry wanted to show me his writing space he was building. He pointed out where his mama lived, this and that road or place, landmarks that had shown up in his fiction. . . . It was comfortable just riding around. . . . We watched [Gary Hawkins's dramatization of "Samaritans"], marveling at Will Patton's performance in that piece—and then we watched bits of various interview clips. He kept saying how Mary Annie was the star and I remember the two of them joking back and forth about that; she was in there in the kitchen just as she was in the film and we were talking and laughing the whole time. Larry gave her a lot of credit and praise for all that she did both in her presence and not. . . . They were funny teasing and interacting with each other, too.

Brown also spent the first months of 1999 revising *Fay*. In early January, after his two-month hiatus from working on the novel, he reacted to Shannon Ravenel's latest round of suggestions: he made Sam a bit less saintly by introducing his affair with Allesandra, a plot twist that "is going to create more tension for Sam through the rest of the book." In addition, Sam and Aaron now met, a revision suggested by Mary Annie Brown (LB to SR, Algonquin Files). Ravenel was "impressed" with the latest changes and saw Fay as "coming through much more clearly in this version as is Sam" (Algonquin Files). Ravenel's response "elated" Brown: "I feel so much better now. I guess I was just under the impression that you didn't think much of the whole thing. I reckon I just can't get everything right the first try, and I know that still using a typewriter slows me way down from what I could be doing" (Algonquin Files). He liked the idea of "thinning" and "pruning" rather than cutting whole scenes and sections. On 15 February, he sent her the revised Book II of the novel and was working hard on Book III. He wrote, "Next month'll be three years since I started this thing, and nobody is more anxious to see it finished than me" (LB to SR, Algonquin Files).

By March, Brown related,

> I've written 400 new pages since November, and the novel has stretched to 883 pages. I had the epilogue all done but the ending itself wasn't right. Then the ending came to me this weekend in a parking lot in Austin, Texas.
>
> I had been waiting for it all to click and it finally clicked, like tumblers in a lock. Now the ending is inevitable, perfect, logical. I'm cool now. (Dees, "Writers Series Kicks" 1)

He continued to work on the novel through the summer and finally submitted it to Ravenel at the beginning of September. He had cut the manuscript to "480 pages [but] the typesetter was all bent out of shape because it wasn't on a disc. He had to type the whole thing in. I'm one of the last ones who doesn't use a computer. I guess I'm becoming a thing of the past" ("Writers Series at Library" 1). The book was scheduled for publication on 31 March 2000.

Having finally finished the manuscript on which he had been laboring for three years, Brown moved temporarily to Montana, where he had been invited to spend the fall 1999 semester as the inaugural Kittredge Writer-in-Residence at the University of Montana, Missoula. His friend, Kevin Canty, who taught there, was instrumental in getting Brown the appointment. Montana paid Larry thirty thousand dollars and provided him with housing. His responsibilities involved teaching two graduate courses—a nonfiction workshop and a special topics class of his own design—and giving one public reading. On 5 September, shortly after his arrival in Montana, Brown wrote to Tom Rankin, "School has started and I've met my classes. I hate teaching so bad I don't know why I'm out here again, but I do know, too: money, always the same thing. I wouldn't even do for myself what I do for my family. I don't know, man, [the students are] so hungry, you can see it in their eyes, and they want from me whatever I have, and I can't give it. All I can give them is all my time for three months. Then I skip back home with a last fat paycheck before Christmas" (Rankin Papers). In 2001, Brown recalled taking

> my students at the University of Montana out under the trees next to the liberal arts building on a fine October afternoon. . . . I told them about some writers they possibly didn't know about and stories to read—Robert Stone, Mark Richard, among others. I told them I wasn't going to hold up any students' stories in front of the class and ask the other students what the story was supposed to be about. They, like most students in any other class I've taught, were wary and perhaps even fearful of the possible criticism they were going to encounter from their classmates about their own work. . . . I told them that they weren't going to hear any criticism from me, that I was just going to try to help them with their stories. I told them the reason why—because I had been where they were now, in a creative writing class, and that they needed guidance and help like I did. ("Writing")

Despite his dislike of his teaching responsibilities, Brown generally enjoyed life in Missoula, writing to Rankin,

> I've got a nice place here. Three bedroom apartment, fully furnished, TV and VCR, washer and drier. I took $600 from my first paycheck and bought me a new rig, big Sony receiver and 5-disc changer and some speakers about waist high. Sent the rest home to [Mary Annie]. Got both my guitars up here, play in the living room all the time, can't do that at home. And I'm learning my way around town. . . .
>
> Funniest damn thing happened last night. I was walking home from a party near here and saw a buck and doe, mule deer, going down the street. I followed them over here to my apartment complex and just kept walking along behind them. They'd let me get to within fifty or sixty feet, then they'd step off, tails only lifted about halfway, under people's clotheslines, down their sidewalks, past their back doors. I could've shot them fifty damn times. (Rankin Papers)

Canty remembered that Brown had no difficulty acclimating him-self and "fit in beautifully" in the new environment ("Larry Brown"). He was, however, frustrated with "students of privilege" who lacked the drive to succeed as writers and refused to give themselves fully to the program ("Larry Brown"). According to Canty, Brown's graduate workshop "was known as 'Hanging around with Larry Brown' among the graduate students. . . . It was very informal and people brought stuff in and they talked about their work but they also talked about a lot of other stuff, and it was the kind of thing where he was kind of a genial host rather than a rigorous instructor-type person in the class-room. And the boys and girls loved him. Loved him, loved him, loved him. Especially the boys. They all want to be him, you know."

When he was not teaching, Brown continued to pursue the same activities he favored in Oxford—driving around, listening to music, talking, and smoking, though the university already had banned light-ing up inside its buildings, forcing Brown outside to indulge. And after more than a year on the wagon, he also resumed drinking. Canty re-membered that "after about a month or so [in Montana], after being out there by himself and being kind of isolated—it's a gray winter out there; I don't think he was used to that—that was the point when he started up again" ("Larry Brown").

One of Brown's students, Steve Rinella, recalled that he knew Brown for only four months but that he was a stronger influence than any other teacher ("Larry Brown"). Brown showed faith in Rinella's writ-ing and provided the young author with necessary prodding, helping him to make writing the center of his life—"the greatest gift anybody could have" ("Larry Brown"). According to Rinella, Brown would "pull inspiration out of you" ("Larry Brown"). Brown also got along well with the other members of the writing faculty. He dined on one oc-casion with William Kittredge, Annick Smith, and Jim Welch and told Tom Rankin, "Annick told some good Cormac [McCarthy] stories and I told one or two." However, Brown was also irritated by "somebody, student or faculty, constantly wanting me to dinner or go out. Makes it tough to get my work done. I'm even advising one on a thesis & I'm sure I don't have any business doing that" (Rankin Papers). He formed a particularly strong friendship with "Debra Earling, a Flathead Indian who teaches here. She's really saved me from going nuts. . . . She's extraordinarily beautiful, so much it hurts me to look at her. She'll cry like a baby when I leave and I probably will too" (Rankin Papers). When Earling published a novel, *Perma Red*, in 2002, Brown provided her with a blurb, earning her deep gratitude: "I read it over and over again and it made me cry. It means so much to have your approval. In the face of your achievements and all of your work it humbles me. I don't have words to thank you Larry but send you every blessing, my wish for all good things, for your happiness in all ways and always" (Brown Collections).

In retrospect, Brown found his time in Montana useful: "I certainly got enough material out of four months in Montana to write a couple of stories, at least. I think going somewhere else for a while is good for a writer" ("*PW*" 44). After Brown returned home, Canty told him "that when everybody got up and read their thesis pieces . . . each of them thanked me, and I wasn't even there. I gave them all I had. That's the only way I know how to do it" (LB to JM, Brown Collections). He reiterated that sentiment in a 2001 speech: "Teaching is never a good proposition for me because I always wind up totally neglecting my own work in favor of theirs. I figure this is the way a teacher ought to act" ("Writing").

In the late 1990s, Brown became increasingly involved in the world of alternative contemporary music. During his semester in Montana, Brown bought tickets—"17 including extra ones for the ones who are married" (Rankin Papers)—and took his students to a Missoula concert by an Oxford band, Blue Mountain. Brown's lifelong interest in music had developed into what his friend, Rick Bass, described as a "passion." Bass saw Brown "at his little apartment in Missoula and was struck by how passionately he was throwing himself into music, not even so much the playing of it, as being moved by it, excited about it. Talking about songs and bands, performers he had spent time with, music he loved. Slobberbone, Graham [*sic*] Parsons, Robert Earl Keen." Brown became personally involved with many of these musicians, leading Dave Hoekstra to assert that "not since John Fane (the inspiration behind Sheryl Crowe's 'All I Want to Do') and Charles Bukowski has an American novelist made such an impact on the music community"

("Songwriters"). Jonny Miles saw Brown as "in some ways like a literary patron saint for a whole school of songwriters" ("Larry Brown").

Among the musical groups with which Brown established a connection was Slobberbone, which, Brown told Jake Mills, "has at least one song with a title and lines from 'Kubuku.' They're Texas Rock-and-country rollers. Hard to describe but awesome to listen to." Brown continued, "I've been meeting a lot of musicians. [Bob] Dylan claimed in a *Time* interview that I was his favorite writer. I signed some books for Willie Nelson and Lucinda Williams but I don't know yet whether they've read them or not. Alejandro Escovedo came through town a few months back and we hung out some. I reckon a lot of songwriters like what I do. That's something I'm very happy to hear, especially when I dig what they doing with music" (Brown Collections).

Brown met Keen and his band when they played at Proud Larry's in Oxford, and they subsequently invited Brown to come to Memphis when they played there. Beginning in the late 1990s, Brown attended Keen concerts whenever he could, making trips as far afield as Nashville and Austin in the spring of 1999. In a portrait of Keen that Brown published in *No Depression* in the summer of 2001, he remembered his excitement at having an all-access pass to the Austin show that enabled him to be part of the musical scene ("King"). When Brown was in the audience, Keen was initially "a little nervous, to say the least, but I got over that pretty fast because I looked out there and I saw him and I realized that he was really paying attention . . . hanging onto every note and every word and, as a performer, that makes you feel good. . . . That's the best you can ask for. As a performer I felt that that was a kind of signature thing about him, about coming to a show. He would just sit there and be very patient and listen very intently." For his part, Brown said that "Robert Earl Keen and his band's music take me to a place where I have been over and over and will be again, and it's a place where you go inside a song with the people who are singing it and playing, although different things are passing beside you, whether they be does and fawns standing in tall grass as the sun burns finally down, or a freshly planted cotton field with the tire tracks still showing in the dirt, the words and the melody are like familiar old friends you can hear from any time you want to. And I never get tired of that with them" ("King" 98). Brown also enjoyed visiting with the band members on their bus: as Keen recalled, "He would sit back there and have his slow drawl and his ready laugh and he would have his exotic skinned cowboy boot propped up on his leg and sit back and talk about Billy Ray or Shane or the new gable on his cabin or the transplanting of the hardwoods around the pond."

Brown also began to write and play his own songs. When he sent his friend, Clyde Edgerton, a tape of some of his efforts in the late 1990s, Edgerton thought "I can hardly understand anything he's singing. It sounds like he recorded with the microphone inside the guitar and held the guitar as far from his mouth as he could, while he mumbled the words. But I also thought: these are good songs" ("Larry"). Edgerton used his connections with a music studio in Durham, North Carolina, to arrange a more professional recording session for Brown, and the two men "had a great time for a couple of hours playing, recording, listening, laughing. He was very steady, making few mistakes, not nervous a bit" ("Larry").

After his stay in Montana, Brown returned to Oxford and continued his writers' series, with Canty, Tim McLaurin, and Clyde Edgerton participating during 2000 and Brown enjoying the opportunity to host his friends. When Canty came, for example, Brown took him out to Tula for some fishing: "We caught eight nice crappies out of my pond this afternoon on minnows and I've got them on ice. We were out every night . . . went out for catfish, rode around and drank some beer" (LB to JM, Brown Collections).

In early March, the Mississippi legislature bestowed on Brown the Governor's Award for Excellence in the Arts in the Artist Achievement Award category. The honor came as Brown prepared for the official and long-awaited publication of *Fay*. He had already begun promotional efforts, doing a reading at the University of Texas in February and readings and signings at Lemuria Books in Jackson on 21 March and at Square Books in Oxford three days later. On 15 April, Brown attended the South Carolina Festival of the Book. On 4 May, back in Oxford, Brown read from *Fay* on Thacker Mountain Radio. In addition to author appearances, Algonquin promoted the book with huge advertisements in the March–April edition of the *Oxford American* and in the 4 June *New York Times Book Review*.

More than one hundred reviews of *Fay* appeared in a wide variety of formats, including on the Internet. Prior to the book's publication, *Kirkus Review, Publishers Weekly, Library Journal*, and *Booklist* printed reviews, with features on Brown and the book later appearing in the *Atlanta Journal-Constitution, USA Today, BookPage, Glamour, Time, People, Men's Journal*, and numerous other traditional publications as well as online at BN.com and other Web sites (Algonquin Files). Sybil Steinberg's January 2000 review in *Publishers Weekly* declared the novel a "saga of degradation and violence" that was Brown's "most powerful novel yet" (43). *Kirkus* pronounced *Fay* "stunning" (61). Later reviews were equally enthusiastic. Reviewing the novel in the *Washington Post*, novelist George Peleconos asserted, "*Fay* is proof that important fiction can be gritty, sexy, and deeply moving" (7). Once again, Brown's work earned him favorable comparisons with William Faulkner and Flannery O'Connor (Wright). Effused Jim Laird, "After 489 pages, perhaps, you'll be closer along to an answer to those greatest of questions given to us in William Faulkner's *Absalom, Absalom*: 'Tell about the South. What's it like there'" (31). Still other reviewers applauded Brown's creation of Fay as a believable female protagonist. According to Diann Blakely, "Brown's comprehension of women sets him apart from the crowd." Harry Levins compared Brown to Larry McMurtry in his "knack for getting inside the heads of his female characters" ("Novel" F10). And James Dickerson wrote, "Probably not since F. Scott Fitzgerald's incursions into the female sensibilities of the 1920s and 1930s has there been a writer so successful in crossing that literary minefield."

Several critics, however, liked *Fay* less than Brown's earlier work, primarily because of the new novel's length. Fredric Koeppel wrote, "In *Fay*, Brown . . . abandoned his customary honed verbal and narrative economy and his slithery provocative insight into character for an atypical and often far-fetched heaping of sensationalism atop melodrama" ("Craft" H3). Writing in *Spectator*, Art Taylor facetiously suggested that the novel would have succeeded better as a short story in the *Oxford American* or as a novella ("Fay's"). Drew Jubera called *Fay* "a sometimes breathtaking disappointment, a series of brilliant flashes undone by bloat and a title character who never transcends the author's inability to fully inhabit her" (L12).

By this time, reviewers had developed a tendency to use certain catchphrases when discussing Brown and his work. According to Algonquin publicist Katharine Walton, Brown was amused when *Vanity Fair* called him the "bad boy" novelist, and he laughed about being called the "King of White Trash," telling interviewer Dan Deluca and others, "I kind of like it. I told my LeAnne, 'If I'm the king, that makes you the princess'" (F5). However, he disliked the use of the term *grit lit* about his writing, flinching when Donald Kartiganer used the phrase in introducing Brown at the University of Mississippi's 2000 Faulkner Conference. Louisiana novelist John Dufresne decried such monikers as "ridiculous and reductive designations, attempts to confine this brilliant writer to a regional and cultural niche. This is provincial thinking. All writing is regional, after all. Brown is simply one of our finest writers—honest, courageous, unflinching" ("Yearning" C2).

In making seventeen-year-old Fay Jones the center of consciousness, Brown deliberately sought to counter reviewers who had emphasized the tough masculinity of his earlier characters and had implied that his readership was primarily male. Brown told Dickerson, "This is a real departure for me, to write a book from a woman's point of view. There were things I didn't know, things I had to ask people about women to find out. Their sensitivities are different and their concerns are different." Not surprisingly, Brown's wife, Mary Annie, was one of his primary sources, frequently providing guidance "about such feminine matters as morning sickness" so that Fay's portrayal would "be genuine to women who read it" (O'Brient, "Writer" L1). But Brown also believed that regardless of a character's gender, the writer's real job "is always about getting into someone's head, wearing their clothes, walking in their shoes and you have to live in this person's head for a couple of years sometimes. But that's what is necessary to write a novel" (Robinson). As with his earlier novels, Brown had found the setting for *Fay* in the North Mississippi countryside around Oxford: "One day I just sat down and started writing about [Fay] walking down this dirt road that came out of this ridge over at Tula"; driving through the countryside with Don O'Brient, Brown pointed out the specific road ("Writer" L1, L6). Brown did not consider *Fay* a sequel to *Joe* but rather a new story: "In my mind, it's supposed to be a love story, but a very dark and destructive love story" (Glendenning, "Mississippi" n.p.).

Fay is certainly Brown's most plot-driven novel. That the novel is a clear example of female bildungsroman adds to its appeal. Marianne Gingher wrote, "This is a coming-of-age story of a femme fatale. The book's called Fay because, match after match, she's the one left standing" (4G). The book begins with the title character setting off with only the clothes on her back, two dollars in her purse, a couple of cigarettes, and a boundless desire to reach Biloxi, and readers are immediately captured: What will happen to this ignorant innocent, barely able to read? But although Fay may not know the ways of the modern world, she is more than ready to take on the dangers that lie ahead. As Rodney Welch wrote, "For all her naiveté, Fay is never the victim; rather she's a youthful adventurer who is experiencing the real world with her own dumb courage, and she is at least the equal of the men in her life when it comes to exerting her own sexual power" (3). On the verge of being raped, Fay saves herself by vomiting on her attacker's genitals, escaping again to the road. Virginia Vitzthum compared Fay's resourcefulness with that of Huck Finn, but unlike Mark Twain, Brown does not "cheat by having her pontificate beyond her intellectual horizons." Whether Fay moves toward a more positive life is debatable, but she unquestionably survives and does so without bitterness: in New Orleans, "She mingled with the talking people on Royal and looked at old coins and Civil War muskets or mummies in shop windows and she smiled as she walked" (*Fay* 491).

Class and economic issues lie at the core of the novel, with Fay struggling to leave her migrant worker background to achieve what she hopes will be a better life. Fay evolves as a contemporary representation of Lena Grove in Faulkner's *Light in August*, of Theodore Dreiser's Carrie Meeber, and even Daniel Defoe's Moll Flanders. Although the settings of these novels vary from the eighteenth to the twentieth century, the four female protagonists illustrate the dearth of economic opportunities available for women in all of these times and places. Lacking family support, sufficient education, and, of course, money, these women can do little to better their lives in a manner acceptable to society.

In *Fay*, Brown offers readers a clear and sympathetic picture of life for young women of a class that many middle-class readers find offensive. As in his earlier writings, Brown uses Fay's qualified triumph to build interest, understanding, and respect for members of a relatively unacknowledged class.

With *Fay* published and selling fairly well, Brown returned home to Mississippi. There, he returned to his work on his property at Tula and to organizing the nonfiction collection that would become *Billy Ray's Farm*.

CHAPTER TWELVE

A Return to Nonfiction

Billy Ray's Farm, 1999–2001

In the summer of 1999, Larry Brown began planning the publication of a collection of his short writings, both fiction and nonfiction, over the past seven years. On 26 August, Mary Annie Brown sent Ravenel a number of stories and articles, and in mid-September, Ravenel told Brown that after reading the pieces, she believed that a nonfiction collection highlighting "Larry's life in Mississippi *now*" would work best. She suggested "Billy Ray's Farm" as the collection's centerpiece, with "By the Pond" as the first essay and a piece about the cabin as the last. She thought the writer's voice in "So Much Fish, So Close to Home" was not really Brown's, and she asked for two other new essays, one about Brown's dogs since Sam and one about Larry and Mary Annie (Algonquin Files).

Brown responded to Ravenel's letter on 4 October. He liked her proposed arrangement of the essays and had "started the essay on building the little house," but he thought he would not be able to make much progress on it while he was teaching in Montana. He was less enthusiastic about her other two ideas for essays, since he had not "had any decent dogs since Sam died. . . . And I don't know where to get a handle on one about Mary Annie" (Algonquin Files). Finally, he reacted defensively to her criticism of "So Much Fish, So Close to Home": Thom Jones, Mark Richard, Kevin Canty, Andre Dubus III, Clyde Edgerton, Jill McCorkle, and Tom Rankin "have all read the essay and like it just fine the way it is" (Algonquin Files). By October, Larry had signed a contract with Algonquin/Workman for the collection. He was to get a $112,000 advance—$50,000 when the contract was signed, $32,000 after he submitted the first draft, and $30,000 on completion. Always in need of money, Brown wanted $10,000 immediately (Algonquin Files).

Work on the collection proceeded slowly over the next few months, as Brown found his time consumed by his promotional efforts on behalf of *Fay*, work on his cabin, and other personal matters. In mid-July, Ravenel urged him to finish *Billy Ray's Farm* so that it could appear on Algonquin/Workman's spring 2001 list. She apologized for "slave-driving" him but explained, "we want to strike while the iron's still hot from FAY. (Which has had more coverage than any book we've ever published)" (Algonquin Files). By the time Brown was nearing the end of writing *Fay*, he had reversed his pattern of work and sleep. According to Mary Annie Brown, "His routine now is to get up about six or seven o'clock at night, drink his coffee, mess out in the yard for a while, go to Tula, come back, mess around in the house a little bit, and as we're getting ready to shut our day down, he's starting his day. And he'll write all night long. That's just the way it is; I don't know why" (*RS*). In July 2000, Brown wrote that he "went four months straight at one point, 7PM to 7AM, every night" while finishing *Fay*; now, trying to complete the manuscript of *Billy Ray's Farm*, which Ravenel wanted by early August, he was "back on the night shift, writing all night long, trying to get done, sleeping in the day" (Author's Papers). Brown sent the manuscript to Ravenel on 13 August.

Billy Ray's Farm was the first book that Brown wrote on a computer rather than a typewriter. He had hoped that the computer would enable him to spend more time writing than revising and retyping, but he later reflected that "all this electronic help doesn't change the fact that it's just making up things from your head and turning them into a story, trying to turn names on paper into living and breathing people who can get rained on, drive cars" ("Writing").

Brown finished his book tour for *Fay* and returned to Oxford in the early summer of 2000, in time for the 24 June wedding of his son, Billy Ray, to his high school classmate, Paula Klepzig. Larry was hoping for a "peaceful wedding ceremony. I have a nice new suit. All my children will be there. It should be joyous and tearful"; indeed, he wrote in a subsequent letter, the ceremony was "really nice" (Rankin Papers). Billy Ray was raising beef cattle on the family property in Yocona, and he and his bride moved into a house "right across the driveway" from his parents: Larry told Shannon Ravenel, "We been working on his house for months. . . . Now he and Paula have all new carpet, washing machine, drier, icebox, central air and heat, plumbing, cabinets, everything." (Algonquin Files). But in some respects, Oxford had ceased to be a haven for Brown. He had become somewhat disgruntled by the loss of anonymity that had accompanied success, and he was tired of doing interviews and of having people photograph him: "Sometimes I'm uptown and some tourist grabs his camera and starts snapping pictures, like I'm some monkey in a zoo. So I don't get out like I used to. [Norman] Mailer says they get a little of your soul each time they take one. If that's true I ain't got much left" (Author's Papers).

In addition to writing, organizing, revising, and editing the essays that would form *Billy Ray's Farm*, Brown spent the early part of the summer preparing his reading for the Faulkner Conference in late July. Dressed in the new suit he had gotten for Billy Ray's wedding, Brown read "A Roadside Resurrection" on 26 July. The audience included academic conference participants, members of a group of retirees, high school teachers, and local residents; the grotesque yet spiritual story enthralled most of the listeners but put some to sleep in their chairs.

Hollywood had again come calling, and Brown spent part of the summer of 2000 working with Debra Winger and Arliss Howard as they prepared to film a movie version of *Big Bad Love*. Howard had read the collection soon after it came out and found the stories "strange and new and completely familiar" (Howard and Winger). In 1991, Howard and his brother, James, "started working and we got a script together pretty quickly" (Neumar, "Arliss").

Arliss Howard ultimately let his option on the book expire as he became involved with other projects but took up the script again in January 2000, with plans to begin filming later that year. Working with a crew of more than one hundred, filming in Holly Springs and Oxford, and using locals as extras, the Howards made the movie in just thirty-two days (Neumar, "Debra"). In addition to Arliss Howard and Winger, the cast included Paul Le Mat, who played Leon Barlow's best friend, Monroe; Rosanna Arquette, who portrayed Monroe's wife; Angie Dickinson, who played Leon Barlow's mother; and Brown himself. He wrote to Ravenel, "I got a part in the movie. Arliss Howard wants me to play Leon's dead daddy, lying in a chest deep freeze. Here's the scene: Leon's in Mr. Aaron's store with Monroe and goes over to the freezer to get a bag of ice to ice down his beer. He lifts the lid and his dead daddy's lying in there (me) and he says, 'Take the high road, son. Take the high road.' I told him I'd do it" (Algonquin Files). Both Winger and Howard described Brown as not interfering with the moviemaking process, although Winger was "shocked" that he was on the set every day with his cup, a folding chair, and cigarettes; she described him as "truly a collaborator" (Howard and Winger).

With publication of *Billy Ray's Farm* scheduled for 1 April 2001, Katharine Walton and the rest of Algonquin's publicity staff began to plan the promotion of the volume. In deference to Brown's dislike of touring, Walton suggested that he make only four stops, beginning with his hometown on 21 April. In the other three cities—Lexington, Kentucky; Chicago; and New York—Brown would be appearing with "legendary singer-songwriter Alejandro Escovedo, who will be promoting his upcoming album *A Man under the Influence*. The events will be a cross market effort between bookstores and music stores (or bookstores that have a music section) in cities that have both a strong music and literary scene" (Algonquin Files). According to Escovedo, someone at his label, Bloodshot Records, "mentioned that Larry was going on a book tour and was interested in having some music. I volunteered, of course, to do it. . . . But it was like we didn't have any plan. We just hung out, singing songs; he'd read and I'd play along, while he was reading. Then I'd sing a song. . . . We had the time of our lives" ("Larry Brown"). On another occasion, Escovedo recalled that he would "try to keep up with the mood [Brown would] be creating with his reading and then I'd play a song. It was wonderful. With Larry there was no rehearsal. We just went for it" (Caligiuri). Algonquin also offered a "signed, limited edition excerpt from the title essay available to key buyers and the media" (Algonquin Files).

As a work of nonfiction, *Billy Ray's Farm* received fewer reviews than Brown's fiction writings, but most commentators were positive if tepid.

Joe Hartlaub's review called the book "a brief but deep collection from an author who should be seriously considered a national treasure." The *Washington Post's* Jonathan Yardley called Brown "a relatively minor voice in American literature" but nevertheless declared, "At a time when even the most ostensibly 'Southern' writers turn out upon close inspection to be cookie-cutter products of the writing school, with all their deadening and sanitizing influences, Brown is the real thing: a self-taught country boy who may make the rounds of the writing conferences but whose heart is obviously, and wholly, in the country he loves" (CO2). Jeff Kunerth found *Billy Ray's Farm* "a nice counterpoint to [Brown's] fiction. For those who have never read Brown, it's a nice way to get acquainted." Jean Charbonneau thought that "*Billy Ray's Farm* will be a treat for Brown's many fans and admirers, but compared with his novels and collections of stories, it is a minor opus" (F5). Reviewers also noted approvingly Brown's acknowledgment of his debts to other writers: Yardley and others declared the essay on Harry Crews the collection's best, and Jere Real commented on Brown's "kind tribute" to Madison Jones, which "should make anyone want to read Madison Jones' work" (n.p.). Although all of the essays except "Shack" had previously been published elsewhere, it appears that none of these reviewers had read the pieces before they came out in the book.

In keeping with Ravenel's suggestions, the collection is carefully structured with the middle essays framed by a prologue in which Brown talks about his years as a writer. The opening essay, "By the Pond," tells of his desire to create an Edenic sanctuary on his Tula property, while the final essay, "Shack," provides a detailed account of the construction of the nearly completed cabin. In between, the essays deal with family issues, Brown's feelings regarding animals, his love for writing, and the changes in North Mississippi over the preceding half century.

According to Brown, the essays collected in *Billy Ray's Farm* evolved over time as he reacted to events in his or others' lives (Harty 13). He found nonfiction a much easier genre to write than fiction because "I can use the language in a lot of interesting ways [and] you've already got the story. You don't have to create the whole thing. It just depends on how you tell the story. An essay always arises out of something I saw or did that affected me. The hard thing is trying to recreate it by memory because your memory can play tricks on you" (13).

The prologue begins with a description of a road "that stretched from Oxford to Toccopola, a distance of about sixteen miles" (*BRF* 1). When Brown was a boy, one lane of the road was paved, while the other was gravel: "That road has been gone for a long time, but I still remember the swaying of the car as my father went from one side of the road to the other. Everybody did it and nobody ever thought anything about it" (1). Oxford had changed in many ways over the preceding thirty years, and William Faulkner "would probably be flabbergasted to know that there are several bars on the Square now, and that blues music can often be heard wailing out of the open doors on hot summer nights" (2). Brown then goes on to ponder the question of why Oxford produces so many writers: "Oxford produces writers for the same reason that New York does, or Knoxville, or Milledgeville, or Bangor. You can't pick where you're born or raised. You take what you're given, whether it's the cornfields of the Midwest or the coal mines of West Virginia, and you make your fiction out of it. It's all you have. And somehow, wherever you are, it always seems to be enough" (5). After the prologue and "By the Pond" (discussed in chapter 9) comes "Thicker than Blood," in which Brown relates how the older men in Tula taught him to hunt after his father's death: "Maybe in some unspoken way they took care of me because of us losing Daddy so early" (16).

In the next essay, "Harry Crews: Mentor and Friend," Brown pays tribute to the Florida author as both literary role model and personal friend. Brown first read Crews's novel, *A Feast of Snakes*, about 1980 and was immediately taken with Crews's writing: "I didn't know a man could invent characters like Joe Lon Mackey, or his sister, Beeder, or Buddy Matlow, the peg-legged sheriff. It was a combination of hilarity and stark reality and beauty and sadness" (*BRF* 18–19). At the time, Brown "was in the process of trying to find mentors, writers whose work I could look up to and gain inspiration from" (18). In the mid-1980s, when Brown was frustrated by his inability to get his work published, he encouraged himself by recalling Crews's long apprenticeship: "I could get one of Harry's books of essays and read again about what he had gone through, how he had worked for years with no success. It was comforting somehow to know that a man of his great talent had not been born to it, but had learned it, and had possessed the perseverance or stubbornness or internal character or whatever it was that he possessed that allowed him to keep on writing in the face of rejection" (19–20). Brown and Crews came to know each other personally after Crews published a glowing review of *Big Bad Love* in the *Los Angeles Times* and Brown wrote to thank him. Brown came to value Crews as an exemplar who taught an important lesson: "Do the best work you can, whatever it takes to do it, whatever the price is that you have to pay" (28).

In "Chattanooga Nights," Brown writes about his first appearance at a major literary gathering, the Arts and Education Council of Chattanooga's 1989 Conference on Southern Literature, where the Fellowship of Southern Writers was formed. Brown was simultaneously excited to have been invited and intimidated about appearing in public among big-name writers. He and Mary Annie stayed at "the big old Radisson downtown, one that was occupied by Union troops during the Civil War, and coming from our country home we were mightily impressed" (*BRF* 31). Brown returned to Chattanooga in 1995, this time accompanied not only by Mary Annie but also by their daughter, LeAnne, whom he wanted to meet some of his literary heroes. He now felt less in awe of the crowd and accepted and realized his connection with other southern writers: "I thought about how much alike we all were, whether we lived in Tennessee or Georgia, Alabama or North Carolina. What we had in common was that we loved the land and the people we came from, and that our calling was to write about it as well as we could" (37).

"Billy Ray's Farm" deals with the challenges Billy Ray Brown encounters in fulfilling his dream of becoming a successful cattle farmer, graphically describing the problems that arise in such an endeavor. Much of the detail covers Larry Brown's ineptitude as he tries to help while his son is away at school or off showing his prized bull, Oscar, at competitions. Brown sees his son's dream as a version of his own fantasies, a perspective that leads to his willingness to support Billy Ray's vision. Although readers from rural backgrounds may well find Billy

Ray's efforts both fascinating and heartrending, more urban readers may find the essay less engrossing. Jean Charbonneau called it the "most flawed [piece] in the book. . . . [T]hings take way too long to unfold, and it's hard not to lose interest after a while" (F5).

"Fishing with Charlie" is another tribute essay—in this case, a eulogy for Brown's friend, Charlie Jacobs, a jazz saxophonist from Mississippi who died in New Orleans in 1997 of heart failure, probably brought on by a drug overdose. Brown met Jacobs when his group, the Tangents, played in Oxford in the late 1980s and early 1990s. Brown wrote the piece on Jacobs "and kept it in a drawer for a year. The fishing trip and all that, it's just something I had to write down. . . . Sometimes when things are beyond your control you need to write them down to deal with it" (Harty 13). Jacobs came to visit Brown in the mid-1990s, when Jacobs had been clean for thirteen months, and the two men fished on Brown's beloved Yocona pond. Brown treasured a photograph that Tom Rankin took of Brown and Jacobs "on the dock I'd built with my own hands" (*BRF* 86). In the wake of Jacobs's death, Brown remembered "Charlie standing on the stage . . . his whole head and hair slicked back with sweat, blowing on that saxophone and the whole house rocking. And then he'd start singing in this old black man's voice, low down and dirty, and he could wail. He loved my books and I loved his music. The Tangents were the house band of Mississippi. . . . They were the best I ever heard" (87).

The next essay, "So Much Fish, So Close to Home: An Improv," is in some ways the most intriguing in the collection. It is Charbonneau's favorite because it most resembles a short story, telling "of three events taking place over the course of a hectic 24 hours: a stray bull that needs to be retrieved, an all-night party, and some sort of variation on the theme of the fish miracle. Subtitled 'an improv,' it has the rhythm and the dislocated structure of a jazz piece. . . . There's a surreal, dreamlike quality to this essay that only fiction normally possesses" (F5). The essay also provides great insight into the sensibilities of its author, giving readers glimpses of Larry Brown, part-time farmer and full-time writer; Larry Brown, Oxford partier; Larry Brown, catfish lover; and Larry Brown, proud North Mississippi native upset about the changes outsiders are bringing to his home area.

Farmer Brown details his difficulties with his bull, Omar, who has broken through a neighbor's fence and remains at large throughout the twenty-four hours of the account. In this essay, Brown reveals his writerly skills in unusual ways; one is the use of a series of riffs that interrupt the flow of the narrative, adding information or allowing Brown to go off on tangents in the same way that a musician in a jazz performance might go off on his or her own. Another disconcerting technique is his use of false names for real people, which makes a nonfiction essay seem fictional: Billy Ray becomes "Bobby Ray"; Mary Annie is "Marlana Antonia"; and LeAnne becomes "Louisa Latigo."

Brown the partier appears in the scenes he describes at Proud Larry's, where he and his friends listen to a performance of the Kudzu Kings. As in the first episode, he uses pseudonyms, but in this case, they are based on the names of writers or other puns: Cervantes, Bukowski, Tolstoy, Rimbaud, Dos Passos, Salinger, Melville, Guitar Bojangles, Mustapha, K-martwanda, and Paddy Chayovsky. There also seem to be inside jokes in the essay that only members of his clique would understand. Brown was drinking only soda that evening, enabling him to give a good picture of Proud Larry's—of the small area where only people in the front row can see the performance and of the audience of local music enthusiasts as well as drunk college students. When Proud Larry's closes at two o'clock in the morning, Brown and his friends end the evening at Murff's, where he learns about the "fish grab" scheduled for the next day at Enid Spillway, about thirty miles from Oxford.

The scene at the spillway showcases Brown the nature lover. About once every five years, the water in the spillway is lowered so that officials can check for cracks in the concrete, a process that strands thousands of fish. Authorities allow people to come into the basin and grab as many fish as they can for their frying pans and freezers. Brown is eager to get his share of the catfish, but he also empathizes with fish being robbed of their natural environment, feeling particular sorrow for those that will end up as fertilizer. He also shows the greed that impels people to try to get something for nothing. Because of his long night of partying and the trouble with the bull, Brown is too late to get any fish, but the trip to the countryside enables him to comment on changes in the area. When he tries to find a country store to get a sandwich for lunch, he finds only fake versions of the stores he remembers from his boyhood, buying nothing and continuing his search for a more authentic bologna and cheese sandwich.

Brown returns to expressing his feelings about publicizing his work in the next essay, "The Whore in Me." He writes about the annoyances of travel—planes that are late, poor food, crowds at book signings, and separation from his family. The most interesting and readable part of the essay is the description of Brown's reunion with his friend, Mark Richard, in California: "Talking to Mark is one of the best things about being out here, sharing ideas, sharing secrets, talking about plans and work" (*BRF* 150). In addition to its downside, book promotion has enabled Brown to make and renew friendships.

The penultimate story in *Billy Ray's Farm*, "Goatsongs," again shows Brown's dichotomized attitude toward the animal world. He treasures Nanette's incestuously created kids and feels murderous rage against the coyotes that carry them away one by one. But Brown undercuts any sentimentality regarding his animals with self-deprecating humor and irony: "Nanette got sick and died. I found her. I found her. . . . I keep one of Nanette's horns in my desk drawer. . . . The horn, hollow and fluted, is a spook, a talisman, a key. I keep it here to remind me of what a man can go through for goats. It reminds me of what is possible in this life in the country, and sometimes what is not" (*BRF* 171–72). Yardley summed up Brown's view of animals as "part utilitarian, part cold-eyed realist, part romantic. He knows that a steer will end up on the chopping block and then be ground into hamburger, he knows that that's the way of the world, and he hates it anyway" (CO2).

Jeff Kunerth called "Shack," the final essay in the collection, the best: "Brown writes about the experience [of building the cabin] with a tranquility that matches the setting of the house itself" ("Writer"). The care Brown gave to building his "shack" is analogous to the care with which Brown wrote.

The film version of *Big Bad Love* premiered at the Cannes Film Festival in May 2001 before being shown in Toronto in September, Denver in October, and St. Louis in November. Brown did not travel to France but was otherwise active in promoting the movie. He was in

Toronto for the 10 September showing and was stuck there for four days when all North American flights were grounded after the attacks on the World Trade Center and the Pentagon the following day. He "wound up catching a Greyhound to New York City. Then, I got a flight out of LaGuardia two days later. The weirdest thing about it was that the second day after it happened, I was out walking around in Toronto, kind of depressed, I guess everybody was, and I was hunting for a liquor store when this fine gritty dust started falling out of the sky. And everybody just stopped and started looking at it. And I know damn well it was all that powdered concrete that blew up and went to the jet stream, because I'd never seen anything like that fall out of the sky before" (Fitten and Hetrick 33). Brown was also touched by the kindness Canadians showed to him during that time: "Bartenders, desk clerks, doormen, the limousine driver, the people who brought my food and cleaned my room wanted me to know that they were our neighbors and friends and would stand by us" ("Writing"). When he finally returned home from what he called the "sadness of the Big Apple," he wrote to Tom Rankin, "I'm just so damn glad to be here and to be alive and back with my family that I don't know what to do. I'm thankful every day. I'm getting up early every day and fixing a good breakfast and coming out here and staying all afternoon writing and then smoking a little bowl every evening and getting a few cold beers and a little bit of schnapps and lowriding down Old Union Road and cutting through over to Old Dallas and listening to some music, to come home to eat supper and work again. Then read" (Rankin Papers).

Men's Journal asked Brown to write about his time in New York City. The result was "The Special Breed," a brief but powerful essay in which the former fireman paid tribute to his brethren who had died while trying to save others in the Twin Towers:

> What kind of person does it take to go up when everybody else is going down? What kind of person goes willingly where death may wait? No single group of American firefighters has ever faced the amount of carnage that was seen on September 11, and nobody but another firefighter can truly understand the total disregard they showed for their own personal safety. . . . When the time came, when their worst nightmare

was suddenly in front of them and they knew that they all might die together, they didn't stop. They just kept going up.

It's hard to imagine bravery like that. (84)

Just a few weeks later, in early October, Brown traveled to Chapel Hill, North Carolina, where he received the Thomas Wolfe Prize, which recognizes contemporary writers with distinguished bodies of work. In honor of the occasion, he gave a speech, "The Writing Life," in which he covered many of the same subjects that he had often explored in interviews and public readings: his early life in Memphis, his love of reading, and the perseverance and hard work required to become a writer. Brown also explained how he used one of his literary heroes when teaching creative writing students:

> I tell them about a novel called *Suttree* by a man named Cormac McCarthy. I tell them it's about a guy named Buddy who lives on a houseboat and fishes on the Tennessee River in Knoxville in 1951 and that it covers just about eight years of his life. I know that doesn't make it sound like a real thriller, but of all the novels I've read in my life, that's probably my favorite, not only for the beauty and flawless use of the language and the astonishment it causes for the writer as well as the reader but also because of the humor, the tragedy, and the terrible ugliness of some of the things that happen in it, but mostly because it is an accurate re-creation of Buddy's life those few years. There is no tightly switched plot driving it. . . . Fiction is merely a re-creation of life. What Mr. McCarthy does in all his novels is create believable characters, characters who are real people with fears, hopes, and flaws. To me, the more flaws the better, because the flawed characters always wrestle much harder for [their] existence in the world. ("Writing")

Brown closed his speech with some observations on how he viewed the world: "I'm also much more aware these last few years, looking up to my fiftieth birthday, about the great, never-ending circle of life in the world. I see it in the memories of my grandmothers' faces and the memories and pictures of my children, who are now grown men and women. I've seen now and probably in these last three weeks even more so, that the appreciation of life is the main thing, to take each day and savor it for the immeasurable pleasures of being alive in the world" ("Writing").

The fall of 2001 also brought about a meeting between Brown and Silas House, who had just published his first novel, *Clay's Quilt*. Just as Brown had been awed when he met his literary idols, House "was completely in awe" of Brown. But the more experienced author quickly put the young man at ease: the two men went out to a restaurant and found themselves talking not about writing but "about fishing and squirrel hunting and knives. [Brown] said, 'You know it's so good to meet a writer who knows how to smoke a Marlboro, how to fish blue-gill, and how to hunt squirrels.' Our whole relationship was built on that" (D. Brown). Brown soon took House under his wing, just as Barry Hannah and others had done for Brown when he was just starting out: House recalled, Brown "was real concerned that book touring would eat me up. He was always telling me to pace myself, to find ways to be still, to not drink too much on the road. . . . He also wasn't too trusting of publishers and was always telling me to make sure I didn't let any of them take advantage of me. . . . He also gave me a lot of advice about being a father and being married and just the whole process of being a man" ("Remembering Larry"). Brown subsequently wrote blurbs for House as well as for such other young authors as Chris Offutt, Steve Yarbrough, and Tim Gautreaux.

As 2001 drew to a close, Brown set his sights on his next writing project. But perhaps because of the tensions between Brown and Ravenel/Algonquin that had begun with *Joe* and continued through her criticisms of *Fay*, he turned to another publisher.

CHAPTER THIRTEEN

Leaving Algonquin

The Rabbit Factory, 2002–2003

On 22 February 2002, almost ten years after the publication of Larry Brown's short story collection, *Big Bad Love*, Arliss Howard and Debra Winger's film version had its commercial release, opening in New York City. Brown and his wife, Mary Annie, received free plane tickets for the trip and attended a "big" pre-premiere party (Rankin Papers). Although the movie had been shown at several film festivals the preceding year and had garnered lukewarm reviews, the wide release generally received critical scorn. Wrote Roger Ebert in the *Chicago Sun-Times*, "It all comes down to whether you can tolerate Leon Barlow. I can't. *Big Bad Love* can and is filled with characters who love and accept him, even though he is a full-time, gold-plated pain in the can. [He is] tiresome and obnoxious. The movie has patience with his narcissistic self-pity. My diagnosis: Send Barlow to rehab, haul him to some AA meetings, and find out in a year if he has anything worth saying." The *Seattle Post-Intelligencer*'s Christy Lemire felt that the film "catalogs Leon's self-destructive behavior without hinting at its origin. We're simply expected to accept that that's the way he is, which makes it difficult to sympathize or connect with him on any level." Part of the problem arose from the film's transplantation of Leon Barlow from working-class origins to a middle-class background. Since both Leon and his friend, Monroe, are portrayed as less economically down-and-out, they seem less sympathetic. Despite their good intentions, the filmmakers missed Brown's main point: art can transcend poverty and need. The story is turned into something of a soap opera, far from

Brown's literary intentions. The film grossed just $5,293 during its opening weekend, and by April 2002, it had earned a mere $100,420 ("Debra Winger").

Despite the film's lack of commercial success and the general negative reviews, several commentators, including Lemire, praised the musical score. Brown agreed: "These songs merge flawlessly with some images that formed in my mind first and then in another mind later, one that belongs to a guy named Arliss Howard" ("Big Bad Love" online). Among the artists whose work can be heard in the movie are Mississippi musicians R. L. Burnside, Junior Kimbrough, Robert Belfour, Asie Payton, and T-Model Ford as well as Tom Waits, Tom Verlaine and the Kronos Quartet, Bob Dylan, and Steve Earle.

Though the movie version of *Big Bad Love* may not have been well received in the wider world, the film's first screening in Brown's hometown, on 11 April 2002 at the Oxford Conference for the Book, created major excitement. Howard and Winger came to Oxford for the event, discussed the film on Thacker Mountain Radio before the showing, and then participated in a discussion panel chaired by local writer Jim Dees. According to Jamie Kornegay, Fulton Chapel on the Ole Miss campus was packed with "a crowd of curious locals and conference-goers" who wanted to see the movie. Brown was among the excited attendees, writing to his friend, Tom Rankin, "There was a huge crowd in Fulton Chapel and [Ole Miss chancellor] Robert Khayat introduced the movie and Arliss and Debra and me. Had all my family there. . . . We sat in the front row and I think the movie looks even better now" (Rankin Papers). Brown also attended a reception after the showing but left to go hear musician Duff Dorrough play at a club (Rankin Papers).

Though not an official part of the Oxford Conference for the Book, the town's first showing of Gary Hawkins's *The Rough South of Larry Brown* took place at the Oxford–Lafayette County Library on 13 April, while the conference was in session. Hawkins and actress Natalie Canerday came to town for the event, and Brown took them fishing at his Tula pond. He told Rankin, "She kept throwing her minnow off and getting it up in a tree. It embarrassed her but I told her that was okay, I did it all the time. I kept baiting her hook. I really like her. . . . I had the guitars out there and me and Hawkins played a little. Then we went to the library and he showed the movie, small crowd. Square Books had had a cocktail party at 6:30, so I suspect most folks went to the bar to eat after that" (Rankin Papers). The film had had its premiere a few days earlier at the Full Frame Documentary Film Festival in Durham, North Carolina.

The Rough South of Larry Brown has extraordinary power, partly because Hawkins elicited sincere and revealing comments from both Larry and Mary Annie Brown. Near the end of the film, Larry admits that he still feels in awe of his literary heroes—William Faulkner, Flannery O'Connor, Cormac McCarthy, Raymond Carver, and Harry Crews— but nevertheless takes pride in his success. Mary Annie Brown, however, makes clear the sacrifices she and their three children made so that her husband could become a published author. Writing in the *Oxford American*, Jeff Baker asserts, "Their forthrightness—along with a variety of visual resources including home movies, photographs, interview footage, and shots of rural Mississippi that evoke Brown's life and work—is responsible for the intimate tone of the film" (43); the magazine declared it one of "thirteen essential southern documentaries." Both Larry and Mary Annie Brown liked the final product. Larry said, "Hawkins put a lot of work into it and I think it's very well done. His use of different film stocks and different cameras works effectively. His adaptations of the stories are true to them. And he was able to capture a good impression of our life as it was then." Mary Annie Brown believes that Hawkins "did an excellent job of capturing Larry as an individual and as a writer. He showed Larry as he really is. I loved the way Gary intertwined Larry's work with our lives."

Hawkins subsequently entered *The Rough South of Larry Brown* in a number of film festivals, among them the Los Angeles Film Festival (June 2002), the Indie Memphis Film Festival (October 2002), the Savannah Film and Video Festival (October–November 2002), the Ohio Independent Film Festival (November 2002), the RiverRun International Film Festival in Winston-Salem, North Carolina (April 2003), and Brown's hometown Oxford Film Festival (April 2003). At both Savannah and Ohio, the movie was declared best feature; in Winston-Salem, it received the award for best cinematography; and in Oxford it was named best documentary. In October 2002, Hawkins also presented the film to an enthusiastic audience at the Southern Festival of Books in Nashville, where Larry and Mary Annie Brown answered questions after the showing.

Reviewer Scott Foundas called *The Rough South of Larry Brown* a "beautifully conceived documentary inquiry into the life and work" of the author, focusing on the writer rather than on secondary opinion. The film highlights at least four distinct themes. First, Hawkins contrasts Brown's working-class background with his literary aims. Second, Hawkins examines the continued agrarian nature of North Mississippi: its farmland, its remoteness, and its torpid heat. Third, the film focuses on Mary Annie Brown—specifically, on her anxieties about being a writer's wife, on what Hawkins called "the conflict of Worldly Calling and Familial Duty" (interview 164). The film's fourth major component is dramatizations of three stories from *Facing the Music*, "Boy and Dog," "Wild Thing," and "Samaritans." Hawkins explained, "'Boy & Dog' is a boy's story, 'Wild Thing' is a young man's story and 'Samaritans' is a middle-aged man's story. I had originally intended to close with 'Sleep,' . . . an old man's story. But we ran out of money and had to stop. Larry's stories tie with certain non-fiction elements, too. 'Boy & Dog' links with Larry's love of dogs, with his days at the fire department and with his willingness to experiment on the page. 'Wild Thing' presents the complement to Mary Annie's [statement that she finds it difficult to be around her husband when he's writing and] also introduces sex as the big troublemaker in Larry's stories. 'Samaritans' presents a beat-up, been-there-done-that protagonist who discovers that some people just can't be helped—one of Larry's more pessimistic beliefs" (interview 168).

Foundas much preferred the dramatizations in *The Rough South of Larry Brown* to the movie version of *Big Bad Love*, which he found replete with "hackneyed surrealism and strained artsiness." Foundas's only criticism of Hawkins's adaptations was that the narrators "don't always speak with the impassioned force Brown's words deserve." Other film critics generally agreed. Baker described "Boy and Dog" as "filmed with a shimmering sepia tone that is suggestive both of magic realism and the heat of a Mississippi summer" (43). Brown wrote "Boy and Dog" as what Hawkins called "a series of stacked sentences, five words to each sentence. The staccato sentences nudged me to present the imagery in a similar way. Instead of the usual flow of action and seamless cut, 'Boy & Dog' leans more towards 'now this, now this, now this.' We shot the film 'spaghetti Western' style in five days. I instructed the sound recordist to get what he could get, but we rarely stopped to slate sound. The result was a stand-alone silent film enhanced by Vic Chesnutt's dreamy narration, some synced dialogue . . . , and Larry's original five-word sentences (in his own hand), dropped digitally onto the images" (interview 166). Hawkins also strove for a "yellowed, comic book look" for "Boy & Dog" (166).

Hawkins dramatized "Wild Thing" with a still-photo technique because he "didn't have enough money to make it any other way. . . . I liked the black & white mood (actually it's sepia). The story is so sad. The hero is so addicted to sex and female attention—he's not just flawed, he's addicted. I could've emphasized the sadness and shot the story another way. But the allure of the young woman, the erotic promise of the night, the sweetness of the countryside, I wanted to get all that across. I wanted to sell it. I wanted viewers, male viewers anyway, to be thinking, 'Sure it's sad, but I don't blame him.' I thought the black & white still would help me sell the erotic promise, give the material an almost pornographic, forbidden fruit feel" (interview 166). "Samaritans" is the most sophisticated of the three films, partly because Hawkins hired a Hollywood actor (and South Carolina native), Will Patton, to play the main character, while Natalie Canerday, an Arkansan, plays the down-and-out woman. Brown thought highly of this adaptation of "Samaritans," describing it as "the best piece in there. . . . The dialogue was lifted straight from the story, so all they had to do was say what I'd written. But to see it on the screen like that, that was pretty awesome."

The 2003 Oxford Film Festival also included a performance of a radio play Brown had written, "a crazy cowboy poet thing, set in a saloon in a slightly altered Old West. We're going to do it live on the courthouse lawn to open the film festival. . . . We get to do all the sound effects I put in, tinkling pianos, drunk barmaids yelling, gunshots, horses falling, all that. I think it's going to take about fifteen people to do it.

We've never done anything like this before." Rainy weather forced the production inside to the Ford Performing Arts Center on the Ole Miss campus, where it was viewed by a crowd that Brown's friend, George Kehoe, who acted in the show, estimated at four hundred. The production was also broadcast on Thacker Mountain Radio.

By early 2002, Brown was completing the manuscript that would become *The Rabbit Factory*. In 2003, he recalled, "I actually started writing this book in 1994. It was actually a short story then, and it got too long for a short story, and I quit on it for a while . . . for a long time. I wrote *Father and Son* and *Fay* and then picked [*The Rabbit Factory*] back up about [2000], and what I'd written still looked pretty good. And I thought I'd turn it into a novella and started working on it some more and it went past a hundred pages pretty soon and it turned into a novel" (Englander). By this time in his career, Brown had turned his focus almost exclusively to novels: writing short stories had become more difficult for him "because I get so involved in characters and they go into novels" (Englander). For *The Rabbit Factory*, "Arthur was the first character who came to me. It was just an image of an old guy trying to catch a wild kitten in a cage trap" (Kingsbury).

In November 2001, when Brown had completed 270 pages of the manuscript, he sent it to Shannon Ravenel, his longtime editor at Algonquin. In her words, she "hated" it. Ravenel "read two drafts of *The Rabbit Factory* and Larry and I had many conversations about it and about why I didn't like it. The reason was that, to me, it read as if it had been written with Larry's tongue firmly in his cheek. That stance struck me as unfortunate. We couldn't agree on much of anything about the novel except that it might be better edited by someone else" (Kenyon, Ravenel interview). When Ravenel "first saw the novel, it was set in New York City, and we worked together a little bit back and forth, and I said 'You don't know anything about New York City: people do not have driveways, and they do not have backyards.' And he acceded to that and . . . decided to set it in Memphis. He didn't want to do to it the huge amount of stuff that I wanted him to do, and I don't blame him. I basically wanted him to trash it."

Although Brown ultimately agreed that the novel should not be set in New York City, he remained upset about her other objections to the novel, writing angrily to Rankin, "She didn't understand the fucking thing at this point and I guess doesn't believe with even eight books she's edited for me that I can make all this work, so she didn't make an offer, wants to see a whole first draft first. [She] sent me a long e-mail that said in part that all the women were nymphomaniacs with large breasts and that wasn't what the real world sports. She did like the animals. She said it wasn't 'Larry Brown fiction' as my fans know it, but that if I wanted to take this new turn, by all means I should. You can tell she's already worried about the damn reviewers. That seems like putting the cart before the horse" (Rankin Papers). In April 2002, when Ravenel still had not offered an advance for the novel, Brown's agent, Liz Darhansoff, told him that Ravenel "wanted to publish my book pretty bad so I told her tonight that was cool but if she didn't offer what I wanted, I wanted to show it to somebody else" (Rankin Papers). At around the same time, Brown told Rankin,

> I've got to make up my mind what I'm going to do, and do it. [Ravenel's] got all these ideas that are so wrongheaded and so numerous I won't even go into them. She thinks the ending with this kitten I've got is brilliant and a brilliant way to end the book. She obviously loves a great deal of it, thinks it's some of the best I've ever done, but she has these reservations about some of the sex stuff. . . . She's got no business trying to write some of my novel. . . . I think the shit's gonna hit the fan. She wants me to keep writing her about all this stuff so that she knows how to suggest revisions. She finds it hard to believe that a black deputy sheriff can have a set of 46 DD breasts. Or that a little dog could jump from the roof of a house into a squirrel nest. It's like it's too much for her, and she is very uncertain. I think she probably knows she could fuck this up. She's got to be aware that other people are ready to publish me. (Rankin Papers)

On 5 May, Brown told Elisabeth Scharlatt at Workman in New York that he could not take Algonquin's offer and would try to find another publisher: "I wrote her nothing with animosity, didn't fire any parting shot in anger. Originally I *wrote* a few parting shots but took them out. I figured there was no need" (Rankin Papers). He planned to send the book to eight other publishers, including Knopf, Houghton Mifflin, and the Free Press (Rankin Papers). Ultimately, the "Free Press just made up their mind they were going to have it at whatever cost, and that was good for me" (Fitten and Hetrick 181). That cost was an advance of about three hundred thousand dollars (Brown Collections).

Brown explained his decision to leave in an e-mail to Ravenel, and she responded that she "might have broken down in tears . . . if I hadn't known that it was a decision that had been made very carefully and—most importantly—wisely, by you and Liz. Like you, I am enormously proud of the work we have done together" (Brown Collections). Brown also looked back fondly on their association, thanking Ravenel "personally for all your help through the years. I feel this move is right now, even feel in some way that it has your blessing" (Algonquin Files).

Brown had first considered leaving Algonquin/Workman a dozen years earlier, when he almost signed with Seymour Lawrence while writing *Joe*. In September 1999, Brown had written to Rankin that he and Ravenel "ain't in tune no more I don't think. We're two badly tuned and mismatched guitars, one with a capo, one without. And I believe we're having our last dance about now" (Rankin Papers). Looking back, Brown's friend, Richard Howorth, recalled that "in the beginning, [Algonquin was] a good place for him to be. He was well cared for; he was respected; he was edited carefully, treated well. I don't know specifically what the money was, but . . . it was fairly good." But over the years, "there was a lot of mothering that went on at Algonquin that Larry rebelled against at times and a lot of it had to do with Larry wanting to [keep] things in his books that sometimes . . . Shannon objected to. . . . She was probably thinking of what was best for his work and his readers . . . but he was probably thinking 'She's a prude.'" According to Howorth, the close friendship between Ravenel and Darhansoff sometimes made Brown feel that "he was being ganged up on" by the two women, and he disliked the two-book arrangement that the company created: "As soon as he finished the first book, they were working on the next two-book contract; he kept wanting to break the ties with Shannon and go elsewhere, but every time he started thinking like that, they would be there with the next advance for the next contract, and he felt a bit sharecropped at times." Howorth's wife, Lisa, also a close friend of Brown's, thought that he made a mistake in leaving Algonquin: "I was never that enthusiastic about the new publisher. They didn't go the extra mile with him like Algonquin." But another friend, Glennray Tutor, enthusiastically approved: when he read *The Rabbit Factory*, he thought, "This is Larry before Ravenel gets her hands on his manuscript."

The Rabbit Factory contained the largest cast of characters Brown ever created: "My whole idea was to tell parallel stories, stories about people that would stand on their own, people who had connections, sometimes very tenuous" (Englander). The "main problem was just trying to figure out how to keep all these different stories parallel and in the same time frame and have a resolution for each one" (Koeppel, "Brown"). Brown put great effort into structuring the novel: "It was kind of like a juggling act, and I wanted it in 100 segments—not chapters, but segments—and that's just the way I tried to put it all together. I had three charts going of how many sections each character had, and I was trying to even it out. The hardest thing was trying to tie it all up at the ending and give everything resolution. It started with the kid. I knew it had to end with the kid. That's the way I tried to do it. It took me fifteen months to write it" (Blanchard 16). Brown borrowed a strategy from William Faulkner, who when writing *A Fable* kept a day-by-day chronology of the novel on his wall: "I just had a bunch of post-its stuck up in my office, just listing how many scenes each character had, and that was the way I kept them balanced. . . . That was the whole thing I was trying to pull off, but I just had to kind of keep it listed there to kind of give all of them equal time on the page" (Englander).

The Rabbit Factory overlaps fact and fiction. Brown explained, "Everything that I use comes out of my life, my memory, the things that are around me. Most of it is made up, but there are actual things that go on all the time. But that's what you do. You draw on your material; you draw on what you know best. . . . I live in Mississippi, so I wrote novels about Mississippi" (Englander). One of the novel's pivotal settings is the Peabody Hotel, where Brown stayed in 1970 when he went to Memphis for his U.S. Marine Corps physical: "Back then, it was run down—and old, shabby, poorly lit, wormy," but it had been refurbished by the time Brown wrote *The Rabbit Factory*, and "all I had to do was go back up there a couple of times and check that I had everything right about the lobby . . . the bar and some hotel rooms" (Fitten and Hetrick 185).

One character in the novel, Anjalee, was based on a woman Brown met "in a strip bar in Memphis" while he was a firefighter. He recalled, "Her grandmother lived over at Toccopola, which is about ten or fifteen miles down the road from me. . . . I never did forget about her, and when it came time to put this girl in a strip club and put her in this novel, that's where I placed her home" (Englander).

The novel includes a menagerie of animals—a cat, dogs, lions, a monkey, and a whale—because Brown "wanted to say something about the relationships that people have with animals; you don't see that much in fiction. . . . I just wanted to say something about how animals influence people's lives" (Englander). The mixed-breed dogs raised by Eric's father as well as another dog, Jada Pinkett, also originated in Brown's real-life experiences: "I was riding by this preacher's house one night and these weird looking dogs ran out. I was writing all this stuff about the character Eric and his daddy and all the dogs he had, and these dogs looked like they might have been a mix between a pit bull and a Dachshund. I said, 'Damn, I'm gonna use that.' So, stuff just pops up everywhere, and I just lift that stuff and use it" (Blanchard 16). And Mr. Hamburger's little dog was modeled after Mack, a shih tzu owned by Brown's daughter-in-law; Brown "just kind of imbued him with these qualities where he could get in and out of anything," an idea Brown borrowed from a Welsh corgi owned by a friend (Englander). Brown makes Hamburger's dog the central character in several episodes in *The Rabbit Factory*: the author

> figured that I would have to use a point of view for the dog, just like I used a point of view for a person, except that the dog could not articulate what he was thinking. I could use only images. . . . So I kind of rolled it out that way without trying to go over the edge and make the dog actually think. But who knows what goes through the brains of animals? Anyone who's been around dogs knows that they have all kinds of human qualities. They have jealousy, fear, and anger. All kinds

of emotions live in dogs, just like they do in people. They're just not able to articulate what they feel except through their actions: either love toward you, or growling at somebody they don't like. They're able to communicate, but not on the same level that we are. (Blanchard 16)

Brown's firefighting experience also helped him conceive of the little dog's rescue after it jumps from the upper-story window of a house into a nearby tree (Englander).

The idea of using lions and the rabbit factory also came from North Mississippi: according to Brown, "There's some people down in Lafayette County where I live who adopted a bunch of lions that were abused in Texas or somewhere like that and built a compound for them, and a couple of them got out a couple of times. One of them killed somebody's dog, and the sheriff's deputy had to shoot it. You could hear them roaring at night down the road. . . . So I kind of lifted these lions and put them in my book. There are actually a lot of things in the book that are really based on fact, like the rabbit factory. The rabbit pen is about two miles from where I live. These guys have these beagles and run [the rabbits] in this field" (Englander). The whale story, however, "just kind of came out of left field. I was wondering if there had ever been an instance when a Navy ship hit a whale" (Fitten and Hetrick 184). Brown initially published the whale story as "The Whale Road"; Walter Mosley wanted to publish it in the 2003 edition of *The Best American Short Stories*, but Brown told the editor, Katrina Kineson, that "it wasn't a short story. Which killed it. 750 bucks, too."

Most of the novel's human characters emerge as fully developed in spite of the number of scenes in which they appear. The inclusion of the Ole Miss professor, Merlot, and his short-term lover, Penelope, represents new territory for Brown, since they are of different races and of different social backgrounds. Brown initially did not think that Merlot "was going to turn into such a major character, or Penelope. Their story got to be really important to me, as all the stories did" (Blanchard 16). Brown included parallel descriptions of one scene from Merlot's perspective and then from Penelope's because he "wanted the reader to see [that] what he was seeing on her face was not even close to what was really going through her head. She was thinking about the kid she gave up for adoption, how badly she wanted to find him, and he was worried about Candy. The reader doesn't even know at that point who Candy is, and he's spending all this time worried about her. All that stuff, when you get into characters' heads is just a way of getting to know the character better, giving them history, families and backgrounds" (16).

Brown spent the fall of 2002 revising *The Rabbit Factory* in response to the suggestions offered by his new editor at the Free Press, Dominick Anfuso. Now that he was using a computer, the revision process was much easier, and he cut the manuscript from 642 pages to 513 in six weeks (Fitten and Hetrick 180). Brown completed the revisions and returned the galleys to the Free Press by late December, although the book was not slated for publication for another nine months. During that time, the press sent out review copies, including one to Richard Howorth at Oxford's Square Books. When Brown saw the "badly uncorrected" version that Howorth had received, he was not happy: "It was too messy for me to want anybody at all to see it like that. The review copies should be in a lot better shape. Suffice it to say that they messed up the ms. in New York transferring it to another disk, lost all the italics and inserted hundreds of spaces that shouldn't have been there, and I had to copyedit it four times. Just when you think you've seen it all, you see something new. I hope we got it all right that last time."

The Rabbit Factory's official publication date was 9 September 2003, with an initial printing of thirty-five thousand hardback copies. Within a week, Brown embarked on a wide-ranging promotional tour. In September, he read and signed at Square Books before moving on to Austin, Texas; Memphis, Tennessee; Blythedale, Arkansas; Jekyll Island, Georgia (the Southeastern Booksellers Association trade show); Birmingham, Alabama; Jackson, Mississippi; Asheville, North Carolina; and Louisville and Lexington, Kentucky. October took him first to Atlanta and then Milledgeville, Georgia, where he read "A Roadside Resurrection" at a conference on Flannery O'Connor. According to conference organizer Sarah Gordon, Brown received roughly a seven-thousand-dollar appearance fee, which he said would allow him to buy a new guitar; in addition, traveling to Milledgeville would give him the chance to "visit some of his drinking buddies in Athens." The reading was a success, and many of the attendees, most of whom were academics, flocked to buy his books. Another conference planner, Bruce Gentry, recalled that Brown "gave a wonderful reading using an impressive speaking voice that made the different characters come alive for me." However, Gordon was disappointed that Brown made little effort to interact with either other writers or conference participants, describing him as "distant" and with "little to say to me or anybody. . . . He seemed distracted and somehow sad."

From Milledgeville, Brown traveled west to Seattle, Los Angeles, and San Francisco before heading back to Iowa City and Minneapolis, where he stayed an extra day to do a reading with musician Ben Weaver, whom Brown described as "simply one of the finest young singers and songwriters I've run into in years" (Kingsbury). Rick Bass had put Weaver and Brown in touch with each other a few years earlier, and Brown helped arrange an appearance for Weaver on Thacker Mountain Radio. According to Weaver, the two men "didn't meet face to face until after the show finished. He came backstage, and I won't forget his smile and how genuinely happy he seemed to be meeting me. He took me up to City Grocery, and then we had dinner at Ajax. Later we went to the show at Proud Larry's. I remember that he really wanted to make sure I had a good time. There was no bullshit about him like with other notable people I have met. When I came to his town it felt like he put his entire life on hold to show me around, to show me his town, to make me feel at home, and ensure a good time." The next day, Brown invited Weaver out to Tula, where they "had a low ride and talked about music and writers."

In Iowa City, Weaver and Brown performed together at what John Kenyon described as "a typical, dingy rock club with a two-foot-high stage at one end of a long room. . . . Weaver sat on a chair and played his guitar while Brown stood at a microphone and read. . . . Weaver would play a bit and then drop the volume to leave room for Brown to read, playing quietly behind him. It seemed fairly unrehearsed and folksy." Brown also came to Minneapolis, Weaver's home turf, where they performed together and Weaver took the opportunity to repay Brown's hospitality. The two men went "for a long drive along the

St. Croix River. [Brown] really loved that. We stopped at a bridge over-looking Taylor's Falls. He kept saying how beautiful it was. . . . [T]his waterfall that was essentially in the middle of the city, which I had seen countless times while growing [up] and held in no high esteem, he seemed to hold in the same light as the Grand Canyon."

After the appearances in the Midwest, Brown finished the book tour in New York City. Despite the rigors of the travel, Brown saw ben-efits to promotional tours: "It's real good to see people who have read your books again and again in other cities. You look forward to eating in favorite restaurants in Seattle, and giving a reading. . . . There's no telling who may show up. I've got friends all over, and they turn out when you hit their town. It's a wide world with a lot of good people in it" (Kingsbury).

In addition to Brown's personal appearances, the Free Press's pro-motional efforts for *The Rabbit Factory* included an extensive media campaign involving both radio and print. Before the book's publica-tion, advertisements ran in *Publishers Weekly*, the *New Yorker*, and the *New York Times Book Review*. Moreover, Brown signed "1700 sheets of paper for a signed edition of 1500 copies . . . to be sent to booksellers around the country."

Many reviewers compared *The Rabbit Factory* unfavorably with Brown's previous fiction. *Publishers Weekly* declared that "the book fails to deliver the punch of his earlier works" and labeled the charac-ters "self-absorbed and incessantly whiny, [with] their obsessive ram-bling thoughts . . . recounted in numbing detail." More favorably, the *Jackson Clarion-Ledger*'s Connor Ennis wrote, "With each new publica-tion, Brown seems to take more chances, challenging himself and his readers with increasingly complex plots, structures and narratives put forth with the same terse writing style that seems simplistic but often reveals itself as much more." *The Rabbit Factory* reminded Jeff Kunerth "what a great short-story writer Brown is. The book tells six stories at once, weaving back and forth as the novel unfolds. . . . The book is six short stories chopped into pieces and sewn back together in alternat-ing order" ("'Rabbit'"). Several reviewers noted the novel's cinematic quality, with both Ennis and John Freeman comparing *The Rabbit Fac-*

tory to Robert Altman's film, *Short Cuts*, an adaptation of Raymond Carver stories. Evan Gillespie compared Brown's work with the films not only of Altman but also of Quentin Tarantino.

The Rabbit Factory's reviewers put most emphasis on Brown's characters and the newfound humor he used in depicting them. According to Jay McDonald, Brown "shows hitherto unknown gifts for comic timing in this fast-paced black farce. The change in tone allows readers to enjoy Brown's unfailing ear for dialog and keen eye for life's absurdities without the emotional baggage of his earlier, darker fiction." Fred Grimm found the humor of the novel "strange" and "savage" yet full of "all manner of pathos" that the reader must confront "while struggling not to laugh." Brad Vice wrote that Brown's prose had always featured "a sly, comic undertow beneath the surface," but in *The Rabbit Factory*, "it becomes more urgent and engaging: one might call it mean-spirited if the reader did not identify so fully with the lusts and anxieties of each character" (M2).

Despite the book's unusual (for Brown) Memphis setting, nearly all of the dozen-plus characters have roots in North Mississippi. In the words of Pam Kingsbury, "Many of his characters grew up in the small towns along the Natchez Trace and migrated to Memphis is search of steady work, stable marriages, and middle-class lifestyles. Unfortunately, their urges for security never quite overcome the wanderlust inherent in their D.N.A. Each character when given a choice and/or a second chance, fumbles, goofs or blunders." Moreover, the characters "live on the fringes of acceptable society" and "seem largely unaware of the thriving mainstream around them" (Gillespie). Though "always searching for something better, they too often settle for something less. Their stories are about love and loss, and the sexual ache of the unsatisfied" (Kunerth, "'Rabbit'"). Brown draws only tentative connections among the characters, probably to make the point that each of us lives primarily in isolation. As Ennis wrote, "Brown's characters brush up against each other in bars, on the road, at work, and even during carjacking investigations. Some profoundly affect each other while others simply interact quickly and move on with their separate lives." Several reviewers, among them Ennis and Vice, found aspects of the novel uneven. In novelist Carolyn See's summation, "This is a strange novel. It has no plot. . . . There are no particular characters to talk about" (CO2).

The novel's central issues, as a reviewer for *Kirkus* wrote, are "relationships between people and animals and the hopes of both species that 'love is out there for everybody, if they could just find it'" (923). In Brown's words, "I think what I was trying to say was about the connections that hook people together, in some cases very tenuous connections" (Englander). But as Richard Gaughran points out, all of the characters suffer "physical limitations or deformities" that make connecting difficult (101). These liabilities also reflect human shortcomings, those weaknesses that clearly limit the options of humans and animals both in the novel and in the real world: Arthur is impotent; Helen is alcoholic; Miss Muffett lacks a leg; Mr. Hamburger has lost his penis to a post-hole digger; Wayne has chronic headaches; Merlot has "skinny legs"; Jada Pickett is aging and traumatized by the brutality she has experienced; Candy is barely alive; Bobby's disease-ridden monkey is near death; some of the lions on the Yocona farm lack legs; and the whale suffers an ultimately fatal injury. Such a catalog of impairment, simultaneously horrible and funny, is as applicable to the human condition as it is to Brown's animals.

Nevertheless, Brown's characters strive toward connection. Arthur hopes to reconnect with his wife, Helen, while she seeks sexual connection elsewhere. Eric seeks to recover a warm family life. Merlot and Penelope strive but fail to connect. Anjalee, like Brown's earlier creation, Fay, needs a financial connection, uses her body to survive, and ends up in deep trouble. Wayne Stubbock, the navy boxer, seeks union with Anjalee. And Miss Muffett has tried to connect with the human world in spite of her handicap. With the possible exceptions of Arthur and Eric and Anjalee and Wayne, however, none of Brown's characters connect. The characters' physical impairments represent the human inability that prohibits many people from connecting with others in meaningful and enduring ways. Brown's disaster-plagued vignettes seem to say that humans are destined to suffer physically, emotionally, and intellectually.

Brown personally found an antidote to life's bleakness in his work and in the pleasures of family life. With their children grown and married, Larry and Mary Annie Brown welcomed the arrival of their first granddaughter, Molly, born to Billy Ray and his wife, Paula, on 2 September 2002. In November of that year, he wrote to Rankin of visiting with his sister, Joy Brown Mooney, and other family members:

> I went over to my sister's today and had a bunch of good food, some of the best gravy I ever had my whole life, all my family was there, and then Billy Ray and Paula came in and brought Molly, and she was asleep, so I sat around waiting for her to wake up, which I knew she would when my little brother picked up her carrier and brought her in the kitchen and set her on the kitchen table right in the middle of everybody talking. And of course I didn't get to hold her when she woke up. Too many other people wanting to hold her. But that's okay. I see her over here five times a week. Which is pretty sweet since she's pretty sweet.
>
> This child has made a big difference in my life. She makes me want to do better. She certainly makes me very happy and grateful to be here and kind of finally makes me understand why I'm here. The great wheel of life. She knows me already. She smiles when she sees me. (Rankin Papers)

Though Brown did not like farming, he also took pleasure in Billy Ray's successes, answering enthusiastically when a member of the audience in Iowa City asked him to comment on the current state of the cattle business (Englander).

The year 2003 also saw Brown make several more unsuccessful attempts at working with Hollywood. For several years, musician Tim McGraw held an option to produce a film version of *Father and Son*, and McGraw's agent contacted Brown about helping McGraw write a book about fatherhood. Neither project came to fruition. Brown also began writing a screenplay for a movie about Hank Williams, of whom Brown had "always been a big fan" (Teresa Weaver Q4). Actor Billy Bob Thornton and director Ben Myron were planning the film and had contacted Brown about writing the script in 2001. He began writing it in January 2003, with hopes of finishing in ninety days. At the end of that period, however, he found that he "wasn't halfway through" (Fitten and Hetrick 187). Brown did extensive and time-consuming research and ended up working on the project "just about every night for eight months. It was the most intensive period of work that I've done in a long time, including finishing *The Rabbit Factory*. . . . My first draft, I turned in 548 pages. That's what I come up with. There will be two more drafts, and we'll size it down from there. It's supposed to be 120 ideally" (187–88). The movie was never made.

CHAPTER FOURTEEN

Writing and Building, 2004

In the fall of 2003, Larry Brown signed a new two-book contract with the Free Press that included a 1 October 2004 deadline for submitting the first book. Brown spent most of the following year at home in Lafayette County, writing the novel he planned to call *A Miracle of Catfish* and finishing his cabin. In the fall of 2003, he reflected, "Writing helps me stay straight. It gives me something to focus on every day, a place I gotta be, and I feel good about myself when I work steadily. If I don't work, I get down on myself. But there's other stuff I have to take care of, stuff around the house. I've got to bush-hog my pasture, and do all this physical labor all the time. I have to do some of that every day" (Teresa Weaver Q4).

In June 2004, Brown was "working hard, at all things. 400 pages into the novel" (e-mail to Orman Day). He interrupted his work to give a written interview to Orman Day, a former student of Brown's at Bread Loaf. Brown told Day that working-class literature was important "to document these lives and the times these people lived in and to tell who they were. To leave something indelible behind. To let people know other people they would never come to know personally in their lives. To let them know they are human beings just like everybody else" (195). Brown also related one of the downsides of fame: "I get all kinds of comments. I truly cannot remember how many times I've been told by somebody (always a woman) that she's my number one fan. Makes you think of [Stephen King's novel,] *Misery*, of course. I swear before God, I was in a mall parking lot in Jackson last weekend . . . when a woman in a white car slowed down, rolled down the window, and said, 'Brown, I'm your number one fan.' Don't know who in the hell she was" (195).

Brown finished the shack in early August 2004: soon thereafter, he wrote, "I moved a little furniture in and I've been enjoying working on the novel in longhand over there, then transcribing it [at his house] onto the computer. There's nothing but crickets and splashing fish and music I play to hear over there at Tula. It makes a tremendous difference. I made me a big NO VISITORS sign like the one Raymond Carver kept in his driveway, and hung it on a sawhorse. I turn it the other way if I'm just fishing. Company can come then. I'm enjoying entertaining friends over there already. All I have is candles to light it, but everybody agrees that the ambience is good."

Later in August, Silas House came to Oxford for a book signing and took the opportunity to visit with Brown. The two men "sat in City Grocery and drank a couple of beers before the reading," and they later "went back to the house and he had a big spread laid out for supper. Mary Annie was gone to Memphis for the day, but she had left some barbeque and coleslaw, so Larry got that out, and he opened a loaf of bread. . . . It was really moving to me, because I realized that he was feeding me, making sure I ate after my reading. About the time we finished eating, dusk moved in and Larry wanted to go out to Tula. So he put some Buds in a little cooler and we got in his little truck and headed over there." Listening to a Ben Weaver CD, Brown and House were "tooling along Hwy 334 on what must have been the hottest day of the year and all at once Larry just slammed on the brakes and came to a dead stop in the middle of the road. He peered out the windshield, nodding his chin toward the horizon, where the sunset was spread out red and orange. 'There really is something about the light in August,' he said, referring to the title of the Faulkner novel. 'Music like that and sky like that,' he said. 'Don't get no better, bro.'" The next month, Brown participated with Ellen Douglas and John Grisham in a "panel of readings and remarks" in honor of Square Books's twenty-fifth anniversary (Schechner).

In early October, Brown took another major break from writing when his daughter, LeAnne, married James Bradley Bonds. Mary Annie went to great lengths to plan the wedding, and the affair plunged the Brown household into chaos. Ben Weaver came to Oxford to perform shortly before the ceremony and asked if he could stay with the Browns since he had no money. Brown told Weaver that the demands of the wedding meant that they could not put him up but instead paid for the young musician's room at a local hotel. The day after Weaver's performance, Brown invited him out to Tula, and they went fishing and ate Mary Annie's fried chicken. The day ended with the two men sitting on the dock with Brown using a flashlight to read aloud from his new novel and from the Hank Williams script.

After the wedding, Brown immediately returned to his writing and construction projects. On 11 October, he wrote to Tom Rankin that he planned to improve the pond at Tula by pulling down a tree that had fallen on the levee "and excavate that cove some, over by the shack, over the winter. Make the water a little deeper there since that's where the deck will be" (Rankin Papers). Brown also included parts of his new manuscript, explaining to Rankin what he still planned to write and describing his overall vision for the novel: "I think I've figured out that the book is about the relationships parents have with children, and how varied they can be. . . . It's huge already and is going to be huger by the time I get done. I guess I'll get back to work writing the rest of it next week" (Rankin Papers).

On the evening of Tuesday, 23 November 2004, recalled Mary Annie Brown, "It was pouring down rain, really hard, and Larry decided he would cook hamburgers on the grill. And for some odd reason—I had never done it before—I went to Paula's and got Molly and brought her home with me—in the rain." Larry and his granddaughter played together for a while, and then he said, "'I know what you want,' and he went and got a bowl of ice cream and he fed her ice cream." After Mary Annie took Molly home, "Billy Ray stopped by, which was unusual. Then Larry and I went into the den and ate supper together. . . . Larry read the paper like he always did, and I sat there watching TV. He looked over at me and said, 'I just don't want to write tonight,' and I said, 'I don't want to sew.' That's what I would do while he was writing. . . . We sat on the love seat together, held hands, and watched *Law and Order*. About midnight he said, 'I'm ready to go to bed. . . . Life's good now, ain't it?'" Brown died of a heart attack the next morning, his death mirroring that of his father, Knox Brown, nearly forty years earlier.

Larry Brown had seldom mentioned his personal health in his many letters to his friends, and he rarely went to see doctors. But Rankin recalled that on one occasion in the late 1990s, he was dining with Larry and Mary Annie Brown when Larry began to experience chest pains so severe that had to leave the restaurant to lie down in the car. In a 2002 letter to Tim McLaurin, who was again suffering from cancer, Brown confessed that he had been hospitalized for two days because of

high blood pressure brought on by alcohol poisoning, and I've had it four or five times before, only they all thought it was a heart attack or a stroke.

It looked like it. I threw up, broke out in a cold sweat, got dizzy and disoriented, and in just a few minutes sweated through my underwear and t-shirt. It looked just like what happened to my daddy when he died. Except I didn't have any chest pain.

. . . I had an EKG run, an ultra-sound on my heart and carotid arteries, two MRIs, a CAT-scan, another EKG, a full chest X-ray, and then they put that isotope in my veins and hooked me up to a blood pressure monitor and stuck about eight wires on my chest and put me on the treadmill with the heart doctor lady standing right there watching me and they couldn't push my heart rate to 170 even with the machine running at 85%, which was a little job for me in my house shoes and pajamas, for several minutes, so I didn't have a heart attack, or a stroke, I have no blockages in my arteries, my chest and brain are clear, but my blood pressure did go that night to 199 over 115, which is getting up there kind of close to stroke country. He's got it down way low now and I have new medicine and some nerve pills too and I'm trying to quit smoking and have some stuff to help me with it and I guess since the booze finally landed me in the hospital for the first time I better lay that shit down, too, for good. (Rankin Papers)

Brown underwent another series of tests during the summer of 2004 but had received no negative reports.

According to Mary Annie, her husband had appeared unwell in photographs taken at LeAnne's wedding, but "mostly he just looked old, and he wasn't old." When Mary Annie and other family members read Larry's last journal, they learned that he had been experiencing chest pains in the days just before his death.

Brown's widow, children, mother, and siblings planned what Mary Annie later described as a "Larry funeral." The viewing took place on the evening of 26 November at the Coleman Funeral Home in Oxford, with a service the following afternoon at Yocona's New Prospect Baptist Church and burial on his cherished Tula property. When Jim Dees arrived at the viewing, "a fire truck was pulling out of the parking lot, E-2 painted on its side. The truck briefly sounded its siren as it left. Once inside . . . Blue Mountain blared from the speakers, then Slobberbone, then John Prine, then Robert Earl Keen, Bonnie Raitt" ("Long" 13). Katharine Walton, Brown's former publicist at Algonquin, attended the viewing alone, "the only person from book publishing that had come there that day," though Shannon Ravenel attended the following day's ceremonies. Walton "had known him for years—a decade—but I had never known any of the town people. It was odd. I was in this line that went all over . . . spilled out into the parking lot; it took an hour to get close to Mary Annie. . . . I had never met his mother, his brothers. . . . It was very moving."

The day of the funeral was "dark and foreboding, the smoky clouds churned low enough to touch and intermittent drizzle fell" (Dees, "Long" 13). With the church filled to capacity, the service began with Clint Jordan playing "Old Rugged Cross." A local minister, Donnie Bobo, gave the welcome and blessing, followed by tributes from Richard Howorth and Arliss Howard. After Mississippi musician Duff Dorrough performed "Take My Hand, Precious Lord," Mark Richard, Tom Rankin, and Clyde Edgerton spoke. The ceremony then closed with remarks by another local minister, James Richardson, and with Jordan's rendition of "Angels Flying Too Close to the Ground" (*In Memory*).

As the funeral procession made its way from Yocona to Tula, according to Dees, "Well over 100 cars with their lights on snaked through the winding road to Larry's land. After various curves, when a vantage point was achieved one could look back and see a truly epic sight: cars as far as the eye could see, reaching all the way out to the very end of the dark, rainy horizon. There was another sight one rarely sees anymore, people in the other lane pulled off to the side of the road in a show of respect" ("Long" 13). The graveside ceremony included a performance of "Amazing Grace" by Dorrough; a prayer by Brown's brother, Darrell; and "I'll Fly Away" performed by Dorrough and Jordan before concluding with "Taps." Carved into the back of his gravestone are the names of his children and grandchildren—Billy Ray and his daughters, Molly and Sarah, and son, Harris; Shane and his son, Maddux, and daughter, Rilee; LeAnne and her sons, Larry Miles (named in honor of her father and of Jonny Miles) and Preston McClain; and Jonny Miles, whom Larry Brown considered his son. When Miles learned that Mary Annie planned to include his name, he at first objected, but she, Billy Ray, Shane, and LeAnne insisted.

Gary Hawkins attended both the viewing and the burial. He recalled that he "tried to film the proceedings and the result was borderline disastrous. . . . Before the casket closed for the last time the family took turns saying goodbye, and when it came Mary Annie's turn I thought she was going to crawl in. I didn't dare lower the camera, that shield that abstracts even the coarsest grief. If I lowered it, I'd never get it back up, so I held it to my eye and framed the drenched gathering, listened to the hymns and then I saw, slightly out of focus, just over the umbrellas and across the pond, the roof of the Shack. I thought, This death came out of the blue, like wild coyotes" ("Just" 143).

The *Oxford Eagle* published front-page stories on Brown's death on 24 and 25 November. Writing in the *Memphis Commercial Appeal*, Fredric Koeppel, who previously had reviewed all of Brown's books, described his voice as "a blunt, sometimes brutal style of plainspoken lyricism" ("Oxford"). Adam Bernstein's 25 November *Washington Post* obituary identified Brown "as a writer of grim and Gothic fiction" (B6). The following day's *New York Times* carried a piece in which Edward Wyatt traced Brown's rise from firefighter to writer and mentioned the constant comparisons between Brown and Faulkner; Wyatt, however, believed that Brown's work was "perhaps better compared to Carver or Hemingway" (C6). National Public Radio and the University of Mississippi's student newspaper, the *Daily Mississippian*, also covered Brown's death.

People closer to Brown also made public statements regarding the loss. In the *Oxford Eagle*, Billy Ray Brown said that his father left behind his belief that "everybody deep down had a heart as good as his" (Schultz, "Larry Brown" A1). Shane Brown remembered that he "always thought I was on top of the world when he'd be up there reading in front of people. I would think, that's my dad" (A1). Ellen Douglas told the *Daily Mississippian*, "There was something wonderful about [Brown's] dry wit and humor. I enjoyed it and admired it. . . . He was good at what he did, and he was committed to it. He had certainly done well" (Newsom 7). Ron Shapiro, the former operator of Oxford's Hoka Theater, remembered Brown as "kind and really funny and always unpretentious. Even as he became so successful, he never changed" (7). Richard Howorth, Brown's close friend and advocate from the beginning, wrote that "Larry Brown was a great friend to Square Books and its booksellers, and he met and communicated with many of his grateful readers through the bookstore. Of all the writers who have been associated recently with this community, he was the one most deeply of it, and his work that most vividly and truthfully portrayed this place and its people. . . . Larry Brown's characters, for whom he elicited, no matter their ugliness or evil, such sympathy and understanding, were people we knew" ("Larry Brown").

Mary Annie Brown soon established the Larry Brown Creative Arts Award, bestowed annually on a student from Lafayette High School who shows special talent in creative writing. The 2006 issue of the *Yalobusha Review* was dedicated to Brown's memory. Among the pieces included were Barry Hannah's "Larry Brown: Passion to Brilliance" (later published as the foreword to *A Miracle of Catfish*), in which Hannah wrote, "Brown was an example of an *élan vital*, the creative force about which the philosopher Bergson wrote. . . . Passion begat brilliance in Larry Brown. . . . My throat is raw from teaching the life of Brown to students. Work work. The pleasure deeper than fun. It gets good when you turn pro" (11). Hannah added, "Not once did a bad word pass between us. There was no time for that. You always felt this with Larry, who considered himself a late bloomer, a late guest at the table" (10). In 2007, Hannah told novelist Steve Yarbrough, "'You know, I think I wrote better when he was around.'"

CHAPTER FIFTEEN

Remembering Larry and *A Miracle of Catfish,* 2004–2007

In the wake of Larry Brown's death, Mary Annie Brown sent the unfinished manuscript of *A Miracle of Catfish* to the Free Press via her late husband's agent, Liz Darhansoff. With the author unable to promote the book, the press was not enthusiastic about publishing the novel, and Mary Annie asked to have the manuscript returned. She began to think about submitting it to Shannon Ravenel: Mary Annie "just felt like with this book, Larry needed to go back home to Algonquin" (Watkins, "Editing" 2F). On 11 April 2005, after reading the manuscript, Ravenel e-mailed Darhansoff, "There's so much wonderful stuff in it that it makes me even sadder that he's dead and not able to give this novel its due. I believe this was a novel that meant a lot to him and that he was intent on putting a great deal of himself into the characters and into their lives in the part of the world he knew and loved and never cared to leave" (Algonquin Files). Ravenel hated the "silliness" of the chapter titles and felt that Brown had created them just to have fun as he wrote, but "what's not silly is the novel's overriding insistence on the importance of fatherhood." Each of the central characters "has some of Larry Brown in them and, for me, understanding that added stature to the book. . . . I think Larry was also writing a hymn to his corner of Mississippi and the life he had led there" (Algonquin Files). Ravenel suggested that Algonquin publish the novel as a work in progress.

During that spring, Mary Annie asked several of her husband's closest friends to go through his papers, an experience that Tom Rankin described as "difficult and strange at times, magical and incredibly revealing" (Rankin to SR, Algonquin Files). Among the items he found was a "little map of the landscape of the Miracle of Catfish," which he sent to Ravenel.

Brown's papers also contained what may have been Brown's earliest piece of nonfiction, a discovery that "totally floored" Jonny Miles (Watkins, "Editing" 2F). Brown had sent the essay to *Outdoor Life* in the early 1980s with a cover letter that read, "I don't know your editorial requirements or if you even print stories written by unpublished writers, but I am trying to get a start. This is not my first work, but it is the first true story I have written. If you like it, I have a large storehouse of memories that I can draw on for more interesting, sad or funny stories, all of which concern hunting and fishing" (N. White 9). *Outdoor Life* had not published the piece, but Miles submitted the story to *Field and Stream*, which published it as "The White Coon" in October 2006. In the story, Brown describes an incident that occurred when he was in high school and went coon hunting with a Tula man who had become one of his surrogate fathers: "I honestly believe I loved coonhunting as much as any man could. The voices of the dogs as they tore through a cotton patch or creek bottom, going all out, so close you could hear their bodies crashing through the brush, filled me with a thrill like no other endeavor, certainly not homework or school" (92) The two men treed three coons, one of them the white coon of the story's title. After Brown climbed the tree to dislodge the animals, he and the other man, Mr. Richard, decided to free the brown coons but allowed the dogs to kill the white coon, planning to keep the hide as a trophy. Since it was late at night, however, and the men had work and school the next morning, Brown dropped the corpse of the exotic coon into a "slough filled with icy black water" rather than carry it home. Brown reflected, "I don't suppose I'll ever be lucky enough to see another one like him because I don't figure God makes very many of his kind. But if I did, I wonder what I'd do this time. I like to think I'd turn my light off and carefully back down out of his way in the darkness, hoping he wouldn't jump out before I reached the ground. Maybe then the debt would be paid" (95). In October 2006, the American Society of Magazine Editors nominated "The White Coon" as one of the year's best pieces of sportswriting, and David Maraniss included the essay in the 2007 edition of *The Best American Sports Writing*.

During the spring of 2005, Mary Annie Brown and Darhansoff worked with the Free Press and Ravenel to transfer the publishing rights to *A Miracle of Catfish* to Algonquin. By 10 June, Ravenel e-mailed Mary Annie Brown, "All parties seem to be in agreement that Algonquin should publish it and that I should edit it. I won't try, of course, to . . . really change it. All I would do is cut it a bit to get rid of some repetition and the kind of stuff that gets into a first draft that the author means to fix before it comes out in print. It's still all a little fuzzy, but I think you can count on the novel being published by Algonquin" (Algonquin Files). After reading Ravenel's e-mail, Mary Annie "went out on the patio to think it over. I had a feeling come over me that this would be what Larry would want. It's really hard trying to make decisions for Larry. He was, as you know, very stubborn when it came to his work. My first priority is doing what I think Larry would want and I'm very positive he would want to be back with you and Algonquin" (Algonquin Files).

In July 2005, Algonquin owner Peter Workman agreed to publish *A Miracle of Catfish*, with Ravenel "overseeing and pulling it into shape"; he also "suggested an advance of around $10,000" (Elisabeth Scharlatt to SR, Algonquin Files). Moreover, Algonquin staffers believed that "if we can make something of the novel, and give a push to the paperbacks, then we might be able to make a case for doing something like a Larry Brown Reader down the road" (Elisabeth Scharlatt to SR, Algonquin Files).

Ravenel consulted with Algonquin cofounder Louis Rubin about editing the manuscript. Ravenel told Algonquin's managing editor, Brunson Hoole, that they had concluded "1) all I can do is cut; and 2) the cuts have to be indicated in the printed text" (Algonquin Files). She then began the process of cutting the 714-page manuscript to approximately 550 pages. Ravenel found the manuscript "beautifully conceived and written—perhaps the most stylistically successful of all Larry's books. But it needed tightening. There were a couple of characters who didn't seem to fill their weight either thematically or narratively and who appeared only once each. The decision to cut those was fairly easy." Ravenel also believed that Brown had extended numerous scenes "beyond their natural endings. Thinning those scenes was also easy and accounted for most of the cut pages in the end. Larry loved writing so much that he sometimes got into a groove and kept going just for the pure fun of it. He was used to my suggestions for thinning over-long scenes and didn't often balk. So I cut. And that was all I did." Ravenel believes that Brown "would have been mad at me because I cut one character . . . a fireman. He was only in there because he was a fireman. . . . It was all about him and his wife, their sex, and it was really Larry having a good time, so I cut it, and he would not have gone with me on that."

With only the first draft of the novel and Brown's sketchy notes on the last few chapters, Ravenel completed her final editing by early April 2006. She told Mary Annie that during the editing process, "I had Larry just behind me and talking in his quiet way in my ear. He grumbled a little bit every now and then about my cuts . . . but now that I've finished the work, I feel pretty comfortable that he would have approved most if not all the ones I've made" (Algonquin Files). She marked all of her deletions with bracketed ellipses. In addition to the cuts, Ravenel planned a few other changes: the inclusion of a tribute to Brown and of his map of the novel's setting as part of the front matter and of an editor's note; the removal of Brown's subtitle, "(or) Jimmy's Daddy Gave Him the Go-Kart"; the deletion of Brown's glib table of contents as well as all chapter titles within the body of the novel. She also inserted "a handful of single words where meanings were unclear, where I felt a word had been inadvertently left out," and made a few corrections in dialogue. And in response to Mary Annie's request, made in accordance with Brown's wishes, Ravenel added a special acknowledgment of Larry and Mary Annie's daughter-in-law, Paula Klepzig Brown, who had been instrumental in the creation of the character of Albert and had reviewed other parts of the manuscript for Brown.

Ravenel initially offered Brown's literary hero, Cormac McCarthy, three thousand dollars to write an introduction for *A Miracle of Catfish*. McCarthy refused, however, asserting that he had never written about another writer and still had no inclination to do so (SR to Liz Darhansoff, Algonquin Files). Miles suggested the use of Barry Hannah's tribute to Brown from the spring 2006 *Yalobusha Review*, and Hannah agreed (Jonny Miles to Liz Darhansoff, Algonquin Files). Miles also proposed that Algonquin/Workman solicit blurbs from musicians who had been Brown's friends—Robert Earl Keen, Tim McGraw, Alejandro Escovedo, Steve Earle, Tom Waits, Willie Nelson, and Bob Dylan (Jonny Miles to Liz Darhansoff, Algonquin Files). Ravenel contacted those musicians, but her efforts brought no responses, and she ultimately procured blurbs from Jim Harrison, John Grisham, Martin Clark, Charles Frazier, and Tom Franklin.

Algonquin/Workman decided to release the novel in March 2007, to coincide with the Oxford Conference for the Book dedicated to Brown's memory. As part of the press's advance promotion, Darhansoff presented the novel at the London Book Fair in March 2006. In addition, Algonquin publicity director Michael Taeckens issued a promotional packet that included photographs of the author, a brief biography, a sheet of comments on Brown's earlier works, and copies of obituaries of Brown that had appeared in the *Washington Post*, the *New York Times*, and *USA Today*. The publicity materials also announced that Bloodshot Records would be releasing *Just One More: A Musical Tribute to Larry Brown* in May 2007.

Algonquin teamed up with *Shelf-Awareness*, an online newsletter of the book trade, to stage a contest for booksellers that offered as a prize a trip to the Oxford Conference for the Book focusing on Brown. In addition to attending the conference, the winners received a food tour of Memphis; a visit to William Faulkner's home, Rowan Oak; a meal at one of Brown's favorite places, Taylor Grocery; and a guided tour of Brown's writing shack and a chance to fish on his pond.

When *A Miracle of Catfish* appeared in March 2007, it received reviews in the *New York Times Book Review*, *USA Today*, *Newsweek*, and the *Southern Review*, among other periodicals. Early sales for the novel were strong, with the book ranking fifth on the *New York Times* bestseller list for the week ending 21 April. However, according to Darhansoff, only 9,500 hardback copies sold; it has never been released in paperback, although it is available as an electronic download.

By and large, reviewers praised the novel. Several, including John

Railey and Mary Jane Park, lamented the fact that *A Miracle of Catfish* would be Brown's final work. Other commentators applauded Brown's characterizations: according to Edward Nawotka, Brown "generates tremendous pathos for his people, rendering them far more human than mere caricatures. He's equally adept at incorporating infrequent and surprising picaresque elements, especially in the form of anthropomorphized animals, such as a pair of crows that talk in African American patois, and a behemoth catfish named Ursula who shares Sharp's pond with 3,000 smaller catfish" (E-15). John Kenyon described Brown's characters as "three-dimensional" and felt that "their various motivations and interactions truly resonate" (review). In Park's view, "For the most part, Catfish is the story of men who do not always abide by traditional codes of honor and ethics. His female characters are as complex and as damaged."

Most reviewers sympathized with the bildungsroman hero, Jimmy, "a 9-year-old heartbreaker with rotten teeth and a good but confused heart" (Minzesheimer, "'Catfish'"). David Abrams saw Jimmy as "a naive dreamer who always looks on the sunny side of life even as he's literally being beaten down. He's a simple, almost unbelievably ignorant boy, but we're drawn to him, rotten teeth and all." Mary McCoy writes that "Jimmy's daddy takes sorry blood to a level far beyond any of Brown's previous characters. He fails at marriage, fatherhood, and work, but he's bad at his hobbies, too. What makes the character most pathetic is the fact he really *tries* to do well, particularly where Jimmy is concerned." He buys Jimmy a cheap go-cart but sells it without consulting his son. When he takes Jimmy to a "swap meet," Jimmy's daddy ends up with a DUI. Jimmy's daddy (the only name by which he is known) somewhat resembles Wade Jones, the unsavory father in Brown's earlier novel, *Joe*. Unlike Wade, however, Jimmy's daddy realizes and worries about his problems, though he can never produce the right solutions. In addition, Brown rarely takes readers inside Wade's sensibility, while much of the narration regarding Jimmy's daddy is interior: we see that he knows what he is and wants to change but lacks the intelligence and strength of will to improve his life or that of his son. Jimmy is a bit like Gary Jones in the earlier novel—a young boy of intelligence and potential. *A Miracle of Catfish* bears similarities to Faulkner's *The Hamlet*. Cortez Sharp is an updated Will Varner, Lucinda is a more sophisticated Eula, and Jimmy's daddy incorporates some of the worst qualities of the Snopeses. But Brown's final work is more hopeful; the characters' violent actions seem somehow offset by what Jimmy brings to the community and to the reader.

Like nearly all of Brown's fiction, *A Miracle of Catfish* explores relationships between parents and children. "Old Frank and Jesus" from *Facing the Music* features a father who believes that he has failed to raise his children properly. Walter James from *Dirty Work* has an unsettling relationship with his father. Leon Barlow in "92 Days" values writing over family. Joe Ransom in *Joe* has failed his own children but tries to atone by rescuing Gary Jones. Negative family issues lie at the core of *Father and Son*. Fay Jones in *Fay* seeks to find or create a positive family to compensate for the horrific one she has abandoned. Most of the characters in *The Rabbit Factory* search for the kind of connection a positive family provides. In *A Miracle of Catfish*, Brown examines the topic of fatherhood not only with regard to Jimmy and his father but also in the lives of Cortez Sharp and Cleve. Brown uses this variety of perspectives to make the point that age does not stifle the desire for life and family connection. Art Taylor pondered, "What does it mean to be a father? A husband? What are the responsibilities, and how should a man fulfill them? And what does it say about a man if he doesn't? . . . I think Brown has a real insight into such questions: a true and often uncomfortable grappling with those issues, sensitivity to examining such struggles (both internal and external) and their consequences, and a generosity in many cases toward the foibles and failures of his characters. It's hard to fault a writer with such a sense of humanity and the gift to articulate his vision of humanity on the page" ("Larry").

Some reviewers were less enthusiastic about the novel. Chris McCann was disturbed by the editing: "Ravenel affirms that she didn't cut anything essential. But what about the inessential? . . . Ravenel's ellipses are tantalizing and ultimately a bit frustrating."

Several other critics voiced reservations about the book. Gaylord Dold declared the "novel itself a failure, a book at once rambling, melodramatic and undisciplined. . . . [T]here is neither metaphysic nor transcendence . . . just big bad love, cold Budweiser and dirty finger-nails." According to Leonard Gill, the novel is too uncontrolled, with plot tangents left unresolved ("Loose"). Art Taylor wrote that the novel suffered from the same "overabundance of details and some degree of repetitiousness of actions and emotions" that characterized *Fay* ("Larry Brown's"). And Adam Sobsey asserted, "It's tempting to glamorize Brown. He was beloved of rock musicians and died young, like one; and, at least geographically and dipsomaniacally, he was the literary heir of William Faulkner." In Sobsey's view, however, Brown is not comparable in literary stature to Faulkner, Flannery O'Connor, or Walker Percy.

Brown undoubtedly would not have wanted *A Miracle of Catfish* published in this form. He would have spent at least another six months paring the manuscript and clarifying certain issues, ultimately producing a novel that is episodic like *The Rabbit Factory* but more cohesively constructed than that novel.

Since Brown's death, there have been two other attempts to bring his work to the screen. In 2006, director Terry Kinney and Steppenwolf Films made an eighteen-minute movie version of "Kubuku Rides (This Is It)" starring JoNell Kennedy as Angel, Morocco Omari as Alan, and Brandon Ratcliff as Randy. The actors, particularly Kennedy and Omari, are quite effective, but the story is told from the perspective of Randy, weakening the emotional impact of Angel's struggle. In the same year, Lionsgate Studio officially optioned *The Rabbit Factory*, but according to Darhansoff, the option expired with no film having been made. Also in 2006, Gary Hawkins added some new footage to *The Rough South of Larry Brown*, including an interview he conducted with Mary Annie Brown about ten months after her husband's death. Hawkins first showed the revised version of the film at the North Carolina Festival of the Book on 30 April 2006, with Mary Annie and Billy Ray Brown in attendance.

Brown was unquestionably a successful author, though he never achieved massive sales. As of 2001, Algonquin estimated that 7,000 copies of *Facing the Music* had been sold, as had 12,000 copies of *Big Bad Love*; 25,000 copies of *Dirty Work*, *Joe*, and *On Fire*; 28,000 copies of *Father and Son*; and 40,000 copies of *Fay* (Algonquin Files). According to Darhansoff, Brown's works have also been published in France, Britain, Sweden, Norway, Brazil, Holland, and Denmark.

Brown's writings have become increasingly accepted by the literary establishment and have consequently acquired more readers. In 2007, Jay Watson published *Conversations with Larry Brown*, a compilation of nearly every interview Brown gave about his life and work between 1998 and 2004. Brown talked extensively about his family history (though he ultimately became protective of his mother and siblings, who did not particularly like to be reminded of their rough early years), his years as a fireman and the other jobs he held, his love of his home area, and his determination to become a writer. In later interviews, he talked about his attempts to transform his land at Tula into a southern Walden and about his pride in his children. Taken as a whole, the interviews provide a full introduction to Brown and his writing, both fiction and nonfiction.

The March 2007 Oxford Conference for the Book represented another major step toward giving Brown the popular and academic recognition that his work deserves. In addition to members of Brown's family and his friends from Oxford, participants in the conference included his early teachers, Ellen Douglas and John Osier. Steve Yarbrough, Margaret Love Denman, and I talked about teaching Brown's work. Shannon Ravenel spoke about her relationship with Brown. And writers Clyde Edgerton, Rick Bass, Jill McCorkle, Kevin Canty, Andre Dubus III, William Gay, and Steven Rinella paid tribute to Brown, as did Brown's musician friends Robert Earl Keen, Bill Whitbeck, Alejandro Escovedo, Vic Chesnutt, Tim Lee, and Ben Weaver. Escovedo, Brent Best, Lee, Duff Dorrough, and Clint Jordan performed on Thacker Mountain Radio; that group, along with Keen, also performed at Proud Larry's. The conference included screenings of *Big Bad Love*, *The Rough South of Larry Brown* (revised version), *100 Proof*, and *The Rough South of Harry Crews* and drew filmmakers Richard Corley, Gary Hawkins, Arliss Howard, and Debra Winger to Oxford.

Just One More, the title for the tribute CD compiled by Tim Lee, came from a phrase Brown liked to use toward the end of a night out with friends—one more drink, one more cigarette, or one more song.

Lee wrote in the *Knoxville Voice* that he decided "that the greatest tribute anyone could pay to Larry would be a CD featuring some of his
friends, favorites, fans, and admirers. Surely it couldn't be that hard
to come up with an album's worth of material from all the folks he
knew and who knew him." Although the idea was embraced not only
by Mary Annie Brown but also by Rankin and by the musicians Lee
contacted, the project languished until the summer of 2006, when Lee
learned about the plans to honor Brown at the following year's Oxford
Conference for the Book. Rankin and Lee decided that the CD honor-
ing Brown's memory should come out at the same time as the conference. Over the next six months, the two men worked with Lee's wife,
Susan Baer Lee, and Jonny Miles to put together the eighteen-song
collection. Tim Lee told an interviewer, "The simple concept of this
disc was to put together a mix tape of sorts, the type of thing that
Larry would have enjoyed listening to as he drove his little truck into
the gloam with a cooler full of beer and an ass pocket of something
that burns a little bit on the way down" ("Bloodshot").

Cary Hudson submitted one of the first selections, "Song in C,"
which describes low riding through the countryside with Brown and
which Lee described as "set[ting] the tone for the project from the
onset." Other Mississippi musicians who appear on the CD include
Duff Dorrough and Tate Moore. Ben Weaver offered "Here's to My Disgrace," inspired by *Big Bad Love*, and Brent Best wrote "Robert Cole"
with Brown's "Boy and Dog" in mind. Caroline Herring added "Song
for Fay" after learning that one of her "CDs was in the stack next to
his computer when he died. . . . I thought that if he could write a short
story for my radio show [Thacker Mountain Radio], then I could write
a song for him" (Caligiuri). Other tracks include Scott Miller's "Thirsty
Fingers," Madison Smartt Bell's "Going Down with Larry Brown," Vic
Chesnutt's "Fish," Alejandro Escovedo's "Baby's Got New Plans" (which
had been one of Brown's favorites), and Robert Earl Keen's "Count-
ing on You." The album closes with "Don't Let the Door," which Brown
wrote and recorded with Clyde Edgerton's help a few years earlier.

Reviewers of the album saw *Just One More* as a fitting tribute to
Brown. Wayne Bledsoe described the compilation as "filled with music that is personable, human and instantly lovable—characteristics

attributed to Brown's writing and the author himself." Carolyn Espe wrote that the selections "interweave the genres of blues, folk and salt of the earth lyrics—seeming much like Brown's characters, who were honest and pained, but eternally real." Brown would have been moved by the songs and thrilled to have these singer-songwriters perform in his honor.

Brown's writings possess many features found in works by other southern authors. In *Billy Ray's Farm*, Brown writes that he and other southern writers "loved the land and the people we came from, and . . . our calling was to write about it as well as we could, to find our own voices through the years of learning, and to bring forth whole people whose lives surrounded us, whose stories were told by us, and who, for whatever length of time it took to compose a piece of fiction, *were* us" (37–38). Brown never tired "of seeing the seasons and the weather change over" (Ketchin, "Interview" 112). Throughout his life, he took great pleasure in driving through the Mississippi countryside: "I like to look at the trees and the ridges. I like to look at the crops. I like to see the hawks that are out hunting, and you see the rabbits, possum, armadillos. Everything else that's out crossing the road. It's just a very peaceful thing for me; it's just a sort of relaxation, recreation. I always got some music playing. I usually got some beer iced down in my cooler. And I just got this little circuit that I make. It's just about seven miles from my house to my other little place that I got over in Tula. And it's all through hills and wood, stuff like that. It's just a pleasant little drive. . . . I do it a couple of times a week" (Hawkins, unpublished interview). However, Brown also did not shy from depicting the negative changes that had come to his beloved region during his lifetime.

Furthermore, like other southern writers, Brown concerned himself with the importance of family, asserting that loyalty exists even among the most troubled families, such as that of Wade Jones and his abused children in *Joe*. But Brown showed family's importance among members of the lower class. William Faulkner's Flem Snopes, in contrast, has little family loyalty, willing to use his connections to advance his economic aims but unwilling to help family members in need. Moreover, although some reviewers have seen Brown's fiction as too brutal for women readers, his female characters are vital women able to make lives for themselves and their families in spite of poor health, alcoholic partners, and emotional deprivation. His admiration for strong women with extraordinary nurturing powers (often modeled on the two women he knew best, his mother, Leona Barlow Brown, and his wife, Mary Annie Coleman Brown) is apparent throughout his writing.

Southern writers have also inevitably taken on the question of race. Brown grew up in North Mississippi and Tennessee during the civil rights era, and his childhood gave him firsthand experience with racial prejudice. But his time in the U.S. Marines and his work with African Americans at the Oxford Fire Department helped make him more aware of racial injustice. He told Kay Bonetti, "There's one word that's not allowed to be said in my house, and all my children know what that word is. It was common when I was raised, but I said, 'I'm going to change things.' It was simply I think from getting older and getting out of here, and then coming back and seeing things don't have to be this way. Things can be okay. I met all these great black guys on the Fire Department that I worked with, all these guys I really cared about. I think it's just a process of growing and getting older and finding out about the world around you, getting educated" ("Larry Brown"). John Edmiston, who knew Brown when both were in the U.S. Marines, recalled that even at that time, Brown "did not carry the stereotypical racial attitudes . . . associated with a white male from Mississippi." Brown "always treated a person based upon the way they deported themselves and not on the color of their skin. The things that he stated in private conversations revealed that his open-mindedness about race was real." Somewhat like Flannery O'Connor, whose outlook on racial issues has recently received scrutiny (see Andrews; Fowler; O'Gorman; E. White; Whitt; Wray), Brown did not directly explore racial problems in his fiction. In his writings, whatever mars the lives of white characters—poverty, alcoholism, crime, war—also blights the lives of black characters. Brown's black characters are realistic inhabitants of rural Mississippi whose problems are not specifically related to their race.

Finally, as it is for many southern writers, Christianity is a component of Brown's fiction. He held "a very deep faith," even though he was no longer "a compulsive churchgoer" during his adulthood (Bonetti et al. 13). He possessed a "strong belief in God . . . that has gotten deeper over the years. It seems to have developed because of the suffering I see—of mine and others. I believe the suffering is here to make you stronger. See what you can endure" (Ketchin, "Interview" 130). This view accords with O'Connor's statement that "sickness before death is a very appropriate thing and I think those who don't have it miss one of God's mercies" (*Habit* 163). When asked whether he had experienced the emotional impact of personal salvation, Brown replied, "I've felt I've been saved many, many times. No joke" (Ketchin, "Interview" 131). Attending the funeral of a firefighter at a backwoods African American church, Brown was deeply moved when the women of the choir began "singing like angels . . . about Heaven and Jesus and the love of God, and the hair wants to go up on my neck because it is unearthly and beautiful and my ears love it like no singing I've ever heard" (*OF* 90). The titles of "Old Frank and Jesus" and "Samaritans," two stories in *Facing the Music*, point to their Christian content, and although none of Brown's six novels is directly Christian, elements of Christian morality inform all of them.

Brown saw himself as a craftsman, constantly striving to improve his work. In 2000, he said, "I do not see myself as naturally talented. Whatever talent I have has been developed through years of writing. I do not believe that anyone is born with a natural talent to write; I think it has to be developed" (Robinson). Brown also believed that "simple language is most effective" (Robinson) and that a writer needs to "hook your reader early" (Pond 68). Moreover, writers must always be concerned about the effect of their words on the reader: "I want him to be right in the middle. I want it to be like a movie he's watching in his head and I'm the one who's supplying the pictures. I want him to be seeing everything and visualize everything; and whatever happens, I want him to feel it as fully as he can, as much as black words on white paper will transmit that. I want it to be as strong as possible" (LaRue 52–53).

Brown developed definite ideas about his craft as a consequence of his own experience and of his interactions with other writers whom he admired. He came to define a writer as "somebody who tries to recreate human life on the page, as accurately as possible, in fiction. You're putting on an illusion. You're making the person forget he's reading. If you can pull that off, then you've succeeded" (Blanchard 17). He sought to "explore the inner strengths of people, and how much people can take and survive" and to draw readers "into situations that possibly they've never encountered and come away changed by what they've read" (Pond 67, 68). Brown's characters became friends to both the author and his readers. When he was conceiving and writing *Dirty Work*, for example, "Walter and Braiden lived in my head for about two and a half years and I knew the novel was finished when I had helped them as much as I could and there wasn't anything else I could do for them in the story. When the story was over I had to turn them loose, but it was like saying good-bye to two friends because they lived with me all that time. There wasn't a day that went by when I didn't think about them" (Manley 124). But he also believed that writers must restrain their feelings about their characters: "There are two ways you can go. You can be sentimental, or can be hard-hearted. The perfect place is right in the middle. You walk a fine line between weeping over stuff and turning a cold eye to it. You can't fool people. You have to be honest with them" (Bonetti et al. 249).

Brown gradually modified his initial belief that almost any young person with a genuine desire to write could succeed, realizing that in forging a writing career, talent was just as important as hard work: "I used to say that anybody could learn [how to write]. But I've kind of changed my opinion about that over the years, just because I've seen so many people go at it for so long and not be able to do anything with it. . . . It's hard to say what it takes. It's a matter of discipline and dedication, but sometimes that's not enough. I guess there has to be a combination of things, and talent has to be in there" (Teresa Weaver Q4). And, he recognized, even some talented writers would not succeed: "Not every kid has the determination and the discipline to sit down and write a bunch of novels that he or she knows are not going to be published. But that's what it takes, to write stuff and throw it away—to keep failing and to keep going at it" (Fitten and Hetrick 182).

Through his teaching, interviews, and other interactions with would-be authors, Brown sought to pass on the benefits of his apprenticeship and career: "I just try to give a little encouragement to young writers without taking them personally under my wing, although I have taken more than a few and tucked them under there already. But I try to do it in a way that gives them a realistic view of what they're facing if they want to be fiction writers. It is not easy, and I've seen people quit their jobs over it, then fail" (Kingsbury). He warned that the road toward success would inevitably include rejection and mistakes and that no shortcuts could be found:

> You have to learn to write fiction that grabs the reader by the throat and doesn't let him go until you're through with him.
>
> And the only way to do that is to sit down and spend years writing and failing and writing again.
>
> If you quit, nobody's ever going to hear from you. (Kingsbury)

One aspect of Brown's writing that he developed over the course of his career was narrative voice. In *Facing the Music* and *Big Bad Love*, Brown experimented with different approaches, including first-person narration, third-person limited perspective, and stream-of-consciousness narration, and in *Dirty Work*, he used a dual perspective that shows Faulkner's influence. By his final novels, Brown had settled on versions of a shifting third-person limited narration.

Other readers of Brown's work, including Matthew Guinn, have explored his use of literary naturalism. Whether that use is conscious or not remains debatable, primarily because the lives of Brown's characters seem naturalistic to educated readers. If the elements are there, they exist not because Brown intentionally set out to use literary naturalism but because his characters' lives resemble the lives of characters deliberately created by Frank Norris and other writers of literary naturalism.

Brown's work still has yet to receive the serious attention it merits, but his literary contributions will endure. His intelligence, his unique perspective, his precise use of language, and his sympathy with people from the lower strata of society enabled him to produce original, powerful, and substantial fiction and nonfiction. Author Lee Smith has said, "Larry gave a voice to a group of people in the South who have been stereotyped. He illuminated many, many lives of people who aren't writing their own stories" (O'Brient, "Appreciation" D1). Brown did not merely write about these people but wrote through them, thus achieving a reality that surpasses that of other southern writers who have tried to chronicle the lives and travails of the working class. Ultimately, he fulfilled the dream he expressed to Peter Applebome in 1990: he became known as Larry Brown, writer.

Appendix A: Poetry

Larry Brown wrote poems throughout his life, and the Brown Collections at the University of Mississippi contain about a dozen of his verse writings. In 1986, Brown said, "I never did really pay attention to poetry, and I really haven't read much of it until just the last few years. I still don't know enough about it to judge it, whether it's good or bad. I know that I like a lot of Raymond Carver's poetry, and Bukowski's poetry. It just strikes me as good" (Brown Collections). In 1994, Brown explained that he had never tried to publish any of his poetry because "I think it really has to be given the time that it deserves. I don't think that I'm a very good poet. I might have written a couple of halfway decent poems, but there's no way I'd call myself a poet because I've got so much respect for it. Poems are stories, but the poet has it down to its finest parts, to the most beautiful parts of the language" (Manley 123–24).

Sometime during his adult years, Brown wrote a poem about visiting the house where he and his family lived after their return to Tula in 1964.

Yellow Tiger

In the rooms of my old house
I stand with dust motes turned
the hushed bedroom of my youth
where Darrel [sic] and I slept
is smaller than it was
I guess it had grown in my memory
The kitchen is different now, the
Cabinets filled with moldy paper cups
mice pills

forgotten utensils
a broken toaster
old coffee cups I suddenly remember
I want to take it all up in my arms
and carry it home
keep it forever
and pass it on to my children
Here is the bed where mama cried so many nights
Here is the table where she laid the food
for all our hungry friends
The wallpaper is peeling
and everything must go
new tenants are coming in
Aunt Flossie said get what you want
and we select odd items
Little shakers of Morton salt
a favorite skillet
and there is one thing I must have
A small yellow ceramic tiger
forgotten until now
and suddenly back in a rush
broken,
and glued together,
he stood on every coffee table of my childhood
Broken maybe not in drunkenness
but probably so
and suddenly familiar
a monument from the past still living
in this dusty house
with the windows curtained against sunshine
for so many, so many years.
I stand gazing around
as drawers are pulled open
and cabinets looked into
and find a three piece bamboo fishing pole
that I tuck under my arm

My mother is here
much older than she was
my father gone all these many years
my own son older than I was
when I lived here
I pick up the magic tiger
and see his broken feet
the fine lines of glue
that make him whole again
He heard and saw every thing
that is too bad to tell
I carry him across the yard
and set him gently
in the floorboard of my truck
I look at the old house
and feel bad that strangers will come into it
replace the wallpaper
repair the porch
fill it with their own lives
It is mine
I want it to be mine
but it is not
and never has been
just a loan from a kind sister
when the children we were had no place to go
In there is the bed that held me
The beds that held all of us
when we were very different people
I don't want the chair Daddy sat in
when he started to die
The tiger and the fishing pole are enough
I take these small ruins
and go gladly with them,
in the sunlight
home

Appendix B: LB's Chicken Stew

This "recipe" is taken from a document in the Algonquin Files. It also appears in *Square Table*, published by the Yoknapatawpha Arts Council.

You get up early in the morning, about six. It's October, cool, the leaves on the maple are turning yellow. Some honkers may be howling down the early morning sky. Your two black iron pots are already sitting in the front yard on their little sawed-off-pieces-of-two-inch-galvanized-pipe legs, which raises their bellies off the ground just enough to let you shove a little firewood up under there, and also leaves room for a good bed of coals to build up later. You've made sure they're fairly level. The pots are freshly washed and the woodpile is piled. All you have to do at this point is light the wood and bring the water hose and have some coffee. It's too early for beer just yet. You'll have plenty of time for beer later. This day'll probably run about 20 hours.

You put about 20 gallons of water in each pot and now is a good time to get some breakfast, while you can't do anything else but wait for the water to boil. It'll take a while, so you've got time for pancakes and bacon if you want them. Nobody else in the house is up yet. Nobody else has to do anything yet.

After breakfast you take all the chickens and hens and dump them into the sink and cut them out of their plastic bags and open them up, get the little paper packets out of there, chunk everything inside them but the livers. Five whole hens or chickens go into each pot after the water gets to boiling. The idea now is to keep the fire really hot and make those pots rise to a rapid boil. You have to leave the chickens in until they're completely disintegrated. It'll be ten o'clock or so by then. Chicken parts and bones and skins will be rolling in a yellow foaming broth. Once that happens, you pull the wood back from the fire and just let the coals keep the broth hot.

It'll be past lunchtime by the time you pick through all the meat, all the bones, all the skin, all the inedible parts like the joints at the end of the drumsticks, the cartilage in the backbones, that weird-ass wedge-shaped tail part, who wants to eat that? All the meat and about half the skin goes into some clean trays. All the other stuff goes in the garbage. You might be having a beer after all this work. But it'll still be after four before anybody arrives. It's getting close to time for most of the work to start.

If you've got invited helper friends, they'll be there by then. Make sure you have plenty of lawn chairs in the yard. Music is good at this time, guitar playing not so good with those greasy fingers. But don't despair. There'll be plenty of time for fingerpicking later.

If you've got somebody to help you in the kitchen, she'll be working on slicing about 10 or 15 pounds of potatoes and cutting them into chunks, peeling and dicing 4 or 5 big white onions, slicing up 4 or 5 packs of carrots, and it's a lot easier to just get whole frozen okra to dump in later, 4 or 5 or 6 or 7 boxes of that, too. The rest of the stuff is in cans: whole peeled tomatoes, lima beans, kernel corn, English peas. All those cans have to be opened and brought outside, along with everything else. By now the meat is back in and you've built the fires back up but not as high as you had them when you were cooking the meat right off the bone. Just dump everything in, halving it between the two pots. If you have people who can't eat onions, like my mama, who taught me how to make this, you can leave one pot onion-free. It's pretty crucial to have enough tomatoes. You want it red. If it's not red, you've got to get some more tomatoes. If it's not red, it's not chicken stew.

So you let everything cook for a while. You put some Cajun seasoning in it. Tony Chachere's is good. Everything will be cooking together, and it'll be getting on up in the afternoon a little. A few guests might start arriving early, but you'll hopefully have all the coolers full of beer by then.

All this time, while all this has been going on, or ever since you dumped the meat and skin back in, somebody has to have been standing there stirring both pots with a long-handled wooden paddle to keep it from sticking. This is very important and requires the full-time services of an invited helper friend, who can be paid with beer and cornbread or crackers and a few bowls of steaming stew and perhaps a few quarts of it to take home. You wish you could extend this last courtesy to each and every guest, but that would require buying about 200 Ball fruit jars and then giving them all away. Not to mention having to fill them all up.

So along about now everything should be smoking. Invited helpers have set up the tables and chairs, and have spread tablecloths to hold the crackers and plates of cornbread and cakes and cookies and pies the guests will be bringing to the feast. You might want to run inside and change clothes now, while you still have a chance.

Back in the yard in clean duds, a few people have gathered around the pots to witness the transformation. All day long it's been a thin and chunky boiling red combination of vegetables and meat, well, fruit too if you want to count the tomatoes, but along in here at a point in time that's hard to define, but easy to see, the ingredients in the pot somehow come together and maybe meld their molecules or something and they go from being 40 gallons of chicken soup to 40 gallons of chicken stew. It thickens. When it thickens, it's done. A few taste tests are in order and you have to be careful not to burn your lips and tongue, because it is very hot when it comes out of that iron. If it needs any more seasoning, now's the time to do it. You can pull most of the fire back, and just leave a few coals under it. But somebody has to keep stirring.

The sun's hanging low in the sky when the first of the cars and pickups and vans and SUV's start coming up the driveway. Soon the yard will fill with 200 people, and guitars will be hauled out, and friends will laugh and talk and visit, and, most importantly, eat together.

Appendix C: "Larry's Catfish," by Clyde Edgerton

Clyde Edgerton wrote a song, "Larry's Catfish," that commemorates his last visit with his longtime friend at Tula.

Larry's Catfish

Down in Tula, Mississippi, where the heads are hard
Sits a one-room cabin with a catfish pond in the yard.
The cabin was built by a good man, a man who wrote things down,
A man who loved his catfish; his name was Larry Brown.

Larry fed his catfish dog food and now they get to barking at night.
Some crawl up on the dam and howl in the moonlight;
Oh, how they howl in the moonlight!

Now there's a spot beside the cabin, over where the ground is bare
And there on blue moon nights, you can see Larry rockin' in a rockin' chair.
He points with a cigarette, in his hand, down to the dam
And there amongst the catfish, by God, it's his little dog Sam.

Oh Larry fed his catfish dog food and now they get to barkin' at night.
Some crawl up on the dam and howl in the moonlight;
Oh, how they howl in the moonlight!

If one night down in Mississippi, you're haulin' a heavy load,
Cut your lights and by the moonlight, pull your car to the side of the road.
You might hear a lonesome sound, a sound that's brown and blue
But sometimes the sound is funny cause Larry he howls, too.

Oh, Larry fed his catfish dog food and now they get to barkin' at night.
Some crawl up on the dam and howl in the moonlight;
Oh, how they howl, oh, how they howl, Oh, how they howl in the moonlight!

Sources

I have conducted the following interviews and correspondence with Brown, members of his, family, and his friends and associates. Unless otherwise indicated, all reminiscences regarding Brown are taken from those sources.

Abadie, Ann. Interviews, 13 July 2005, 21 June 2006, 28 March 2007.

Bass, Rick. E-mail interview, 3 June 2008.

Benedict, Pinckney. E-mail interview, 19 December 2006.

Benson, Lafe. E-mail interview, 22 August 2007; e-mail, 6 July 2008.

Brown, Billy Ray. Interview, 17 December 2008.

Brown, Larry. Letters, 12 July 2000, 3 April, 8 August 2001, 11 August, 23 December 2002, 6 June 2003, 6, 21 August 2004.

Brown, Larry, and Mary Annie Brown. E-mail interview, 21 August 2004.

Brown, Leona Barlow. Interviews, 26 March 2007, 6 June 2008.

Brown, Mary Annie. E-mails, 10 October, 20 November 2008, 8 January 2009, 19 January, 3 May 2010; interviews, 12 July 2005, 27 March 2007.

Brown, Paula Klepzig. Interview, 17 December 2008.

Brown, Shane. Interview, 15 December 2008.

Budy, Andrea Hollander. E-mail interview, 7–8 December 2006.

Canty, Kevin. Interview, 23 March 2007.

Coleman, Paul. Conversation, 26 March 2007.

Corban, LeAnne Brown. Interview, 19 December 2008.

Darhansoff, Liz. E-mail interview, 11 October 2009.

Day, Orman P. E-mails, 29, 31 December 2006.

Douglas, Ellen. Interview, 21 June 2006.

Earling, Debra Magpie. E-mails, 28 January, 22 February 2009.

Edgerton, Clyde. E-mail interview, 4 September 2007; e-mails, 23 January,

9 April, 8, 17, 22 June, 9, 14 July, 7 February, 7 July, 9 August 2008, 26 March, 14 April, 13 May 2009, 19 January, 31 May 2010.

Edmiston, John B. E-mail interview, 1 June 2009.

Evans, John. Interview, 7 June 2008.

Fitts, Dorothy. E-mails, 12, 13 October 2006, 16, 18 March 2007, 22 July 2008; interview, 6 June 2008.

Foster, Mike. Conversation, 26 March 2007.

Gentry, Marshall Bruce. E-mail, 22 August 2007.

Gordon, Sarah. E-mail, 16 June 2008.

Grisham, John. Interview, 27 August 2009.

Hannah, Barry. Interview, July 2006.

Hawkins, Gary. E-mails, 30 October, 11 November 2006, 7 June, 1, 8, 17 July 2007, 20, 21 January, 1 June 2010; interview, 24 January 2007.

Hewlett, Lynn. Interview, 16 November 2006.

House, Silas. E-mail interview, 8 October 2009.

Howorth, Lisa. Interview, 27 October 2006.

Howorth, Richard. Interviews, 13 July 2005, 27 October 2006.

Kehoe, George. Interviews, 17 November 2006, 20 February 2007.

Kenyon, John. E-mails, 3, 5, 17 March 2008.

McCorkle, Jill. E-mail, 21 June 2008.

Miles, Jonathan. E-mails, 27 July 2009, 31 August 2009; Interview, 25 July 2008.

Miller, Scott. E-mail, 3 October 2008.

Moser, Barry. E-mail, 11 May 2008; interview, 2 April 2008.

Moses, John Taylor. Interview, 28 September 2007.

Nordan, Lewis. E-mails, 21, 22 July 2008.

Odell, Anne. Interview, 25 October 2006.

Pace, Patsy Clark. Interview, 14 July 2005.

Panning, Anne. E-mail interview, 30 November 2006.

Rankin, Tom. E-mail, 16 June 2008; interview, 10 June 2008.

Ravenel, Shannon. Interview, 22 January 2007.

Rinella, Steven. Conversation, 23 March 2007.

Rubin, Louis D., Jr. E-mail, 13 July 2008.

Tutor, Glennray. Interviews, 20 June, 27 October 2006.

Walton, Katherine. Interview, 23 January 2007.

Weaver, Ben. E-mail interview, 20 March 2009.

Wilson, Jenny. Interview, 26 March 2007.
Yarbrough, Steve. Interview, 24 March 2007.

I have also used the following collections of documents.

Algonquin Books. Files. Chapel Hill, North Carolina (abbreviated in text as Algonquin Files)
Larry Brown Collections (MUM00049 and MUM00051). Department of Archives and Special Collections, J. D. Williams Library, University of Mississippi, Oxford (abbreviated in text as Brown Collections)

With the exception of "All God's Children," which Brown burned, copies of all of Brown's unpublished novels and many of his unpublished stories are in the Larry Brown Collections at the University of Mississippi. Unless otherwise noted, the collections are also the source of all other unpublished writings by Brown, including poems and his journal from Bowling Green. "And How Are You," the unpublished story Brown wrote with Clyde Edgerton, is in Folder 1114, Clyde Edgerton Papers, 1918–2004, Collection 04616, Southern Historical Collection, University of North Carolina at Chapel Hill. A copy of Brown's speech at the 13 April 1997 dedication of the Oxford–Lafayette County Library is available in the library's Mississippi Writers Room.

The following people allowed me access to their personal collections of documents relating to Larry Brown:

Leona B. Brown, Yocona, Mississippi
Clyde Edgerton, Wilmington, North Carolina
Gary Hawkins, Thomasville, North Carolina
Anne Odell, Oxford, Mississippi
Tom Rankin, Durham, North Carolina
Glennray Tutor, Oxford, Mississippi

The following abbreviations appear in the text citations.

BBL   *Big Bad Love*
BRF   *Billy Ray's Farm*

FM	*Facing the Music*
JM	Jake Mills
LB	Larry Brown
LS	*A Late Start*
OF	*On Fire*
RS	Hawkins, *Rough South*
SR	Shannon Ravenel

Published Works by Larry Brown

"And Another Thing." In *Reb Fiction '90*, ed. Barry Hannah, 7–11. Oxford, Miss.: Southern Reader, 1990.

"Big Bad Love." *Big Bad Love Online*. Web site no longer available.

"Big Bad Love." *Chattahoochee Review* 10.1 (Fall 1989): 1–9.

"Billy Ray's Farm." *Oxford American*, May–June 1995, 98–113.

Billy Ray's Farm: Essays from a Place Called Tula. Chapel Hill: Algonquin/Workman, 2001.

"A Birthday Party." *Southern Review* 28 (Autumn 1992): 715–22.

"Boy and Dog." *Fiction International* 15.2 (Fall 1984): 1–8.

"By the Pond." *Glamour*, October 1995, 254.

"Chattanooga Nights." *Chattahoochee Review*, Fall 1996, 33–37.

"The Crying." In *Reb Fiction '90*, ed. Barry Hannah, 155–67. Oxford, Miss.: Southern Reader, 1990.

Dirty Work. Chapel Hill: Algonquin/Workman, 1989.

"Discipline." In *They Write among Us: New Stories and Essays from the Best of Oxford Writers*, ed. Jim Dees, 177–90. Oxford, Miss.: Jefferson Press, 2003.

"Facing the Music." *Mississippi Review*, Fall–Winter 1986, 21–26. Rpt. in *New American Short Stories*, ed. Gloria Norris. New York: New American Library, 1989.

Facing the Music. Chapel Hill: Algonquin, 1988.

Father and Son. Chapel Hill: Algonquin/Workman, 1996.

"Faulkner's Legacy in Oxford, MS." *Algonkian*, June 1996.

Fay. Chapel Hill: Algonquin/Workman, 2000.

"A Fireman's Sketches." *North American Review*, November–December 1993, 38–44.

"Fire Notes." *Oxford American*, Spring 1992, 15–22.

"Fishing with Charlie." *Oxford American*, Summer 1999, 52–53.

Foreword to *Faulkner's World: The Photographs of Martin J. Dain*, ed. Tom Rankin, 7–8. Jackson: University Press of Mississippi, 1997.

Foreword to "Photographs by Tom Rankin." *Oxford American* 3 (1993): 27.

"The Baby Goat Murders." *Men's Journal*, July 2000, 86–90.

(with Liz Darhansoff, Richard Howorth, Shannon Ravenel, and Ina Stern) "'Go, Little Book . . .': Getting a Book to Readers." *Publishing Research Quarterly* 9.4 (1993–94): 41–52.

"Harry Crews: Mentor and Friend." *Southern Quarterly*, Fall 1998, 8–13. "Interview." In Barbara Shoup and Margaret Love Denman, *Novel Ideas: Contemporary Authors Share the Creative Process*, 83–96. Indianapolis: Alpha, 2001.

"Interview: Larry Brown." In Kay Bonetti et al., *Conversations with American Novelists*, 234–53. Columbia: University of Missouri Press, 1997.

Joe. Chapel Hill: Algonquin/Workman, 1991.

"King of Y'allternative." *Oxford American*, July–August 2000, 40.

"Kubuku Rides (This Is It)." *Greensboro Review* 43 (Winter 1987–88): 3–16. Rpt. in *Best American Short Stories*, ed. Margaret Atwood and Shannon Ravenel, 60–74. New York: Houghton Mifflin, 1989.

"Larry Brown: A Conversation with Kay Bonetti" (audiotape). Columbia, Mo.: American Audio Prose, 1995.

A Late Start. Chapel Hill: Algonquin, 1989.

"LB's Chicken Stew." In *Square Table*, 122–23. Oxford, Miss.: Yoknapatawpha Arts Council, 2005.

Liner Notes. *Homegrown*, by Blue Mountain. Roadrunner, 1996.

Liner Notes. *Shake Hands with Shorty*, by the North Mississippi All Stars. Tone-Cool Records, 2000.

"Little Big Band." *Oxford Town*, 18–24 June 1998, 9.

"Merry Christmas, Scotty." *Oxford Town*, 23–30 December 1998, 4–7. Rpt. in *Christmas in the South: Holiday Stories from the South's Best Writers*, ed. Charline McCord, 213–24. Chapel Hill: Algonquin, 2004.

A Miracle of Catfish. Chapel Hill: Algonquin/Workman, 2007.

"Nightmare." *Twilight Zone* 4.6 (January–February 1985): 91–92.

On Fire: A Personal Account of Life and Death and Choices. Chapel Hill: Algonquin/Workman, 1994.

"Plant Growin' Problems." *Easyrider*, June 1982, 12, 84–93.

"Preface: Home of My Father, and Grandfathers, and Great-Grandfathers."
In *New Stories from the South*, ed. Shannon Ravenel, vii–xii. Chapel Hill:
Algonquin, 2002.

The Rabbit Factory. New York: Free Press, 2003.

"Remembering Tim: Friends and Family Recall One of the Literary Community's Most Beloved and Colorful Figures." *Indyweek*, 24 July 2002. http://
www.indyweek.com/indyweek/remembering-tim/Content?oid=1187035.

"The Rich." *Mississippi Review* 13.3 (1985): 28–32.

"A Roadside Resurrection." *Paris Review* 33 (1991): 12–39. Rpt. in *The Christ-
Haunted Landscape: Faith and Doubt in Southern Fiction*, ed. Susan Ketchin,
102–25. Jackson: University Press of Mississippi, 1994; and in *Stories from
the Blue Moon Café II*, ed. Sonny Brewer, 5–29. San Francisco: MacAdam/
Cage, 2003.

"Samaritans." *St. Andrews Review* 34 (1988): 3–10.

"Sleep." *Carolina Quarterly* 42.1 (1989): 62–64.

"So Much Fish, So Close to Home: An Improv." *Chattahoochee Review*, Winter
2001, 7–33.

"Southern Comfort." *Men's Journal*, May 2001, 49.

"Southern Genius, the New Breed." *Oxford Town*, 25 September–1 October
1997, 11.

"Southern Women We Love: Shannon Ravenel." *Oxford American*, March–
May 1999, 26.

"The Special Breed." *Men's Journal*, November 2001, 84.

"Thicker Than Blood." *Outside*, August 1999, 60–62.

"Tim." In "A Tribute to . . . Tim McLaurin," comp. Joe Mandel. *Pembroke Magazine* 36 (2004): 67–68.

"Tiny Love." In *Writer's Harvest*, ed. William H. Shore, 154–79. San Diego:
Harcourt Brace, 1994.

"A Tribute to William Faulkner." In *Faulkner at 100: Retrospect and Prospect*,
ed. Donald M. Kartiganer and Ann J. Abadie, 267–71. Jackson: University
Press of Mississippi, 2000.

"The Whale Road." *Southern Review* 38.4 (September 2002): 794–808.

"The White Coon." *Field and Stream*, October 2006, 90–95. Rpt. in *The Best
American Sports Writing 2007*, ed. David Maraniss, 1–6. Boston: Houghton
Mifflin: 2007.

"The Whole World's out There to Write About." *No Depression*, July–August
2001, 94–105.

"The Whore in Me." *AOL: The Book Report*. No longer available.

Wings. In *Mississippi Writers: An Anthology*, 4th ed., ed. Dorothy Abbott, 48–94. Jackson: University Press of Mississippi, 1991.

"The Writing Life." Thomas Wolfe Prize and Lecture, University of North Carolina, Chapel Hill, 2 October 2001. Available on DVD.

Other Sources

Abrams, David. "A Long Goodbye." Rev. of *A Miracle of Catfish*. *January Magazine*, May 2007. http://januarymagazine.com/fiction/catfish.html.

"About the Author: Larry Brown." Algonquin Books of Chapel Hill Online. 1 February 2001.

Ackerman, Karl. Rev. of *On Fire*. *Smithsonian*, April 1994, 145.

Ahlport, Dan. "'Music' Is Vital, Entertaining." Rev. of *Facing the Music*. *Greensboro News and Record*, 8 January 1989, E5.

Andrews, Charles. "Colored Man: The Ambiguous White Male Body in 'Parker's Back.'" *Flannery O'Connor Review* 6 (2008): 70–80.

Applebome, Peter. "Larry Brown's Long, Hard Journey on the Road to Acclaim as a Writer." *New York Times*, 5 March 1990, B1.

Atkinson, Ted. "Redeeming Violence: Postmodern Masculinity in Larry Brown's *Father and Son*." Paper presented at the American Literature Association Conference, Boston, 26 May 2007.

Aumen, Adrian. "Brown's Literary Career Is Starting to Heat Up." *Oxford Scene*, 11 January 1990, 3.

Baker, Jeff. "The Rough South of Larry Brown (2002)." In "Thirteen Essential Southern Documentaries." *Oxford American* 42 (Winter 2002): 43.

Barnes, Allison. Rev. of *The Rabbit Factory*. *Southern Living*, October 2003, 56.

Barnett, Sheena. "Upcoming Album a Lovely Tribute to Larry Brown." *Scene: North Mississippi's Entertainment Guide*, 19–25 April 2007, 5E.

"Barry Hannah, Brad Watson, and Larry Brown: The Radio Session (1997)." In *Conversations with Larry Brown*, ed. Jay Watson, 124–46. Jackson: University Press of Mississippi, 2007.

Bass, Rick. "Foreword: A Tribute to Larry Brown." In *Larry Brown and the Blue-Collar South*, ed. Jean W. Cash and Keith Perry, vii–xvii. Jackson: University Press of Mississippi, 2008.

———. "Heart of Fire." Rev. of *Father and Son*. *Boston Globe*, 20 October 1996, M16–17.

————. "In the Hospital, Waiting for a Savior." Rev. of *Dirty Work*. *New York Times Book Review*, 1 October 1989, 15.

Bell, Madison Smartt. "He Could Stand the Heat." Rev. of *On Fire*. *New York Times Book Review*, 6 February 1994, 38.

Becker, William H. Rev. of *Dirty Work*, by Larry Brown, and *The Acquittal of God: A Theology for Vietnam Veterans*, by Uwe Siemon-Netto. *Theology Today* 47 (1990): 212–15.

Benson, Lafe. "Larry Brown—The Late and Great Southern American Writer." 11 April 2005. http://olelafe.blogspot.com/.

Bernstein, Adam. "Larry Brown, 53; Southern Novelist." *Washington Post*, 25 November 2004, B6.

Beuka, Robert A. "Larry Brown." In *Dictionary of Literary Biography*, vol. 234, *American Short-Story Writers since World War II*, ed. Patrick Meanor and Richard E. Lee, 57–63. New York: Gale, 2001.

Blakely, Diann. "Shades of Brown: Mississippi Writer's Latest Novel Affirms His Depth as a Story Teller." Rev. of *Fay*. *Nashville Scene Online*, 14 August 2000.

Blanchard, Charles. "Pulled Out of a Hat: An Interview with Larry Brown." *Oxford Town*, 11–17 September 2003, 16–17.

Bledsoe, Erik. "The Rise of the Southern Redneck and White Trash Writers." *Southern Cultures* 6.1 (2000): 68–90.

Bledsoe, Wayne. "Lees Had No Trouble Culling Artists for Tribute to Writer." *Knoxville News Online*, 20 May 2007.

"Bloodshot Records to Release 'Just One More,' a Musical Tribute to Larry Brown, Celebrating a Great American Writer." *Modern Guitars*, 1 February 2007.

Bonetti, Kay, et al. *Conversations with American Novelists*. Columbia: University of Missouri Press, 1997.

Bostick, Alan. "Southern Writer's 'Rough' Life Examined." *Nashville Tennessean Online*, 12 October 2002.

Boylan, Roger. Rev. of *Fay*. *Boston Review Online*, April–May 2000.

Brooks, Cleanth. *An Affair of Honor: Larry Brown's Joe*. Chapel Hill: Algonquin/Workman, 1991.

Brown, Billy Ray. "Remembering Larry Brown." Presentation at the Fourteenth Oxford Conference for the Book, University of Mississippi, Oxford, 22–24 March 2007. Available on DVD.

Brown, Dale. "Silas House: Incredibly Blessed." *Southern Ledger*, November 2006. www.southernledger.com. Rpt. as "Silas House, Ruralist." In *Conversations with American Writers: The Doubt, the Faith, and the In-Between*, ed. Dale Brown, 177–221. Grand Rapids, Mich.: Eerdmans, 2008.

Brown, Shane. "Larry Brown on Music." Presentation at the Fourteenth Oxford Conference for the Book, University of Mississippi, Oxford, 22–24 March 2007. Available on DVD.

Bussey, Jane. "Hitchhiking down 55 to a New Life." Rev. of *Fay*. *Miami Herald*, 23 April 2000, M10.

Caligiuri, Jim. "Earache! Austin Music Blog, 'Just One More.'" *Austin Chronicle Online*, 4 June 2007.

Campbell, McCoy. "Two War Veterans Form a Bond of Love." Rev. of *Dirty Work*. *Chattanooga Times*, 6 September 1989, G5.

Campbell, Steven. "The Larry Brown Interview." *Oxford Town*, 17–23 November 1994, 5, 8, 19.

———. "Larry Brown's Joe Comes to the Hoka Stage." *Oxford Town*, 17–23 November 1994, 4.

Canty, Kevin. "Larry Brown: Writers and Friends." Presentation at the Fourteenth Oxford Conference for the Book, University of Mississippi, Oxford, 22–24 March 2007. Available on DVD.

Cash, Jean W. "Combining Reality and Fiction: Gary Hawkins's *The Rough South of Larry Brown*." Paper presented at the annual meeting of the American Culture Association of the South/Popular Culture Association of the South, New Orleans, September 2004.

———. "Evangelical Fervor and Gothic Horror: Reflections of Flannery O'Connor in Larry Brown's 'A Roadside Resurrection.'" Paper presented at the annual meeting of the Philological Association of the Carolinas, Charleston, South Carolina, March 2001.

———. "Evangelical Fervor, Gothic Horror, and Redemption: Reflections of Flannery O'Connor in Larry Brown's Fiction." *Flannery O'Connor Review* 1 (2000–2001): 37–48.

———. "Larry Brown." In *Dictionary of Literary Biography*, vol. 292, *Twenty-first-Century American Novelists*, ed. Lisa Abney and Suzanne Disheroon Green, 24–33. New York: Gale, 2004.

———. "Larry Brown." In *The New Encyclopedia of Southern Culture*, ed. Charles Reagan Wilson, vol. 9, *Literature*, ed. M. Thomas Inge, 198–201. Chapel Hill: University of North Carolina Press, 2008.

———. "Larry Brown: A Rough Beginning." Paper presented at the annual meeting of the American Culture Association of the South/Popular Culture Association of the South, Savannah, October 2006.

———. "Larry Brown and Bruce Springsteen: The Dissolution of the Contemporary Family." Paper presented at the annual meeting of the American Culture Association of the South/Popular Culture Association of the South, Roanoke, Virginia, October 1999.

———. "Larry Brown and Music: I Don't Like to Write without It . . . .'" *Studies in American Culture* 33.1 (October 2010): 37–52. Shorter version also presented at the annual meeting of the American Culture Association of the South/Popular Culture Association of the South, Savannah, October 2010.

———. "Larry Brown and William Faulkner: A Shared Reverence for Rural Mississippi." Paper presented at the annual meeting of the American Culture Association of the South/Popular Culture Association of the South, Jacksonville, Florida, October 2005.

———. "Larry Brown as Creative Writing Teacher: 'I Gave It All I Had. That's the Only Way I Know How to Do It.'" Paper presented at the annual meeting of the American Culture Association of the South/Popular Culture Association of the South, Jacksonville, September 2007.

———. "Larry Brown: From Fireman to Literary Artist." Panel at the annual meeting of the College English Association, St. Louis, March 2008.

———. "Larry Brown: Humanity Overrides Race." Paper presented at the annual meeting of the Southwest/Texas Popular Culture Association/American Culture Association, Albuquerque, New Mexico, February 2002.

———. "Larry Brown: Voice of the Yeoman South." Paper presented at the annual meeting of the College English Association, Richmond, April 2004.

———. "Larry Brown's *Father and Son*: Food and Family." Paper presented at the annual meeting of the College English Association, Memphis, April 2001.

———. "Larry Brown's *Fay*." In *Still in Print: The Southern Novel Today*, ed. Jan Nordby Gretlund, 105–18. Columbia: University of South Carolina Press, 2010.

———. "Larry Brown's *Fay* and Defoe's *Moll Flanders*: Unlikely Feminist Heroines." Paper presented at the annual meeting of the Philological Association of the Carolinas, Myrtle Beach, South Carolina, March 2005.

———. "Larry Brown's Literary Apprenticeship—1980–1988." *Studies in American Culture* 30.1 (October 2007): 95–128.

———. Rev. of *A Miracle of Catfish*. *Studies in American Culture* 30.1 (October 2007): 162–65.

———. "Saving Them from Their Lives: Storytelling and Self-Fulfillment in *Big Bad Love*." In *Larry Brown and the Blue-Collar South*, ed. Jean W. Cash and Keith Perry, 36–48. Jackson: University Press of Mississippi, 2008.

———. "Teaching Larry Brown." Paper presented at the Oxford Conference for the Book, Oxford, Mississippi, March 2007.

———. "Two Biographies [Flannery O'Connor, Larry Brown], Different Approaches." Paper presented at the annual meeting of the American Literature Association, Boston, May 2009.

Cash, Jean W., and Keith Perry, eds. *Larry Brown and the Blue-Collar South*. Jackson: University Press of Mississippi, 2008.

"Casting Call for *Big Bad Love*." *Oxford Town*, 10–16 August 2000, 5.

Charbonneau, Jean. "Essay Collection Isn't Larry Brown at His Best." Rev. of *Billy Ray's Farm*. *Denver Post*, 16 April 2001, F5.

Childers, Doug. "Brown's Last Novel Appears, 3 Years after His Death." Rev. of *A Miracle of Catfish*. *Richmond Times-Dispatch*, 18 March 2007, 1.

Crews, Harry. "Perfectly Shaped Stones." Rev. of *Big Bad Love*. *Los Angeles Times*, 21 October 1990, 3.

Crowley, Brian E. "Larry Brown, Author of 'Joe' Provides a Literary Voice for the Poor." Rev. of *Joe*. *New York Times*, 30 September 1991.

Darhansoff, Liz. "Darhansoff, Verrill, Feldman, Highlights, London Book Fair, 2006." Web site no longer available.

Day, Orman P. "That Secret Code: Interview with Larry Brown, Dan Chaon, John McNally, Susan Straight." In *Conversations with Larry Brown*, ed. Jay Watson, 190–96. Jackson: University Press of Mississippi, 2007.

Dean, Darren. "Interview with Clyde Edgerton—Director's Cut." *The Rough South: Grit Lit Composition Online*, 29 August 2007. Web site no longer available.

"Debra Winger and Arliss Howard Named as 2005 Festival Guests." *Port Townsend Film Festival News Online*. August 2005. http://www.ptfilmfest.com/news/archive/2005.08.html#01.

Dees, Jim. "Bard of the Bottoms." *Oxford Town*, 19–25 September 1996, 14–15.

————. "Hometown Hero, Larry Brown Shucks Mountain Goat Meatballs for Southern Elevation." *Oxford Town*, 16–22 December 1999, 5.

————. "In Oxford, a Reverent Toast." *Oxford Eagle*, 25 September 1997, 1A, 16A.

————. Introduction to *They Write among Us*, ed. Jim Dees. Oxford, Miss.: Jefferson, 2003.

————. "Long Way Home: Larry's Light in the Darkness." *Oxford Town*, 2–8 December 2004, 12–15.

————. "The Rough Road of Larry Brown: Smith and Wesson Meets Smith and Corona." In *Conversations with Larry Brown*, ed. Jay Watson, 163–67. Jackson: University Press of Mississippi, 2007.

————. "UM names Brown Creative Writing Instructor." *Oxford Eagle*, 29 October 1997, 1A.

————. "Writers Series at Library Saturday, Jill McCorkle." *Oxford Eagle*, 21 September 1999, 1.

————. "Writers Series Kicks Off Saturday at Library." *Oxford Eagle*, 26 March 1999, 1, 20.

————. "Writers Series Welcomes Richard." *Oxford Eagle*, 20 May 1999, 1.

Deluca, Dan. "Author Larry Brown Goes and Stares at Human Fires." *Philadelphia Inquirer*, 18 April 2000, F1, F5.

Dewan, Shaila. "Long Way Home: A 'Rough South' Lion Honored in His Old Lair." *New York Times*, 26 March 2007.

Dickerson, James L. "America's 'Bad Boy Novelist' Enters Virgin Territory with *Fay*." *BookPage Online*. April 2000.

Dickie, Elizabeth D. "'Joe' Proves That Brown Just Keeps Getting Better." Rev. of *Joe. Richmond Times-Dispatch*, 3 November 1991, F4.

Dirga, Nik. "Cold Mountain Is a Breathtakingly Good First Novel." Rev. of *Cold Mountain*, by Charles Frazier. *Oxford Town*, 19–25 June 1997, 7–8.

Dold, Gaylord. "'Catfish' Is Not So Miraculous: The Late Larry Brown's Last Novel Is Rambling and Melodramatic." Rev. of *A Miracle of Catfish. Wichita Eagle*, 20 May 2007.

Donahoo, Robert. "Implicating the Reader: *Dirty Work* and the Burdens of Southern History." In *Larry Brown and the Blue-Collar South*, ed. Jean W. Cash and Keith Perry, 18–35. Jackson: University Press of Mississippi, 2008.

Douglas, Ellen. "Larry Brown: Friends and Writers." Presentation at the Fourteenth Oxford Conference for the Book, University of Mississippi, Oxford, 22–24 March 2007. Available on DVD.

Dufresne, John. "Hard Luck, Hard Living in Brown's Corner of the South." Rev. of *A Miracle of Catfish. Boston Globe*, 22 April 2007.

———. "Yearning for a Future." Rev. of *Fay. Boston Globe*, 26 March 2000, C1–2.

Ebert, Roger. Rev. of *Big Bad Love*, dir. Arliss Howard. *Chicago Sun-Times*, 15 March 2002.

Edgerton, Clyde. "Larry, Music, and Me." *Just One More*, liner notes. Bloodshot Records, 2007.

Englander, Julie. *Live from Prairie Lights* (interview with Larry Brown). 20 October 2003. http://www.prairielights.com.

Ennis, Connor. "Brown Returns with Violent, Bawdy Novel." Rev. of *The Rabbit Factory. Jackson (Mississippi) Clarion-Ledger*, 4 January 2004.

Escovedo, Alejandro. "Larry Brown on Music." Presentation at the Fourteenth Oxford Conference for the Book, University of Mississippi, Oxford, 22–24 March 2007. Available on DVD.

Espe, Carolyn. "Various Artists—Just One More: A Musical Tribute to Larry Brown." *Feminist Review Online*, 24 June 2007.

Farmer, Joy. "The Sound and the Fury of Larry Brown's 'Waiting for the Ladies.'" *Studies in Short Fiction* 29.3 (1992): 315–22.

Fisher, Ann H. Rev. of *Big Bad Love. Library Journal*, 1 August 1990, 139.

Fitten, Marc, and Lawrence Hetrick. "An Interview with Larry Brown—2003." In *Conversations with Larry Brown*, ed. Jay Watson, 180–89. Jackson: University Press of Mississippi, 2007.

Ford, Richard. *The Ultimate Good Luck*. 1981; New York: Vintage, 1986.

Foundas, Scott. "The Rough South of Larry Brown." *Variety*, 21 April 2002.

Fowler, Doreen. "Writing and Rewriting Race: Flannery O'Connor's 'The Geranium' and 'Judgment Day.'" *Flannery O'Connor Review* 2 (2003–4): 31–39.

Foyston, John. "Code for a Meandering Craftsman Writer: 'A Miracle of Catfish.'" Rev. of *A Miracle of Catfish. Oregonian*, 25 March 2007.

Freeland, Tom. "Alejandro Escovedo Brings the Tex-Soul to Double Decker." *Oxford Town*, 27 April–3 May 2000, 5.

Freeman, John. "Harebrained Ideas Hop into Sexy Story, Southern Characters Wonderfully Done." Rev. of *The Rabbit Factory. Denver Post*, 25 September 2003.

Gaughran, Richard. "*The Rabbit Factory*: Escaping the Isolation of the Cage." In *Larry Brown and the Blue-Collar South*, ed. Jean W. Cash and Keith Perry, 99–110. Jackson: University Press of Mississippi, 2008.

Geary, Robert F. "The Firehouse Bard." Rev. of *Joe*. *The World and I*, January 1992, 417–23.

Gill, Leonard. "Animal Planet: Taking a Beating in Memphis, in North Mississippi." *Memphis Flyer*, 17 September 2003.

———. "Loose Ends: Larry Brown: Down to the Finish." Rev. of *A Miracle of Catfish*. *Memphis: The City Magazine*, July 2007. http://www.memphismag azine.com/gyrobase/Magazine/Content?oid=oid%3A1341426.

Gillespie, Evan. Rev. of *The Rabbit Factory*. *Whatzup: Heartland Art, Entertainment, and Recreation*, 2004. http://www.whatzup.com/Features/br012204 .html.

Gingher, Marianne. "Sweet and Innocent." Rev. of *Fay*. *Raleigh (North Carolina) News and Observer*, 9 April 2000, 4G.

Glendenning, Karin. "Booklovers, Browsers, and Buyers Flock to Booksellers Convention." *Chattanooga News–Free Press*, 18 June 1989, L6–7.

———. "Mississippi Writer Larry Brown Hard at Work on New Novel." *Chattanooga Times Daily*, 7 February 1999.

Goodrich, Chris. "Books from Oxford and Algonquin Question Idea of a 'Good War.'" *Publishers Weekly*, 23 June 1989, 31–32.

Goolsby, Nina. "Local Author to Have Short Stories Printed." *Oxford Eagle*, 27 June 1988, 1.

Gray, Stanfield. "Barry and Larry: Local Scribes Read for Benefit." *Oxford Town*, 23–29 October 1997, 12.

———. "We Got Book: The Fifth Oxford Conference for the Book." *Oxford Town*, 12–18 March 1998, 10.

Gretlund, Jan Nordby. "The Man by the Jukebox: Larry Brown's Haunted Voices." In *Frames of the Southern Mind: Reflections on the Stoic, Bi-Racial, and Existential South*, ed. Jan Nordby Gretlund, 231–41. Odense, Denmark: Odense University Press, 1998.

Grimm, Fred. "Tall Tales, Sad Stories on Coffee Shop Menu." Rev. of *The Rabbit Factory*. *Miami Herald*, 7 September 2003.

Gross, Terry. *Fresh Air* (interview with Larry Brown). 1990. http://www.npr .org/player/v2/mediaPlayer.html?action=1&t=1&islist=false&id=4190546 &m=4190547.

Guinn, Matthew. *After Southern Modernism: Fiction of the Contemporary South.* Jackson: University Press of Mississippi, 2000.

Gurwitt, Rob. "Light in Oxford: How the Vision of One Independent Bookseller Has Revitalized the Heart of Faulkner's Mississippi." *Mother Jones,* May–June 2000.

Hahn, Tina. "Grishams Fund Two Programs for Southern Writers." *Southern Register,* Fall 1993, 15.

Hannah, Barry. "Larry Brown: Passion to Brilliance." *Yalobusha Review* 11 (2006): 9–12.

———. Preface to *Reb Fiction '90.* Oxford, Miss.: Southern Reader, 1990.

Hanson, Ron. Rev. of *Father and Son. America,* 5 April 1997, 32.

Harris, Chico. "Larry Brown, *On Fire*: A Personal Account of Life and Death and Choices." *Oxford Town,* 3–9 February 1994, 3, 5.

Harris, Jana. Rev. of *Facing the Music. Seattle Post-Intelligencer,* 8 January 1989, L7.

Hartlaub, Joe. "Interview with Larry Brown." *Bookreporter Online,* 28 April 2000. http://www.bookreporter.com/authors/au-brown-larry.asp.

———. Rev. of *Fay. Bookreporter Online,* 28 April 2000. http://www.bookreporter.com/reviews/0743205383.asp.

———. Rev. of *Billy Ray's Farm. Bookreporter Online,* 15 May 2001. http://www.bookreporter.com/reviews/0743225244.asp.

Harty, Kristen. "Down on the Farm." *Oxford Town,* 19–25 April 2001, 12–13.

Hawkins, Gary. Interview with Katherine Powell. In *Larry Brown and the Blue-Collar South,* ed. Jean W. Cash and Keith Perry, 157–73. Jackson: University Press of Mississippi, 2008.

———. "Just One More, Larry Brown (1951–2004)." *Oxford American,* Spring 2005, 138–43.

———. "Praise for the First Annual Oxford Film Festival (2003)." http://www.oxfordfilmfest.com/.

——— *The Rough South of Harry Crews* (VHS). Chapel Hill: North Carolina Public Television, 1991.

———. *The Rough South of Larry Brown* (DVD). Blue Moon Film Productions and Down Home Entertainment, 2002.

———. Unpublished interview with Larry Brown. October 1991. In possession of Gary Hawkins.

———. "What Makes a Movie Southern? Chicken House Cinema." *Oxford American*, Winter 2002, 24–33.

Herbst, Linda Peal. "The Larry Brown Writer's Series." *Oxford Eagle*, 4 March 1999, 8.

Hodges, Sam. Rev. of *Billy Ray's Farm*. *Bookreporter Online*, 15 May 2001.

———. "These Plot Twists Stretch Credibility." Rev. of *Dirty Work*. *Orlando Sentinel*, 17 September 1989.

Hoekstra, Dave. "Rhythm and Blues: Larry Brown Has Created a World Both Bleak and Lyrical." Rev. of *A Miracle of Catfish*. *Chicago Sun-Times*, 18 March 2007.

———. "Songwriters Sing Praises of Novelist's Lyrical Prose." *Chicago Sun-Times*, 27 May 2007.

Holditch, Kenneth. "A Mississippi Macho Man from Novelist Larry Brown." Rev. of *Joe*. *Chicago Tribune*, 29 September 1991, 4.

Holland, Gina. "Oxford Firefighter Writes Stories with Southern Flavor." *Memphis Commercial Appeal*, 30 October 1989, B3.

House, Silas. "On God's Creek." *A Country Boy Can Surmise*. 17 February 2008. http://silashouseblog.blogspot.com/2008/02/on-gods-creek_17.html.

———. "Remembering Larry." *Ace Weekly*, 2 December 2004.

———. "Remembering Larry Brown." *No Depression*, January–February 2005, 96.

Howard, Arliss, and Debra Winger. "Larry Brown on Stage and Screen." Presentation at the Fourteenth Oxford Conference for the Book, University of Mississippi, Oxford, 22–24 March 2007. Available on DVD.

Howorth, Richard. "Book Notes." *Oxford Town* 30 December–6 January 1993, 4.

———. "*Big Bad Love*." *Dear Reader*, 1990.

———. "Good Old Boys." Rev. of *Billy Ray's Farm*. *Dear Reader*, March–April 2001.

———. "Friday, March 24 Is *Fay* Day: Larry Brown Returns with Biggest, Best Novel Yet." *Dear Reader*, March–April 2000.

———. "Larry Brown, 1951–2004." *Dear Reader*, January–February 2005.

Hudson, Berkeley. "Country Boy Hits Big Time." *Los Angeles Times*, 17 September 1989, sec. 6, p. 1.

Huntley, Dan. "Billy Ray's Farm: Essays from a Place Called Tula." Rev. of *Billy Ray's Farm*. *Charlotte Observer*, 6 May 2001.

Hynes, James. "Southern Cross: In Rural Mississippi, a World of Anger and Loathing." Rev. of *Father and Son*. *Washington Post*, 26 September 1996, C2.

Ingram, Marit. Rev. of *A Miracle of Catfish*. *Austin (Texas) Chronicle*, 9 March 2007.

In Memory of William Larry Brown, July 9, 1951–November 24, 2004 (program). Coleman Funeral Home, Oxford, Miss. In possession of the author.

James, Susie. "Larry Brown Faces the Music." *Mississippi*, March–April 1989, 79–81.

Jennings, Jay. "Voice Lessons: Stories Capture Faces of the South." Rev. of *Facing the Music*. *Dallas Morning News*, 6 November 1988.

Johnson, Greg. "Stirring Story of Veterans' Painful Lives." Rev. of *Dirty Work*. *Atlanta Journal-Constitution*, 3 September 1989, L10.

———. "Strong Novel Charts a Formidable Terrain between Love and Hate." Rev. of *Father and Son*. *Atlanta Journal-Constitution*, 29 September 1996, L11.

Johnson, Jerry. "Larry Brown: Friends and Writers." Presentation at the Fourteenth Oxford Conference for the Book, University of Mississippi, Oxford, 22–24 March 2007. Available on DVD.

Jones, Suzanne. "Refighting Old Wars: Race Relations and Masculine Conventions in Fiction by Larry Brown and Madison Smartt Bell." In *The Southern State of Mind*, ed. Jan Nordby Gretlund, 107–20. Columbia: University of South Carolina Press, 1999.

Jubera, Drew. "Plodding 'Fay' Has Its Brilliant Moments." Rev. of *Fay*. *Atlanta Journal-Constitution*, 9 April 2000, L12.

Kaplan, Paul. Rev. of *Facing the Music*. *Library Journal*, 15 September 1988, 90.

Keen, Robert Earl. "Larry Brown on Music." Presentation at the Fourteenth Oxford Conference for the Book, University of Mississippi, Oxford, 22–24 March 2007. Available on DVD.

Kenyon, John. Interview with Shannon Ravenel. *Things I'd Rather Be Doing*. 30 April 2007. http://tirbd.com/category/larry-brown-week/.

———. Interview with Tim Lee. *Things I'd Rather Be Doing*. 3 May 2007. http://tirbd.com/category/larry-brown-week/.

———. Rev. of *A Miracle of Catfish*. 1 May 2007. http://tirbd.com/category/larry-brown-week/.

Ketchin, Susan. "Interview with Larry Brown." In *The Christ-Haunted Landscape: Faith and Doubt in Southern Fiction*, ed. Ketchin, 126–39. Jackson: University Press of Mississippi, 1994.

———. "Larry Brown: Proceeding Out from Calamity." In *The Christ-Haunted Landscape: Faith and Doubt in Southern Fiction*, ed. Ketchin, 100–101. Jackson: University Press of Mississippi, 1994.

Kimbrough, Kim. Rev. of *Fay*. *Harbinger Books* (Mobile, Alabama), 22 August 2000. http://www.theharbinger.org/xix/000822/kimbrough.html.

Kingsbury, Pam. "King of Grit Lit: An Interview with Larry Brown." *Southern Scribe*, September 2003. http://www.southernscribe.com/zine/authors/Brown_Larry.htm.

Kirn, Walter. "High, Hard One." Rev. of *Father and Son*. *New York*, 21 October 1996.

Klam, Matt. Rev. of *Big Bad Love*. *Hollins Critic* 29.3 (1992): 16.

"Klepzig, Brown to Wed June 24." *Oxford Eagle*, 7 June 2000, 3.

Klinkowitz, Jerome. "Generating the Story." Rev. of *Minimum of Two*, by Tim Winton; *The Coming Triumph of the Free World*, by Rick DeMarinis; *Moustapha's Eclipse*, by Reginald McKnight; and *Facing the Music*. *North American Review*, March 1989, 69–72.

Knutson, Karen. "Brown Crafts Tales of Mississippi Men." Rev. of *Big Bad Love*. *Arkansas Gazette*, 11 November 1990, 7G.

Koeppel, Fredric. "Art Redeems Tale of Squalor, Degradation." Rev. of *Joe*. *Memphis Commercial Appeal*, 22 September 1991.

———. "Author, His 'Tragedy' Springs from the Same North Miss. Turf." *Memphis Commercial Appeal*, 22 September 1991.

———. "Brown Tours with Rabbit Factory, Novel Set Partially in Memphis." *Memphis Commercial Appeal*, 14 September 2003.

———. "Craft Gives Way to Crassness in Brown's Latest." Rev. of *Fay*. *Memphis Commercial Appeal*, 2 April 2000, H3.

———. "Oxford Writer Larry Brown Dies of Heart Attack." *Memphis Commercial Appeal*, 25 November 2004.

Kornegay, Jamie. "Ninth Oxford Conference for the Book." *Southern Register*. Winter 2002. http://www.olemiss.edu/depts/south/register/winter02/cover.htm.

Kunerth, Jeff. "Brown Paints Fine Portraits in 'Father and Son.'" Rev. of *Father and Son*. *Chicago Tribune*, 9 October 1996, 5.

―――. "'Rabbit Factory' Greater Than the Sum of Its Novel." Rev. of *The Rabbit Factory*. *Milwaukee Journal-Sentinel*, 21 September 2003.

―――. "Writer Passionate about Mississippi Roots." Rev. of *Billy Ray's Farm*. *Orlando Sentinel*, 29 April 2001.

Laird, Jim. "'Fay Transcends Southern-Fried Sturm and Drang." Rev. of *Fay*. *Mississippi Business Journal*, 3 April 2000, 31.

"Larry Brown." *Contemporary Writers Online*. 2000. www.contemporarywrit ers.com/authors/larrybrown.

"Larry Brown Writer's Series, Tim McLaurin." *Oxford Town*, 17–23 August 2000, 5.

Larson, Susan. "Blood Simple." Rev. of *Father and Son*. *New Orleans Times-Picayune*, 6 October 1996, E7.

―――. "Keeper of the Flame." *New Orleans Times-Picayune*, 2 October 1996, E1–2.

LaRue, Dorie. "Interview with Larry Brown: Breadloaf 1992." In *Conversations with Larry Brown*, ed. Jay Watson, 45–61. Jackson: University Press of Mississippi, 2007.

Lee, Tim. "Just One More." *Knoxville Voice*, 8 February 2007.

Leighton, Betty. "No Faulkner: Strong Stories Show Dark, Partial View of Man." Rev. of *Facing the Music*. *Winston-Salem (North Carolina) Journal*, 8 January 1989, H4.

Lemire, Christy. "At the Most, 'Big Bad Love' Is Intoxicatingly Bad." *Seattle Post-Intelligencer*, 29 March 2002.

Levins, Harry. "Novel Provides an Interesting Look at Working-Class White Southerners." Rev. of *Fay*. *St. Louis Post-Dispatch*, 16 April 2000, F10.

―――. "This Year's Best Thriller Has Arrived." Rev. of *Father and Son*. *St. Louis Post-Dispatch*, 22 September 1996, C5.

Lewis, Graham. "Letters from Larry: A Memoir." *Agora*, February 2009. http://castle.eiu.edu/~agora/0902/larryall.htm.

Lowry, Beverly. "The One That Got Away." Rev. of *A Miracle of Catfish*. *New York Times Book Review*, 29 April 2007, 14.

Lyons, Gene. "Bad Behavior." Rev. of *Joe*. *Entertainment Weekly*, 4 October 1991, 56–57.

Lyons, Paul. "Larry Brown's *Joe* and the Uses and Abuses of the 'Region' Concept." *Studies in American Fiction* 25 (1997): 101–24.

Mabe, Chauncey. "Author's Post-Vietnam Novel Reflects Short-Story Style." Rev. of *Dirty Work*. *Fort Lauderdale Sun-Sentinel*, 24 December 1989, 1F, 2F.

Manley, Michael S. "Telling Stories: An Interview with Larry Brown" (1994). In *Conversations with Larry Brown*, ed. Jay Watson, 70–78. Jackson: University Press of Mississippi, 2007.

Mannes-Abbott, Guy. Rev. of *Dirty Work*. *New Statesman and Society* 3 August 1990, 46.

Mantell, Suzanne. "Larry Brown, Son of the Literary South." *Publishers Weekly*, 2 June 1997.

Martin, Philip. "Larry Brown's Big Bad Dream." Rev. of *Fay*. *Arkansas Democrat-Gazette*, 24 September 2000, 1E, 2E.

McCann, Chris. Rev. of *A Miracle of Catfish*. "New in Books." *Seattle Stranger*, 17 April 2007. http://www.thestranger.com/seattle/new-in-books/Content?oid=200911.

McCorkle, Jill. "In the Company of Louis Rubin." *The Journal* (National Book Critics Circle) 31.2 (2005). http://bookcritics.org/images/uploads/2005summer.pdf.

———. "Writers Remember Larry Brown." Presentation at the Fourteenth Oxford Conference for the Book, University of Mississippi, Oxford, 22–24 March 2007. Available on DVD.

McCoy, Mary. Rev. of *A Miracle of Catfish*. *PopMatters*, 7 May 2007. www.popmatters.com.

McDermid, Riley. "Clyde Edgerton to Conduct Writer's Workshop." *Oxford Town*, 21–27 September 2000, 8.

McDonald, Jay. "Comedy Springs from a Dark Place." Rev. of *The Rabbit Factory*. *Fort Myers News-Press*, 17 September 2003.

McKensie, Danny. "Oxford Writer Stays Same while Literary Fires Brightly Burn." *Jackson (Mississippi) Clarion-Ledger*, 6 February 1994, 1B.

McManus, Linda. "Larry Brown Puts Fire in His Fiction." Rev. of *Joe*. *South Bend (Indiana) Tribune*, n.d. Algonquin Books of Chapel Hill Records, 1982–2007. Collection 4736. Southern Historical Collection, University of North Carolina, Chapel Hill.

McMellon, Reba. "Posthumous Book Belongs with Classics of Southern Literature." Rev of *A Miracle of Catfish*. *Pascagoula Mississippi Press*, 1 April 2007.

Menconi, David. "Robert Earl Keen Sings of Cowboys, Onions." *Oakland Tribune*, 17 February 2004.

Miles, Jonathan. *Dear American Airlines*. Boston: Houghton Mifflin, 2008.

———. "The Deer, the Writer, and the Mississippi Gloam." *Sports Afield*, October 1998, 98+.

———. Interview. *Free Bird Books*, 19 August 2008. http://freebirdbooks-events.blogspot.com/.

———. "Larry Brown on Music." Presentation at the Fourteenth Oxford Conference for the Book, University of Mississippi, Oxford, 22–24 March 2007. Available on DVD.

———. "Writers Read in Honor of Inauguration." *Oxford Eagle*, 12 April 1996, 1A, 10A.

———. "Yocona Best Known for Farms, Fishing." *Oxford Eagle*, 12 April 1996, 1A.

Minzesheimer, Bob. "'Catfish' Swims in Endless Waters." Rev. of *A Miracle of Catfish*. *USA Today*, 22 March 2007.

———. "Reluctant Flier Jonathan Miles Takes a Pen to (Un)Friendly Skies. *USA Today*, 30 May 2008.

Mitgang, Herbert. "2 Strangers Telling Each Other Their War Stories." Rev. of *Dirty Work*. *New York Times*, 23 September 1989, A13.

Mobilio, Albert. "Biloxi Bound: A Teenager Hitchhiking in Mississippi Find Life's Highway Full of Bumps." Rev. of *Fay*. *New York Times Book Review*, 16 April 2000, 18.

Morrisey, Larry. "Sing 'Just One More.'" *Jackson (Mississippi) Free Press*, 23 May 2007.

Mort, John. Rev. of *On Fire*. *Booklist*, 15 November 1993, 578.

Moses, John Taylor. "Take Care, Youngblood: Excerpts from Larry Brown's Letters, 1998–2002." *Oxford Town*, 22–28 March 2007, 16–17.

Nawotka, Edward. "Larry Brown's Last, Unfinished Country Epic." *San Francisco Chronicle*, 30 March 2007, E-15.

Neumar, Chris. "Arliss Howard Interview Transcript (November 01)." *Stumped*. http://stumpedmagazine.com/Interviews/arliss-howard-transcript.html.

———. "Debra Winger Transcript (October 01)." *Stumped*. http://stumped magazine.com/Interviews/debra-winger.html.

Newsom, Michael. "Locals Remember Acclaimed Writer." *Daily Mississippian*, 29 November 2004, 1, 7.

Nichols, Bill. "Beauty and Bodies on the Road to Biloxi." Rev. of *Fay*. *USA Today*, 5 April 2000, 7D

Nicholson, David. "A Fireman's Memoirs: Hot Spots." Rev. of *On Fire*. *Washington Post Book World*, 1 March 1994, C2.

"Notes on Current Books: *Big Bad Love*." *Virginia Quarterly Review* 67.3 (1991): 94.

Oates, Nathan, and Amy Day Wilkinson. "An Interview with Frederick Barthelme." *Missouri Review* 27.2 (2004): 39–53.

O'Brient, Don. "An Appreciation, Larry Brown, 1951–2004: Hardscrabble Rural South Gave Novelist His Material." *Atlanta Journal-Constitution*, 27 November 2004, D1.

———. "A Blazing New Southern Voice." *Atlanta Journal-Constitution*, 20 August 1989, L1, L10.

———. "'Love': It's Big, Bad and Wonderful." Rev. of *Big Bad Love*. *Atlanta Journal-Constitution*, 9 September 1990, N8.

———. "Writer Larry Brown in Faulkner's Footsteps." *Atlanta Journal-Constitution*, 9 April 2000, L1, L6, 7.

O'Connor, Flannery. *Collected Works*. Boston: Library of America, 1989.

———. *The Habit of Being*. New York: Farrar, Straus, and Giroux, 1979.

———. *Mystery and Manners*. Ed. Sally and Robert Fitzgerald. New York: Farrar, Straus, and Giroux, 1969.

O'Gorman, Farrell. "White, Black, and Brown: Reading O'Connor after Richard Rodriguez." *Flannery O'Connor Review* 4 (2006): 32–49.

"Ole Miss Archives Acquire Larry Brown Manuscripts." *Foundation News*, 18 July 1996.

Orr, Jay. "Firefighter-Turned-Author Set for Book Fest." *Nashville Banner*, 10 October 1991, C-10.

Osier, John. "Teaching Larry Brown." Presentation at the Fourteenth Oxford Conference for the Book, University of Mississippi, Oxford, 22–24 March 2007. Available on DVD.

Panning, Anne. *Super America: Stories and a Novella*. Athens: University of Georgia Press, 2007.

Park, Mary Jane. "More Than a Fish Story." Rev. of *A Miracle of Catfish*. *St. Petersburg Times*, 8 May 2007.

Parsons, Alexander. "Waiting in the Gloam, an Interview with Author Larry Brown." *Uno Mas*, 14 April 2000. http://www.unomas.com/features/Larrybrown.html.

"Passions of the Trailer-Park." Rev. of *Fay. Economist*, 15 April 2000, 13.

Pearson, Michael. "A Siren Song." Rev. of *On Fire. New Orleans Times-Picayune*, 27 March 1994, E8.

Peat, Isie, and Diane Young. "'What a Wonderful Century and More We Have Had.'" *Southern Living*, May 1990, 87–92.

Pelecanos, George P. "White Trash Dreaming." Rev. of *Fay. Washington Post Book World*, 18 June 2000, 7.

Perry, Keith. "Fireman-Writer, Bad Boy Novelist, King of Grit Lit: 'Building' Larry Brown(s) at Algonquin Books of Chapel Hill." In *Larry Brown and the Blue-Collar South*, ed. Jean W. Cash and Keith Perry, 130–55. Jackson: University Press of Mississippi, 2008.

Pettus, Gary. "Interview with Larry Brown." In *Conversations with Larry Brown*, ed. Jay Watson, 3–14. Jackson: University Press of Mississippi, 2007.

———. "Literary Luncheon Serves Feast of Brown's Words." *Jackson (Mississippi) Clarion-Ledger*, 18 May 1990, 1E.

———. "Writing His Way to the Holy Grail." *Jackson (Mississippi) Clarion-Ledger*, 23 August 1988, 1C, 3C.

Phifer, Martha. "Joe Is Southern Literature at Its Faulknerian Best." Rev. of *Joe. Harrisonburg (Virginia) Daily News-Record*, 7 November 1991, 12.

Plummer, William. Rev. of *Fay. People*, 15 May 2000, 59.

Pohrt, Karl. "South Awareness Tour, Days 1–4." *Shelf Awareness: Daily Enlightenment for the Book Trade*, 27–30 March 2007. http://news.shelf-awareness.com/ar/theshelf/2007-03-28/south_awareness_tour_day_two.html.

Pond, Wayne. "New Southerners: Larry Brown." In *Conversations with Larry Brown*, ed. Jay Watson, 62–69. Jackson: University Press of Mississippi, 2007.

Prescott, Peter S. "Pillow Talk." Rev. of *Dirty Work. Newsweek*, 20 November 1989, 81.

"PW Talks with Larry Brown." *Publishers Weekly*, 10 January 2000, 44.

Quinn, Anthony. "The Summer of Hate." Rev. of *Father and Son. New York Times Book Review*, 22 September 1996, 11.

Railey, John. "Unfinished Novel a Real Southern Gem." Rev. of *A Miracle of Catfish. Winston-Salem (North Carolina) Journal*, 17 March 2007.

Rankin, Tom. "On the Home Front, Larry Brown's Narrative Landscape." *Reckon: The Magazine of Southern Culture*, February 1995, 90–101.

———. "Putting a Bottom under It." *Oxford American*, Spring 2005, 142–53.

Ranney, Dave. "Keen Edge: Straight-Talking Singer-Songwriter Reveals 'What I Really Mean.'" 7 September 2005. Lawrence.com.

Ravenel, Shannon. "Interview with Shannon Ravenel." *Slushpile*, 23 August 2005. http://www.slushpile.net/index.php/2005/08/23/interview-shannon -ravenel/.

———. "Two Artists." *Algonkian*, 1989, 4–5.

———. "Wild with Discovery." *Five Points: A Journal of Literature and Art* 8.2 (n.d.). http://www.webdelsol.com/Five_Points/issues/v8n2/sr.htm.

———. "Writer Larry Brown Shows Us Our Human Side." 25 November 2004. Web site no longer available.

Real, Jere. "Larry Brown Finds Times Are Changing in 'Ole Miss' Oxford." Rev. of *Billy Ray's Farm*. *Richmond Times-Dispatch*, 6 May 2001.

Reeves, Rhonda. "Dead Cow Blues: Larry Brown and Alejandro Escovedo Take You Someplace beyond Lonely." *Ace Weekly*, 19 April 2001. http://www.ace weekly.com/Backissues_ACEWeekly/010419/index.html.

———. "White Trash Gothic: Author Larry Brown Talks about Big Bad Jeeter Love." *Ace*, December 1996, 1–4.

Rev. of *Big Bad Love*. *Virginia Quarterly Review* 67.3 (1991): 94.

Rev. of *Father and Son*. *Antioch Review* 55 (1997): 120.

Rev. of *Father and Son*. *Publishers Weekly*, 24 June 1996, 44.

Rev of *Fay*. *Kirkus Reviews*, 15 January 2000.

Rev. of *On Fire*. *Kirkus Reviews*, 5 November 1993.

Rev. of *On Fire*. *New Yorker*, 18 April 1994, 107.

Rev. of *The Rabbit Factory*. *Kirkus Reviews*, 15 July 2003, 923.

Rev. of *The Rabbit Factory*. *Publishers Weekly*, 9 September 2003.

Richardson, Thomas J. "Larry Brown." In *Contemporary Fiction Writers of the South*, ed. Joseph Flora and Robert Bain, 55–66. Westport, Conn.: Greenwood, 1994.

Rinella, Steven. "Larry Brown: Friends and Writers." Presentation at the Fourteenth Oxford Conference for the Book, University of Mississippi, Oxford, 22–24 March 2007. Available on DVD.

———. "Required Reading." Rev. of *A Miracle of Catfish*. *OutsideOnline*, March 2007. http://outsideonline.com/outside/culture/200703/larry-brown-bill-gifford.html.

Robinson, Charles. "Interview with Larry Brown." Starkville High School Mississippi Writers and Musicians Project. April 2000. http://www.mswriter sandmusicians.com/writers/larry-brown.html.

Ross, Jean W. "Contemporary Authors Interview with Larry Brown." *Contemporary Authors*, vol. 134, ed. Susan M. Trosky, 87–91. Detroit: Gale, 1992.

Rungren, Lawrence. Rev. of *Father and Son*. *Library Journal*, August 1996, 110.

Saldivar, Steve. "'Rabbit' Doesn't Resonate." Rev. of *The Rabbit Factory*. *Daily Californian*, 9 September 2004.

Sampsell, Kevin. "Book Pusher—Following the Ghost of Larry Brown." *Raleigh (North Carolina) News and Observer*, 12 April 2007.

Sayre, Maggie Lee. *"Deaf Maggie Lee Sayre": Photographs of a River Life*. Ed. and intro. Tom Rankin. Jackson: University Press of Mississippi, 1995.

Schechner, Karen. "A Silver Jubilee for Oxford's Square Books." *ABA Bookselling This Week*, 9 September 2004. http://news.bookweb.org/news/silver-jubilee-oxfords-square-books.

Schultz, Lucy. "Larry Brown Remembered for Tough Stories, Tender Heart." *Oxford Eagle*, 25 November 2004, A1.

———. "Renowned Writer Larry Brown Dies at 53." *Oxford Eagle*, 24 November 2004, A1.

Scott, Russell E. "Don't Stop until the Road Ends." Rev. of *The Rabbit Factory*. *PopMatters*, 19 November 2003. http://popmatters.com/books/reviews/r/rabbit-factory.shtml.

Scott, Sid. "Special Delivery: Book Begins New Chapter in the Life of Larry Brown." *Northeast Mississippi Daily Journal*, 2 November 1989, 6F–7F.

Segretto, Mike. "Interview with Kaye Gibbons." *Barnes and Noble Online*, Winter 2006.

"Self-Taught Writer Larry Brown Emerges Muddied but Uncowed." Rev. of *Billy Ray's Farm*. *Staunton (Virginia) News-Leader*, 3 June 2001.

Schragin, Adam. "Book Review: How 'Miracle of Catfish' Came to Be a Miracle in Itself." Rev. of *A Miracle of Catfish*. *San Antonio Express-News*, 22 April 2007.

See, Carolyn. "A Visit to the Land of Character Flaws." Rev. of *The Rabbit Factory*. *Washington Post*, 5 September 2003, C02.

Sermon, Charles. "Dirt, Heat, Passion and Death: Brown's 'Fay' Hits Like a Bullet." Rev. of *Fay*. *Columbia (South Carolina) State*, 9 April 2000.

Shoup, Barbara, and Margaret Love Denman. *Novel Ideas: Contemporary Authors Share the Creative Process*. Indianapolis: Alpha, 2001.

Siegel, Tatiana, "Lionsgate Goes to Larry Brown's 'Rabbit Factory' for Adaptation." *Book Standard*, 21 June 2006. http://www.allbusiness.com/retail trade/miscellaneous-retail-miscellaneous/4404246-1.html.

Sigal, Clancy. "Looking for Love in All the Wrong Places." Rev. of *Big Bad Love*. *Washington Post Book World*, 23 December 1990.

Skube, Michael. "Straight from the Heart." *Atlanta Journal-Constitution*, 29 September 1996, M3.

Slater, Joyce. "'Facing the Music' Has a Firefighter's Searing Perception." *Atlanta Journal-Constitution*, 4 December 1988, K10.

Smith, David. "Fireman Plans to Retire." *Oxford Eagle*, 4 January 1990, 1A.

———. "Local Author Wins Award for Short Story Collection." *Oxford Eagle*, 23 May 1989, 1.

Smith, Lee. "Meet the Author: Lee Smith." *Charlotte-Mecklenburg (North Carolina) Public Library Reader's Club Newsletter*, December 2003. http://www.plcmc.org/readers_club/meetAuthor.asp?author=4.

Sobsey, Adam. "The Final, Unfinished Novel of the Late, Great Larry Brown, Fire Engine Redneck." Rev. of *A Miracle of Catfish*. *Independent Weekly*, 11 April 2007. http://www.indyweek.com/gyrobase/PrintiFriednly?oid%3A73432.

South, Paul. "Remembering Mississippi Literature's Regular Guy." *Oxford Eagle*, 3 December 2004, 4A.

"Stage Debut of 'Dirty Work' Thursday." *Oxford Eagle*, 29 March 1995, 8A.

Stankard, Linda. "Passing the Rabbit Test." Rev of *The Rabbit Factory*. *BookPage Online*, 17 September 2003. http://www.bookpage.com/0309bp/fiction/rabbit_factory.html.

Starr, William W. "Larry Brown Makes Impressive Debut." *Columbia (South Carolina) State*, 11 September 1988.

Steinberg, Sybil. Rev. of *Fay*. *Publishers Weekly*, 10 January 2000, 43.

Sullivan, Pat. "Author Larry Brown Discusses His Writing." *Oxford Scene*, 4 April 1991, 3.

Summer, Bob. "Larry Brown: The Former Firefighter Talks about His Long Apprenticeship as a Writer." *Publishers Weekly*, 11 October 1991, 46.

Sussman, Paul. "Something Nasty in the Woodshed." Rev. of *Father and Son*. *Spectator*, 14 February 1998, 31.

Swaim, Don. "Book Beat Interview with Larry Brown (1989)." In *Conversations with Larry Brown*, ed. Jay Watson, 15–25. Jackson: University Press of Mississippi, 2007.

Talbott, Chris. "Late Mississippi Author's Unfinished Final Novel Published." Rev. of *A Miracle of Catfish*. *Athens (Georgia) Banner-Herald*, 26 March 2007.

Taylor, Art. "Fay's Fate: Larry Brown's Latest Lingers Too Long." Rev. of *Fay*. *Spectator*, 8 April 2000.

———. "Larry Brown's Legacy." Rev. of *A Miracle of Catfish*. *Metro* (Raleigh, North Carolina), March 2007.

Terhark, Chuck. "Rough North: Ben Weaver Tries to Shake His Backwoods-Gothic Image." *Minneapolis Music City Pages*, 9 May 2007. http://www.cit ypages.com/2007-05-09/music/rough-north/2/.

"'That Fellow Can Write a Blue Streak': Lafayette County Author Larry Brown." *Southern Register* (University of Mississippi Center for the Study of Southern Culture), Summer 1988, 7.

Tighe, James. "Amen." *Oxford Town*, 2–8 December 2004, 16.

Tollison, Horhn. Senate Concurrent Resolution No. 575. Mississippi Legislature, Regular Session 2000.

Tripp, Mary Kate. "Tripp: 'Fay' Earns Place in 'Grit Lit' of Southern Writers." *Amarillo (Texas) Globe-News*, 14 May 2000.

Truman, Cheryl. "Silas House Shows Southerners as Eclectic, Not Redneck." 19 February 2008. staugustine.com.

Tucker, Neely. "Novelist Recalls Life with Lapping Flames." Rev. of *On Fire*. *Detroit Free Press*, 20 March 1994.

———. "A Weaving of Love's Sorrow and Pity." Rev. of *Big Bad Love*. *Detroit Free Press*, 19 August 1990, 7G.

Tunis, Walter. "*Just One More: A Musical Tribute to Larry Brown*." *Lexington (Kentucky) Herald-Leader*, 8 June 2007.

Ulin, David L. Rev. of *Joe*. *Bloomsbury Review*, January–February 1992, 18.

Vice, Brad. "Irony and Pathos in Memphis." Rev. of *The Rabbit Factory*. *San Francisco Chronicle*, 14 September 2003, M2.

Vitzthum, Virginia. Rev. of *Fay*. *Salon*, 4 April 2000. http://www.salon.com/books/review/2000/04/04/brown/index.html.

Wallace, Richard. "'A Miracle of Catfish': A Last Novel of Grace, Great Characters." Rev. of *A Miracle of Catfish*. *Seattle Times*, 30 March 2007.

Walters, Barry. "Down on the Farm." Rev. of *Facing the Music*. *Village Voice*, 22 November 1988, 56–57.

"Wanted: Extras for Brown's 'Big Bad Love.'" *Oxford Eagle*, 9 August 2000, 1A.

Warner, Toby. "Feature Interview with Shannon Ravenel." *Boldtype* 46 (August 2007). http://boldtype.com/issues/aug2007/index.html.

Watkins, Billy. "Editing 'Miracle of Catfish' a Real Challenge." *Jackson (Missis-sippi) Clarion-Ledger*, 18 March 2007, 2F.

———. "Hot Career Move." *Jackson (Mississippi) Clarion-Ledger*, 24 December 1996, 1D, 2D.

———. "Nonfiction Work by Late Author Finds Home. *Jackson (Mississippi) Clarion-Ledger*, 6 October 2006, 1E.

Watson, Jay, ed. *Conversations with Larry Brown*. Jackson: University Press of Mississippi, 2007.

———. "Economics of a Cracker Landscape: Poverty as an Environmental Issue in Two Southern Writers." *Mississippi Quarterly* 55 (2002): 497–513; partial rpt. In *Larry Brown and the Blue-Collar South*, ed. Jean W. Cash and Keith Perry, 49–97. Jackson: University Press of Mississippi, 2008.

Weaver, Ben. "Larry Brown on Music." Presentation at the Fourteenth Oxford Conference for the Book, University of Mississippi, Oxford, 22–24 March 2007. Available on DVD.

———. "Tribute." *Things I'd Rather Be Doing*. 4 May 2007. http://tirbd.com/category/larry-brown-week/.

Weaver, Teresa K. "Q&A/Larry Brown: Mounting Tension Is Critical to Story-telling." *Atlanta Journal Constitution*, 28 September 2003, Q4.

Weinraub, Judith. "The Back-Roads Blue-Collar Artiste." *Washington Post*, 9 December 1990, F1, F4.

Welch, Rodney. "Larry Brown's Road Trip." Rev. of *Fay*. *Columbia (South Caroli-na) Free Times Book Review*, 12–19 April 2000. http://www.free-times.com/index.php?cat=121304064644348.

West, Heather. "Bloodshot Records to Release *Just One More: A Musical Trib-ute to Larry Brown*." 29 January 2007. http://www.bloodshotrecords.com/album/just-few-more-musical-tribute-larry-brown-bonus-collection.

Weston, Keith. "WUNC-FM Radio Interview (2002)." In *Conversations with Larry Brown*, ed. Jay Watson, 168–72. Jackson: University Press of Missis-sippi, 2007.

Whitbeck, Bill. "Larry Brown on Music." Presentation at the Fourteenth Ox-ford Conference for the Book, University of Mississippi, Oxford, 22–24 March 2007. Available on DVD.

White, Evelyn C. "Not Deferential to White People: Alice Walker, Flannery O'Connor, and the Art of Biography." *Flannery O'Connor Review* 6 (2008): 81–89.

White, Neil. "'New' Larry Brown Story Published; Manuscript, Cover Letter Discovered." *Oxford Town*, 5–11 October 2006, 9.

Whitt, Margaret Earley. "1963, a Pivotal Year: Flannery O'Connor and the Civil Rights Movement." *Flannery O'Connor Review* 3 (2005): 59–72.

Williams, Don. "Larry Brown's Writing Style Has Roots in Several Phases." *Knoxville News-Sentinel*, 22 October 1991, B1, B4.

Williams, Lynna. "The Late Larry Brown's Last Look at Human Imperfection." *Chicago Tribune*, 14 March 2007, 8.

Wilson, Jenny. "The Sun Goes Down in Tula." Unpublished history of Tula, Mississippi. In possession of the author.

Winders, Glenda. "'Joe' Is Powerfully Poignant, but Unpleasant." Rev. of *Joe*. *San Diego Union*, 3 November 1991.

Winter, Max. Rev. of *Father and Son*. *Boston Book Review*, September 1996.

Wood, Susan. "Writing—The Great Struggle." Rev. of *Big Bad Love*. *Houston Post*, 9 September 1990, C8.

Woodrell, Daniel. "Losers Take All." Rev. of *Joe*. *Washington Post Book World*, 20 November 1991, 9.

Wray, Virginia. "Flannery O'Connor and Lillian Smith: A Missed Opportunity." *Flannery O'Connor Review* 5 (2007): 35–43.

Wright, John. "Larry Brown's 'Fay' Captures Essence of the South, Its People." Rev. of *Fay*. *Decatur (Alabama) Daily*, 7 May 2000.

Wyatt, Edward. "Larry Brown, Author of Spare, Dark Stories, Dies at 53. *New York Times*, 26 November 2004.

Yardley, Jonathan. "Cow Sense." Rev. of *Billy Ray's Farm*. *Washington Post*, 29 March 2001, CO2.

Yow, Dede. Rev. of *Conversations with Larry Brown*, ed. Jay Watson. *Southern Quarterly* 45.2 (2008): 187–88.

Zacharek, Stephanie. Rev. of *Big Bad Love*, dir. Arliss Howard. *Salon*, 22 February 2002. http://www.salon.com/entertainment/movies/review/2002/02/22/big_bad_love/index.html.

Zane, J. Peder. "Author Keeps the Tales Pouring." *Raleigh (North Carolina) News and Observer*, 8 June 2008.

Acknowledgments

My enthusiasm for Larry Brown and his work and the cooperation I have received from his family and friends have made writing this biography a special pleasure. Without the support of Mary Annie Brown, I could not have completed this project. In particular, I appreciate her permission to quote from Larry's unpublished writings, including his numerous letters. My interview with Larry's mother, Leona Barlow Brown, was essential and inspiring. I also thank JoRuth Pruitt, Larry's first cousin, who drove us through "Brown country" in early April 2007 and helped me get the photographs that appear in this book. In addition, my heartfelt gratitude goes to Billy Ray and Paula, Shane, LeAnne, and Jonny.

Among Brown's friends in Oxford, Glennray Tutor was the first to talk with me with complete candor; he also allowed me to use his letters from Larry and supplied several photographs. I also appreciate the help of Ellen Douglas (Josephine Haxton), John Evans, Dorothy Fitts, John Grisham, Barry Hannah, Lynn Hewlett, George Kehoe, Lisa N. Howorth, Richard Howorth, and Anne Odell. Jim Dees urged me to use whatever he had written about Larry in the *Oxford Eagle*. Jay Watson, professor of English at the University of Mississippi, sent me interviews before the publication of his *Conversations with Larry Brown* in 2007. Joan Wylie Hall helped me to track down a photograph.

I owe special thanks to the staff of the Department of Archives and Special Collections at the John D. Williams Library at the University of Mississippi, particularly department head Jennifer Ford and Pamela Williamson, curator of visual collections. At Ole Miss, I also offer special thanks to the Center for the Study of Southern Culture, especially Ann Abadie, for supplying me with DVDs of the 2007 conference dedicated to Brown's work and for allowing me to quote from them.

Larry's friends from outside of Oxford who helped this project along in-

288

clude Rick Bass, Silas House, Jill McCorkle, Jake Mills, and Ben Weaver. Gary Hawkins not only offered information but also provided me with a transcript of *The Rough South of Larry Brown*. His brilliant film and his cooperation made my work much easier.

Shannon Ravenel allowed me access to all of the Brown material at Algonquin Books, including her correspondence with the author. She also answered my questions, bought me lunches in Chapel Hill, and read the entire manuscript. Her candor, kindness, enthusiasm, and sharp editorial eye have enormously benefited this book. Others connected with Algonquin who have offered helpful information include Louis D. Rubin Jr., Ina Stern, and Katharine Walton. Larry's literary agent, Liz Darhansoff, also contributed vital material.

One of Larry's closest literary friends, Clyde Edgerton, did everything possible to make this biography a complete study. He trusted me with his numerous letters from Larry, answered many questions, provided a video of his interview with Gary Hawkins about Larry, gave me photographs, and read the manuscript from start to finish. His song, "Larry's Catfish," has inspired me.

Like Clyde and Shannon, Tom Rankin generously answered my questions; in addition, Tom allowed me to use his many letters from Larry as well as other documents in his possession and contributed several photographs. He and Robert Donahoo served as readers of my manuscript for the University Press of Mississippi, and both men offered much appreciated help. At the press, I owe special thanks to Leila Salisbury, Valerie Jones, and Ellen Goldlust-Gingrich, whose scrupulous editing helped shape the book.

Two others who deserve special recognition are Robert McDonald of Virginia Military Institute and Jan Nordby Gretlund of Denmark, both of whom published material that became part of this book. Rob has published two of my articles, "Larry Brown's Literary Apprenticeship—1980–1988" and "Larry Brown and Music: I Don't Like to Write without It . . . ," in *Studies in American Culture*; he has also printed my reviews of *Conversations with Larry Brown* and *A Miracle of Catfish*. Gretlund included "Larry Brown's *Fay*" in his collection, *Still in Print: The Southern Novel Today*.

Others who contributed in ways major or minor to this volume include Jo Ann Atkins, Ted Atkinson, Pinckney Benedict, Lafe Benson; Andrea Hollander Budy, Paul Coleman, Orman P. Day, Debra Earling; John B. Edmiston;

Timothy J. Evans; Ben Fisher; Mike Foster; Bruce Gentry; Sarah Gordon; Susan H. Irons, Robert Jordan, John Kenyon, Scott Miller, Barry Moser, John Taylor Moses, Lewis Nordan, John Osier, Patsy Clark Pace, Anne Panning, Keith Perry, Steve Rinella, Bes Spangler, Shelby Stephenson, Jimmy Tighe, Alex P. Watson, Jenny Wilson, Virginia Wray, and Steve Yarbrough. I apologize to anyone I have inadvertently omitted.

I thank Jim Benson for his gift of the June 1982 issue of *Easyrider*, still in its original brown paper wrapping. Tim Evans of Steppenwolf films sent me a copy of the film version of "Kubuku Rides (This Is It)." Dorothy Fitts provided me with a copy of Brown's speech at the 1997 dedication of the Oxford–Lafayette County Public Library.

At James Madison University, David Jeffrey, currently dean of the College of Arts and Letters, was instrumental in helping me secure the 2006–7 educational leave that enabled me to make significant progress on this book, and I am grateful both for his help and for the grant itself. Robert V. Hoskins and Mark Parker, chairs of JMU's English department, have provided advice, encouragement, and friendship. I also thank the Interlibrary Loan staff at Carrier Library for their efforts on my behalf. Melissa Van Vuuren was particularly helpful to me in resolving bibliographic issues.

Friends, colleagues, and students who proofread the manuscript include Dabney Bankert, Erin Fearing, Joan Frederick, Richard Gaughran, Judy Good, Dawn Goode, Marcus Hamilton, Michael Harper, Matt Hawkins, David Jeffrey, Emily Langhorne, Joe Loyacano, Mark Parker, Camilla Shelton, and Geraldine Poppke Suter.

My sister, Helen W. Smith, deserves more thanks than I can give her. She has served as my chief editor on this project, reading the entire manuscript at least four times and scouring my writing for errors in content and style. An acute and sensitive reader, she has helped make this book what it has become. My mother, Kathryn E. Wampler, who died in the fall of 2009, followed this project from the beginning, reading nearly all of Brown's work so that she could understand what I was doing. I regret that she did not live to read the finished product. My son, Gordon, has always been my strongest advocate. Finally, my husband, Lloyd, has endured my absence during the many hours I spent in my basement office.

Index